Wallace Jonason

THE AMERICAN CHAIR
Three Centuries of Style

Braced comb-back, continuous-arm Windsor armchair. New England. Ca. 1780. Pine and ash. H. 45¾", W. 25½", D. 19½". The chair is inscribed in punched letters underneath the seat: "Made by D. B. Austin for his cousin Daisy Olive Berry." Underneath the tongue of the seat two intertwined hearts are coupled with the words: "To My Sweetheart." (Mr. and Mrs. John Gordon)

THE AMERICAN CHAIR
Three Centuries of Style

by Robert Bishop
Director of the Museum of American Folk Art

Foreword by
Charles F. Hummel
Deputy Director of Collections, Winterthur Museum

Bonanza Books
New York

This 1983 edition is published by Bonanza Books,
distributed by Crown Publishers, Inc., by arrangement with
E.P. Dutton, Inc.

Manufactured in the United States of America

Library of Congress Cataloging in Publication Data

Bishop, Robert Charles.
   The American Chair: Three Centuries of Style

   Reprint. Originally published: New York : Dutton,
c1972.
   Bibliography: p.
   Includes index.
   1. Chairs—United States.   I. Title.
NK2715.B55   1983   749′.32′0973   83-6001
ISBN: 0-517-413582

h g f e d c b a

Windsor bench. Frederick County, Maryland. Ca. 1740. Oak, ash, hickory. H. 34″,
L. 76¼″, D. 23⅝″. An unusual example of the eighteenth-century Windsor style with
interesting turnings. (The Baltimore Museum of Art)

This book is dedicated to my grandmother

ETHEL BISHOP

who taught me that a chair is more than
just something to sit on!

CONTENTS

ACKNOWLEDGMENTS

The author wishes to express his sincere gratitude to the many individuals and institutions who have generously provided pictorial and textual material for this volume. It gives me pleasure to make a special acknowledgment for their contributions to the book to Charles F. Hummel, Curator, The Henry Francis du Pont Winterthur Museum, who read the manuscript and made so many valuable suggestions; to Cyril I. Nelson of E. P. Dutton & Co., Inc.; and to Patricia Coblentz, who not only served as Associate Editor, but whose countless hours of patient reading and typing have made this book a reality. Special mention should also be made of the fine photographs that have been provided by Charles T. Miller, Carl Malotka, and Rudy Ruzicska of the Henry Ford Museum; and Arthur Vitols of Helga Photo Studio, Geoffrey Clements, and Louis Reems, all of New York City.

PRIVATE COLLECTORS: Mr. and Mrs. David Aldrich; Cary F. Baker, Jr.; Thomas B. Buckles, Jr.; Joseph T. Butler; Freeman Champney; Mr. and Mrs. Samuel Chew; Mr. and Mrs. David Claggett; Mrs. Henry M. Clark; Lammot DuP. Copeland; Cornercopia; Dr. and Mrs. Roger Gerry; Mr. and Mrs. Harry Connelly Groome, Jr.; James Gwynn; Mr. and Mrs. Charles V. Hagler; Mr. and Mrs. W. Denning Harvey; Norman Herreshoff; G. William Holland; Dr. Richard H. Howland; Walter M. Jeffords, Jr.; Edgar Kaufmann, Jr.; Mr. and Mrs. James Keene; Mr. and Mrs. James A. Keillor; Mrs. George Malin Davis Kelly; Felix H. Kuntz; Mr. and Mrs. Terence Leichti; Mrs. Bertram K. Little; Sam Maloof; Edgar de N. Mayhew; Mr. and Mrs. J. Balfour Miller; Paul Nelson; Andrew Oliver; Mr. and Mrs. Joseph K. Ott; Henry J. Prebys; James Ricau; Eric M. Schindler; Mr. and Mrs. Walter E. Simmons; Frances K. Talbot; Mrs. Thomas S. Taylor; Mrs. Cornelia G. Thompson; Mr. and Mrs. Bradford A. Warner; Mrs. C. McGregory Wells.

INSTITUTIONS AND THEIR STAFF MEMBERS: *Abby Aldrich Rockefeller Folk Art Collection, Williamsburg, Virginia:* Jean C. Hildreth; *Albany Institute of History and Art, Albany, New York:* Norman S. Rice, Kenneth R. DeLisle; *Albright-Knox Art Gallery, Buffalo, New York:* Ethel Moore; *The American Museum in England, Bath:* Mrs. M. E. Irwin; *Anglo-American Art Museum, Baton Rouge, Louisiana:* H. Parrott Bacot; *Art Commission of the City of New York:* Donald J. Gormley; *The Art Institute of Chicago, Chicago, Illinois:* Betty R. Saxon, David A. Hanks; *The Baltimore Museum of Art, Baltimore, Maryland:* David McIntyre, William Voss Elder III; *The Bayou Bend Collection, The Museum of Fine Arts, Houston, Texas:* David B. Warren; *Bishop Hill, State of Illinois, Department of Conservation:* Ronald E. Nelson; *The British Museum, London:* P. Warwick, Edward Telesford; *The Brooklyn Museum, Brooklyn, New York:* J. Stewart Johnson; *Chelsea Hotel, New York:* Stanley Burd; *Chicago Historical Society, Chicago, Illinois:* Mary Frances Rhymer; *City Art Museum, St. Louis, Missouri:* Barcy Fox; *Collection of Edgar William and Bernice Chrysler Garbisch, New York:* Clifford W. Schaefer; *Colonial Williamsburg, Williamsburg, Virginia:* Hugh DeSamper, Jane Abbot Tyler; *The Connecticut Historical Society, Hartford, Connecticut:* Thompson R. Harlow, Philip H. Dunbar; *Cooper–Hewitt Museum of Decorative Arts and Design, Smithsonian Institution, New York:* Catherine Lynn Frangiamore; *The Corcoran Gallery of Art, Washington, D.C.:* Ellen H. Gross; *Cranbrook Gallery of Art—The Galleries, Bloomfield Hills, Michigan:* Mary Riordan; *Decorative Accents, New York:* Albert Eisenlan; *The Detroit Institute of Arts, Detroit, Michigan:* William A. Bostick; *De Witt Historical Society of Tompkins County, New York:* Miss Helena Schaber; *Essex Institute, Salem, Massachusetts:* David B. Little, Margaret L. Nelson; *Estate of Stephen Girard:* Kent L. Roberts; *First Unitarian Church, Baltimore, Maryland:* Howard A. Waterhouse; *Folger Shakespeare Library, Washington, D.C.:* Ann Skiff; *Frick Art Reference Library, New York:* Mildred Steinbach; *Ginsburg & Levy, Inc., New York:* Benjamin Ginsburg, Lewis B. Rockwell, Elsie Yamin; *Girard College, Philadelphia, Pennsylvania:* Alfred Moscariello; *Gorham Silver Company, Providence, Rhode Island; Grand Rapids Public Museum, Grand Rapids, Michigan:* W. D. Frankforter, Dorothy Jaqua; *Greenfield Village and Henry Ford Museum, Dearborn, Michigan:* Dr. Donald A. Shelley, Robert G. Wheeler, Katharine B. Hagler, Michael O. Smith; *Harvard University, Carpenter Center for the Visual Arts, Cambridge, Massachusetts:* Jael Nathan; *The Henry Francis du Pont Winterthur Museum, Winterthur, Delaware:* Charles F. Hummel, Karol A. Schmiegel, Nancy Goyne Evans, Elizabeth M. Hill; *Hirschl & Adler Galleries, New York:* Stuart P. Feld; *Historic Deerfield, Inc., Deerfield, Massachusetts:* Maude E. Banta; *Historical Society of York County, Pennsylvania, York, Pennsylvania:* Mrs. A. F. Lynch; *Hitchcock Chair Company, Riverton, Connecticut:* Thomas H. Glennon; *Index of American Design, National Gallery of Art, Washington, D.C.:* Lina A. Steele; *Indianapolis Museum of Art,*

8

Indianapolis, Indiana: Carl J. Weinhardt, Jr., Jeffrey R. Brown; *International Business Machines, New York:* Harold J. Santare; *International Garden Club, Pelham Bay, New York:* Betty W. Culling; *Henry W. Jenkins & Sons Company, Baltimore, Maryland:* Jane K. Kramer; *Knoll International, New York:* Beth Evans; *The Library Company of Philadelphia, Philadelphia, Pennsylvania; The Litchfield Historical Society, Litchfield, Connecticut:* William L. Warren; *The Lockwood-Mathews Mansion, Norwalk, Connecticut:* Mrs. John Sutherland; *Longfellow House, Cambridge, Massachusetts:* Thomas H. deValcourt; *Los Angeles County Museum, Los Angeles, California:* Rexford Stead; *Lyndhurst, National Trust for Historic Preservation, Tarrytown, New York:* John N. Pearce, Gerald L. Fiedler; *The Magazine Antiques, New York:* Alice Winchester, Wendell Garrett, Edith Gaines, Margaret Aspinwall; *Maryland Historical Society, Baltimore, Maryland:* Lois B. McCauley; *Massachusetts Historical Society, Boston, Massachusetts:* Malcolm Freiberg, Stephen T. Riley; *The Metropolitan Museum of Art, New York:* Berry B. Tracy, Mary Glaze, Frances Gruber, Nada Saporiti; *Herman Miller, Inc., Zeeland, Michigan:* Howard Sutton; *Milwaukee Art Center, Milwaukee, Wisconsin:* Thomas Beckman; *Missouri Historical Society, St. Louis, Missouri:* Ruth K. Field; *Monmouth County Historical Association, Freehold, New Jersey:* Millicent Feltus; *The Mount Vernon Ladies' Association of the Union, Mount Vernon, Virginia:* Christine Meadows; *Munson-Williams-Proctor Institute, Utica, New York:* Barbara Franco, Marjorie C. Freytag; *Museum of the City of New York:* Margaret D. Stearns, Charlotte LaRue; *Museum of Fine Arts, Boston, Massachusetts:* Pamela Tosi, Mary E. Maher; *The Museum of Modern Art, New York:* Linda Loving; *Museum of New Mexico, Santa Fe, New Mexico:* Miss E. Boyd, Charles Proctor; *Lillian Nassau, Ltd., New York:* Lillian Nassau; *National Gallery of Art, Washington, D.C.:* Mildred W. Kirshner, Catherine P. Hefling; *National Museum, Athens, Greece:* V. Kallipolitis, E. Thanos; *William Rockhill Nelson Gallery of Art, Atkins Museum of Fine Arts, Kansas City, Missouri:* Ross E. Taggart; *The Newark Museum, Newark, New Jersey:* Wilmot T. Bartle, Mildred Baker; *New Hampshire Historical Society, Concord, New Hampshire:* Margaret W. Sawyer, Mrs. William F. Oakman; *New Mexico State Tourist Bureau, Santa Fe, New Mexico:* Frank Anaya; *Newport Historical Society, Newport, Rhode Island:* Theodore E. Waterbury; *The New-York Historical Society, New York:* James Heslin, William DuPrey, Mary Black; *The New York Public Library, New York:* John P. Baker; *New York Society Library, New York:* Helen Ruskell; *New York State Historical Association, Cooperstown, New York:* Ruby Rogers; *Old Salem, Winston-Salem, North Carolina:* Frank L. Horton; *Old Sturbridge Village, Sturbridge, Massachusetts:* Fred L. Broad, Jr., Jane C. Giffen; *Owens-Thomas House, Savannah, Georgia:* Mrs. J. Allen Tison; *The Peabody Museum of Salem, Salem, Massachusetts:* Philip Chadwick Foster Smith; *Pennsylvania Academy of the Fine Arts, Philadelphia, Pennsylvania:* Teresa R. Wieck; *Pilgrim Hall, Plymouth, Massachusetts:* L. D. Geller; *Philadelphia Museum of Art, Philadelphia, Pennsylvania:* Calvin S. Hathaway, George H. Marcus, Judy Spear; *Providence Art Club, Providence, Rhode Island:* Mrs. Truell; *Preservation Society of Newport County, Newport, Rhode Island:* Monique M. Panaggio; *Rhode Island Historical Society, Providence, Rhode Island:* Frank H. Goodyear, Jr.; *Theodore Roosevelt Birthplace, New York:* Helen MacLachlan; *Israel Sack, Inc., New York:* Harold Sack, Dale S. Herman; *Sagamore Hill, Oyster Bay, New York:* S. Paul Okey; *Saridis of Athens, Greece:* E. Saridis; *Selig Manufacturing Company, New York:* Jerrold A. Wexler; *Shelburne Museum, Inc., Shelburne, Vermont:* Bradley Smith, Nancy Muller; *Sleepy Hollow Restorations, Tarrytown, New York:* Joseph T. Butler; *Smithsonian Institution, Washington, D.C.:* James M. Goode, Anne M. Serio, Herbert R. Collins, Alexis Doster III, Barbara J. Coffee, G. M. Rhoades, Rodris Roth; *David Stockwell, Inc., Wilmington, Delaware:* David Stockwell; *Suffolk Museum, Stony Brook, New York:* Mrs. Robin H. Nelson; *Tennessee State Library and Archives, Nashville, Tennessee:* Wilmot H. Droze; *The Toledo Museum of Art, Toledo, Ohio:* Donna Morrow; *United States Department of State, Washington, D.C.:* Vincent F. Tobin; *Vermont State House, Montpelier, Vermont:* Reide B. Payne; *Village Green Antiques, Richland, Michigan:* Bernard C. Plomp; *Virginia Musuem of Fine Arts, Richmond, Virginia:* Sally Guy Lynch; *Vose Gallery, Boston, Massachusetts:* Robert C. Vose, Jr.; *Wadsworth Atheneum, Hartford, Connecticut:* Henry P. Maynard, Elva B. McCormick; *John S. Walton, Inc., New York:* Joseph C. Lionetti; *White House Historical Association, Washington, D.C.:* Hillory A. Tolson; *Worcester Art Museum, Worcester, Massachusetts:* Mrs. H. B. Crooks; *Yale University Art Gallery, New Haven, Connecticut:* Heather Nary.

FOREWORD

Since the late seventeenth century, chairs have been the most prolific type of furniture form, whether produced by hand craftsmen or factory personnel operating power machinery. Of course, the need for a piece of furniture designed for use and comfort was certainly evident much earlier among the ancient civilizations of Egypt, Greece, and Rome. Charles Darwin apparently did not address any part of his studies of evolution to a consideration of that point in human development when mankind found it necessary to produce seating furniture. But according to *The Oxford English Dictionary*, the word "chair" first appeared in the English language about A.D. 1300. Its importance to humanity, or at least to those who speak English, is made clear by the fact that more than two folio-size pages are devoted to definitions of the term and compound words or phrases employing it.

In fact, the fascination with chairs as a furniture form is perhaps best illustrated by the number of ways in which the word "chair" has been incorporated into so many facets of our daily lives. The seats of empire, government, or of a bishop are recognized terms describing the location of power and strength. *A Dictionary of Americanisms on Historical Principles* reveals that a chairman or chairlady is an important individual because of his or her privilege to convene, or preside over, a meeting. Many colleges and universities have used endowment funds to provide professors' chairs. A dentist's chair instinctively places one more at ease than would the prospect of standing for examination or treatment, or worse, lying in a prone position in an office. For many years when railroads were major forms of transportation, the Pullman Parlour Car was commonly referred to as a "chair" car. The ultimate form of modern punishment for a capital crime is referred to by most Americans as "the chair," explaining perhaps why someone thought to be in great difficulty is on "the hot seat." To prevent chairs from damaging walls, "chair rails" were an important architectural feature of houses built in the eighteenth and nineteenth centuries. Nowhere, however, is there a more delightful example of the use of the word than in *A Dictionary of Slang and Unconventional English*, in which a "chair-warmer" is defined as "a physically attractive woman who does nothing on the stage beyond helping to fill it." While probably pejorative in connotation, this phrase is much kinder than its American relative, "bench-warmer," or the act of being "benched." The Puritan ethic relating to the dangers of idleness and failure are somehow crystallized in that unhappy phrase.

Innumerable books have been written about the provenance of chairs, special types and design, and their age. It is surely immodest for this writer to state that the library of The Henry Francis du Pont Winterthur Museum houses one of the world's best collections relating to the history of American art, especially decorative art, and its European background from 1600 to 1925. The claim is relevant to this foreword, however, because by actual count and measurement, the card catalogue of that library contains over 140 titles of books and articles solely about chairs. Those cards occupy more than two inches of drawer space. If books and articles about American furniture, in which chairs are prominently featured, are added to those statistics, one might quickly conclude, "Why another book about American chairs?"

Having participated in criticism of and comment on Robert Bishop's manuscript, and much later, having examined the galley proofs and design layout for his book, I believe that the answer to that question simply must be it is the best "Beowulf to Virginia Woolf" treatment of this subject that has ever been assembled. Robert Bishop has used the term "chair" in its broadest sense to include most types of seating furniture. In more than 900 illustrations, the whole development of American chair forms from earliest settlement to the age of space exploration becomes readily apparent to a collector and student, or to the casual reader.

It is true, of course, that Wallace Nutting's *Furniture Treasury*, first published in 1928 and still in print, contains over 1,100 pictures of seating forms. A reader of that book, however, must keep in mind Nutting's subtitle disclaimer, "Mostly of American Origin." Also to be considered are the generally poor quality of the original photographs and settings used for illustrations; the always maddening fact to a curator or collector that the size of the illustrations prevents comparison of details; and that there was no attempt to include later nineteenth- or early twentieth-century examples of chairs. None of those problems is to be encountered in Robert Bishop's book.

More impressive, however, is the fact that *Centuries and Styles of the American Chair* is not just another attractive "picture" book to decorate the shelves of a personal library or provide an "accent" for a living-room table. In text and captions, the reader is provided with information about the appearance of forms, use of various types of decoration and ornament, design sources, and specific craftsmen or manufacturers who made the often beautiful, occasionally ugly or bizarre, but always intriguing chairs chosen for illustration by the author. Those who wish to investigate the subject in greater detail will find many helpful titles listed in the bibliography at the end of the volume.

The variety of seating furniture selected is one of the strengths of this book. Rudolph Wittkower, one of the giants of scholarship in the field of art history, once stated that to understand the art of a given culture or society, one must be aware of objects produced at the "high, middle, and low" levels. Without discussing which chairs in this book fit those categories, it is clear that Robert Bishop decided not to assemble only a collection of "masterpieces" for his readers. The result is an accurate view of the almost incredible variety of taste and choice experienced by Americans in their selection of chairs.

Of importance to the art historian, social historian, and collector are the large number of original paintings, drawings, and photographs that are used to illustrate either how Americans have used chairs in their homes and public buildings, or that help to document a type of chair to a specific time and place. While this idea is not novel, of course, the number of previously unpublished examples of source material and their pertinency to surviving examples of seating furniture is a most welcome addition to the literature about American chairs.

A somewhat morbid aspect of the collecting of furniture used to be known as the "waiting game." It was simply a matter of "waiting" until a collector, prominent or otherwise, died and then purchasing the desired object at public or private sale. Further, it is no secret that doctors and morticians were, and still are, among the best sources for finding antiques or "collectibles." Many of the examples pictured in Wallace Nutting's book, however, literally had disappeared into museum collections and no longer formed part of the "waiting game." It is instructive to compare the number of chairs credited to private collections illustrated in *Furniture Treasury* and those now shown by this book to be in public museums. Equally instructive is the discovery that few public institutions are collecting chair forms made in the mid-nineteenth century or later. Private individuals, however, are purchasing not only types of seating furniture manufactured in the mid- and later-nineteenth century, but many are collecting "classic" examples of chairs designed and produced in the twentieth century. This book makes apparent, once again, that museums sometimes place a stamp of approval on art only after courageous and farsighted individuals have shown the way and preserved examples that might otherwise have been destroyed.

It is a strength of this book, therefore, that the "bodies" are disinterred. The author's selection of examples from the widest possible number of museum and private collections should make it possible for interested parties easily to make comparisons of their own chairs to actual examples; and despite obvious views about the importance of this book, there is no substitute for seeing and examining an actual chair. Some criticism might be forthcoming about the author's selection of slightly more than one fifth of the illustrations from the collections of the Henry Ford Museum. In this writer's opinion, however, that is also a virtue of Robert Bishop's survey. The rich and important collections of the Henry Ford Museum are not as well known as they deserve to be, and it should be of great value to the public to learn of the existence of important chair forms in that collection.

At the beginning of this foreword it was attempted in capsule form to show that mankind has always been fascinated by chairs. One of the important historical values of *Centuries and Styles of the American Chair* is the revelation that while chair designs have not exactly "re-invented the wheel" in each generation, there is a persistent use of materials and shapes that should be fascinating to most readers. This insight is usually lost in our own fragmented and compartmentalized society. To know that designers and hand craftsmen like George Nakashima and Sam Maloof are still producing beautiful chairs is comforting to those of us who would like to feel that wood will never go out of style.

It should not be construed from this slight essay that Robert Bishop has produced a perfect book about chairs. Like the subject matter itself, a "perfect" book about chairs may be as impossible as the production of a "perfect" chair. But I believe that all who are interested in the decorative arts will find that as a panoramic view of the American chair this book sets a standard of excellence that will be difficult, if not impossible, to supersede.

CHARLES F. HUMMEL

Winterthur, Delaware

In this book I have endeavored to illustrate the never-ending progression of stylistic change that altered the appearance of the American chair from about 1640, when its form was basically architectural and derived from an inherited European medieval tradition, through a span of almost three-and-a-half centuries to the present, when man can sit in a scientifically engineered molded-plastic chair aboard a space ship bound for the moon.

This parade of successive styles reflects more than just fancy or whim on the part of the craftsmen who fashioned the furniture. Each chair is representative of the way of life, the social structure, and the related customs of the period in which it was created. This book, which is essentially a chronological history of the American chair, attempts to place that form in the lives and homes of our ancestors.

In the first brave New England settlements of the seventeenth century a desire for physical comfort manifested itself almost as soon as temporary shelters were replaced by permanent dwellings. Heavy oak stools and benches were relegated to a secondary position in the homes of the more affluent. The first chairs—sturdy, architectural, and above all, stately—were outmoded by the forms created during the brief flowering of the Cromwellian and, a bit later, the more enduring and flamboyant William and Mary style. The adoption in America of these foreign fashions, almost as soon as they were popular in England, indicates a strong cultural dependence upon the mother country. This dependence was manifested in the colonists' countless attempts to re-create in this hostile new world a way of life not unlike that left behind. Even so, during the first century of settlement in America, few owned much furniture, and fortunate indeed was the man who could boast of possessing more than one or two chairs.

It was not until the triumph of the curve with the emergence of the Queen Anne style, *circa* 1720, that anything more than a bench or at best a slat-back chair could be hoped for by the common man. By 1725 economic conditions improved sufficiently to enable many more people to acquire the niceties of life. Also, joiners and carpenters, now greatly increased in numbers through immigration, were able to devote more of their time to furniture making, since survival and shelter were no longer the prime motivating forces in the colonists' lives. Specialization in woodworking began to emerge, replacing the

INTRODUCTION

1. Above: Frontispiece from *The Whole Psalms in Foure Partes* by John Day. England. 1563. During the sixteenth and seventeenth centuries, there were few chairs, and they were reserved for the men of the family, as shown in this illustration of family worship. (The Folger Shakespeare Library)

age-old "jack-of-all-trades" concept, where a joiner was expected to build ships, construct houses, and make furniture. The great influx of immigrant craftsmen brought with them traditions which, through gradual modification, tended to develop into native regional styles.

In the cosmopolitan areas like Boston, Philadelphia, and to an even greater extent, Williamsburg and other cities in the South, furniture designs closely mirrored those of London. In the back country of the New World less experienced, though often highly gifted, chairmakers borrowed ideas from the city craftsmen and adapted the forms to satisfy the tastes and needs of a more rural society. Throughout the eighteenth century London continued its cultural leadership in matters of furniture, household accessories, and dress. Even the German settlers in Pennsylvania and the Swedish who settled in the Delaware Valley were susceptible to English influences.

In mid-eighteenth-century England a gradual assimilation of the French Rococo resulted in what Thomas Chippendale, an English cabinetmaker and author of *The Gentleman and Cabinet-maker's Director* (1754) called the "Modern" style. His comprehensive furniture manual introduced the currently popular English styles of furniture to craftsmen in America. Here, for the first time, was an extensive collection of drawings and design patterns that could be adapted by most woodworkers. Intricately carved asymmetrical motifs, whimsical elements in the "Chinese taste," the pointed arch and trefoil of the Gothic, and an endless variety of other decorative designs became a new part of the vocabulary of the American chairmaker.

Political conditions changed; economic conditions changed; and American furniture making matured. In 1765 Samuel Morris advised his prominent nephew, Samuel Powel, who was on a trip to London, to refrain from purchasing furnishings there for his newly planned Philadelphia mansion. "Household goods may be had here as cheap and as well made from English patterns. In the humour people are in here [Philadelphia], a man is in danger of becoming invidiously distinguished who buys anything in England which our Tradesmen can furnish. I have heard the joiners here object this against [those] who brought their furniture with them." Mr. Morris's advice mirrored the sentiments of many. An ever-increasing number of newspapers carried a vast assortment of advertisements assuring discriminating customers that American-made goods were comparable in style and quality to European products. The advertisements failed to note, however, that English pattern books were frequently used in the creation of American furniture. They seldom were slavishly copied, but it is easy to establish that our native craftsmen took from these books the elements they felt best suited the taste of their clients, often rearranged them and, with the exercise of personal taste created a distinctly native style—a style that varied as

noticeably from region to region as it did between colony and mother country.

The Rococo style in England, ebbing from fashion in the late 1760's, was slowly replaced by the development of a neoclassical taste that was popular for the next thirty-five years. Robert Adam, master of this neoclassical movement, introduced into English furniture design a new vocabulary of decorative motifs, which included carved pendant husks, urns, draperies, paterae, and sheaves of wheat.

In 1788 George Hepplewhite's pattern book of some three hundred designs was published posthumously by his wife's firm, A. Hepplewhite and Company. *The Cabinet-Maker and Upholsterer's Guide,* twice revised, summarized in visual terms what Adam had accomplished. The heart-back, the shield-back, and the lyreback chair designs in this volume served as models that were endlessly adapted by our ingenious cabinetmakers.

A few years later Thomas Sheraton in his book of designs, *The Cabinet-Maker and Upholsterer's Drawing Book* (1791–1794), made extensive use of chairs with square backs. This publication, like Hepplewhite's *Guide,* was reissued several times, and it too was immensely influential in the Colonies.

Throughout the entire Colonial period Americans looked to England for inspiration in matters of taste; however, toward the end of the eighteenth century, Paris, the first to adapt a kind of pure classical design inspired by the archaeological study of ancient Egypt, Greece, and Rome, replaced London as dictator of European and American taste. American interest in the new style, almost manic at times, manifested itself in many different ways—social attitudes, manner of dress, architecture, but above all, the furniture that fashionables chose to live with.

Parisian furniture design, closely associated with the antique, greatly influenced American furniture makers. During the opening years of the nineteenth century Thomas Seymour of Boston crafted settees and chairs with saber legs—an element of the new fashion. Duncan Phyfe, in his New York City salesrooms, offered seating pieces with motifs from the new Classical style grafted onto the older Sheraton style. Phyfe's furniture of this period, somewhat advanced and yet typical of pieces made a few years later along the entire Eastern seaboard, leaned heavily upon the French for inspiration. Charles-Honoré Lannuier, a French emigré, worked in New York City between 1803 and 1819. His furniture, mostly in the French Directoire style, met with great success in a country clamoring for sophistication. The flowering of Classical America far outlived in its architecture the scant twenty-five years of popularity it enjoyed in the decorative arts.

During the 1830's and 1840's, ornately gilded decoration and rich, bold carvings on American Empire furniture were superseded by flat, scrolled surfaces in veneered mahogany and rosewood. This Pillar-and-Scroll style, with its free use of undulating supports, remained in vogue in various forms throughout the nineteenth century. Gradually it was replaced by newer styles that would help create interiors compatible with the prevailing Romantic Spirit—a spirit that reveled in the construction of thirty-room Gothic "cottages" on the Hudson River and elsewhere across the ever expanding country.

John Henry Belter, the New York City furniture maker who mass-produced seating pieces and other forms in the Rococo style during the 1850's, patented his idea for laminating sheets of wood that were then molded and shaped with the aid of steam and finally ornately carved with naturalistic floral and animal motifs. His methods of construction and his designs were infringed upon by many, and furniture of this style, so reminiscent of the French Rococo of a century earlier, all but dominated the American domestic scene. Its lingering popularity, co-existing with the Grecian, the Gothic, and the spool-and-rope-turned elements of Elizabethan Revival furniture, resulted in chairs that often, by current standards, seem very odd. Elements of these totally disparate styles, often united within a suite or even a single piece of furniture, created truly startling effects.

The first international fair held in America was in the newly constructed Crystal Palace at New York City in 1853. Most of the furniture shown there by European manufacturers was constructed in the Renaissance Revival style, distinguished by mammoth proportions and heavily carved in oak and walnut. This style, because it fitted the nineteenth-century predilection for romantic association, was so fully accepted by furniture manufacturers and the buying public that it dominated American furniture design for the next decade. It was not until the Philadelphia Centennial Exposition in 1876 that its popularity waned in favor of the style favored by the English Arts and Crafts movement.

The Philadelphia Centennial was a supreme catalyst for American furniture designers. It sparked an intense interest in the English style originated by Charles Eastlake which, once established, governed domestic furniture production. The Japanese Pavilion, with its display of artistic products, impressed many critics and found favor with the public. A clamor for exotic decorative accessories from the Orient, not unlike the vogue for chinoiserie of the late seventeenth century, caused many manufacturers to incorporate Japanese motifs into the design of their products. Kimbel and Cabus of New York City and, a bit later, Nimura & Sato of Brooklyn seem to have specialized in the manufacture of such Japanese-inspired furniture. For most visitors to the Exposition, however, it was the "Colonial Kitchen," a display graced by ladies dressed in what were thought to be authentic early American

costumes and by period furniture, that was most popular. This installation kindled an intense interest in America's heritage and triggered an extensive Colonial Revival movement that still flourishes today. Colonial-style houses, modest and otherwise, sprang up everywhere. Colonial furniture, many times exact reproductions, more often, however, vague approximations of the originals, soon flooded the market. People rushed to the attic to resurrect great-grandma's favorite rocking chair. The age of American furniture collecting began.

At the St. Louis Exposition of 1904, a remarkable suite of Turkish frame furniture, constructed with the innovational coil spring, was shown. Other displays boasted the elegant Louis XV style made by both European and American manufacturers. The Art Nouveau Room of the French Pavilion also attracted much attention. While very little Art Nouveau furniture was made in America, approximate versions of this French style were manufactured by Karpen Brothers of Chicago and New York.

Gustav Stickley, Elbert Hubbard, and Will Bradley, in their violent rejection of all revivalist styles, crafted furniture known as Mission. These square-sectioned, square-framed, angular pieces, adapted by the young Frank Lloyd Wright and used in his Robie House in Chicago, represent the beginning of the International style of furniture design.

In the modern period architects and chair manufacturers enjoyed new freedom of design made possible by ever-improving manufacturing methods and the introduction of new materials. Probably the single most famous chair of the twentieth century—the Barcelona chair—was designed by Mies Van Der Rohe to furnish the German Pavilion he designed for the Barcelona International Exhibition of 1929. The International School of Architects in many ways became the International School of Furniture Designers, working first with steel rods and aluminum tubes, then with molded and inflatable plastics and other synthetic materials. Modern interpretations of ancient Grecian seating pieces by T. H. Robsjohn-Gibbings, Oriental-inspired chairs designed by Hans Wegner and George Nakashima, and twentieth-century Windsor chairs hand-crafted by Sam Maloof, are both totally innovational in concept and traditional in form.

Future chair design is in many ways predictable. Comfort will continue to be a prime consideration. Sculptural form and visual appeal will continue to preoccupy furniture designers and, certainly, the traditionalists who are satisfied only with reproductions of "early American" will continue to thrive. What of the twenty-first century? Perhaps the last illustration in this book prophesies the forms to come.

ROBERT BISHOP

CHAPTER 1

THE EARLIEST SETTLERS
1640-1700

Wainscot Chairs

In seventeenth-century Colonial homes, there were few chairs. People sat on joint stools and ate with rude implements from what was called a "long jointed table." Wainscot chairs, known as "great chairs," were seats of authority and the exclusive privilege of the rich and of high-ranking political and religious leaders. These majestic oak forms, essentially of Renaissance design, were named from the Dutch word, *wagonschot*, a fine grade of oak board. The American wainscot chair, like its English prototype made most frequently between 1570 and 1670, was architectural in concept. Elaborately carved, monumental examples, such as those associated with the name of the famed seventeenth-century craftsman, Thomas Dennis (1638–1701), contrast sharply with more modest forms, figures 3 and 4. The richly carved back and the front rail of figure 2 are more typical of English than American work of the period. This is not surprising since Dennis was born in England and received his training as a "joyner" and carver there, prior to his arrival in Portsmouth, New Hampshire, in 1663. In 1668, he is known to have worked at Ipswich, Massachusetts, where wainscot chairs, Bible boxes, chests, and a tape loom, all crisply carved with guilloche, foliated S-scrolls, arcading palmate panels, and strapwork, have descended in the Dennis family.

2. Left: Wainscot armchair. Attributed to Thomas Dennis. Ipswich, Massachusetts. 1660–1675. Oak. H. 48½", W. 25½", D. 15¼". This chair was left by Dennis to his son John, in whose inventory it and a similar chair were listed as "2 wooden Great Chairs carved @ 2/0." The three urn finials are restorations thought to date from the late eighteenth or early nineteenth century. (Bowdoin College Museum of Art)

3. Above: Wainscot armchair. Probably made by Robert Rhea. New Jersey. 1695. Oak. H. 42½", W. 25¾", D. 17½". (Monmouth County Historical Association)

4, 4a. Above: Wainscot armchair. Attributed
to Thomas Dennis. Ipswich. 1690–1700.
Oak. H. 36¼″. Breadth of seat at back 18¾″.
The entire base of this chair below the tapered
square column has been restored. On such an
important piece, accurate restoration is not
only acceptable, but desirable. (Museum of
Fine Arts, Boston)

American wainscot chairs tend to date later than those of English origin. Figure 3, dated 1695 and initialed "R/RI" for Robert and Janet Rhea of Freehold, New Jersey, has a very wide crest like those seen on sixteenth-century English wainscot chairs. The use of spool-turned stretchers is reminiscent of an earlier style, too. Rhea, a Scots Quaker, came to his American "plantation" in 1685. A carpenter and "joyner," he probably made this chair for use in his new home. The boldly carved thistle at the bottom of the panel and the conventionalized tulip-and-rose motif on the crest rail are decorations often found on early Scots furniture.

An English wainscot chair with squared baluster front posts and a double-paneled back topped with a deeply carved crest, brought to America by the Dennis family, is preserved in the collections of the Danvers, Massachusetts, Historical Society. It appears to have served as the prototype for a rare group of chairs, all similar,

5. Above: Wainscot armchair. New England. 1640–1680. Oak. H. 43″, Seat height 18″, D. 14¾″. This wainscot chair was constructed with raised fielded panels in the back. (Yale University Art Gallery)

6. Near right: Wainscot armchair. Possibly made by Kenelm Winslow. Massachusetts. Ca. 1635. Oak. H. 42″, W. 24″, D. 15½″. (Pilgrim Hall)

7. Far right: Wainscot armchair. Connecticut. 1640–1660. Oak. H. 39″, W. 23¼″, D. 19¼″. (Wadsworth Atheneum)

but with variations in the carving, and with a history of ownership common to the Ipswich, Essex County, Massachusetts, area. Figure 4 and the detail, 4a, are from this unusual group and are carved in a manner far superior to most American wainscot chairs. The guilloche motif of intertwined circles enclosing beautifully carved rosettes and the arcaded crest rail are distinctive on so simple a piece. Like all American chairs made in this style, the upper ends of the back rails are tenoned into the enclosing architrave-like crest rail. The feet, restored long ago, are a substitute for the original square-shaped feet seen on the other related examples. Most of these chairs were at one time considered the work of Dennis; however, scholars now attribute some of them to another Ipswich "joyner," William Searle.

John Winthrop, Jr., helped establish the settlement now known as Saybrook, Connecticut. Yale University, with Abraham Pierson as its first rector, was originally located in this infant community. Pierson used the two-paneled-back wainscot chair, figure 5, possibly made by Charles Gillam of Saybrook. Wainscot chairs were always considered important pieces of furniture. It is, therefore, not surprising to discover the names of eminent seventeenth-century Americans often associated with surviving examples. "Joyner" Kenelm Winslow, of Marshfield, Massachusetts, probably made the commanding chair, figure 6, for his more famous brother, Governor Edward Winslow. Bold turnings and sensitive design distinguish this otherwise simple piece.

Originally less satisfying in form, but perhaps even more interesting as a social document, is the unique oak chair, figure 7, once owned by Thomas Robinson of Hartford, who moved to Guilford in 1639. Probably at a somewhat later date, a tape loom was cut into the back panel, a curious arrangement, since, if it were being used for weaving purposes, it would be unusable as a chair. The seat is a later replacement; however, the piece should not be discredited, since its distinctive turnings indicate a very early date of construction.

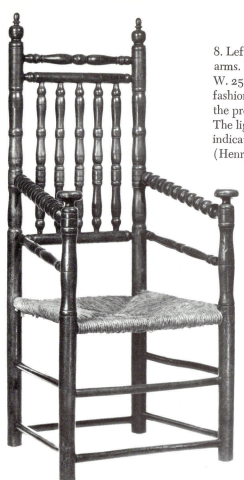

8. Left: Carver armchair with raking spool-turned arms. New England. 1650–1675. Maple. H. 53½″, W. 25″, D. 19″. Turners, the men responsible for fashioning turned chairs, were enthusiastic about the properties of maple and much preferred it to oak. The lightness of the front stretchers on this chair indicates that they have probably been replaced. (Henry Ford Museum)

10. Right: Brewster armchair. Massachusetts. 1650–1660. Hickory, ash. H. 44¾″, W. 32½″, D. 15¾″. The solid wood seat on this chair is made more comfortable through the use of a squab or cushion. This Brewster chair is perhaps the finest example extant. (The Metropolitan Museum of Art)

Brewster,

Carver, and

9. Left: Carver armchair with woven splint seat. New England. Ca. 1650. Maple. H. 41¾″, W. 23¼″, D. 20¾″. The height of many early chairs has been reduced through the loss of a portion of their feet or legs. The stretchers of this chair originally would not have been so close to the floor. (Henry Ford Museum)

11. Right: Brewster armchair. Massachusetts. 1640–1660. Oak. H. 46¼″, W. 24⅞″, D. 18½″. The massive posts and vigorously turned spindles lend a robust air to this distinctive seating piece. The gaps created by two missing spindles in the lower bank under the seat provide an ideal place for the sitter to prop his heels. (Henry Ford Museum)

Turned

Chairs

Brewster, Carver, and other turned chairs were popular throughout the seventeenth century. Such turned pieces were fashioned on a great wheel, or lathe, which was cranked by an apprentice generally called a "turn-wheel." Figure 11 is similar to an example that once belonged to Elder William Brewster (1567–1644) and is now in Pilgrim Hall, Plymouth, Massachusetts. During the nineteenth century, pieces constructed in this form came to be known as "Brewster" chairs. They have banks of turnings in the back and below the arms and seat rails. Brewster, "a very cheerful spirit," was somewhat of a dandy. His dashing wardrobe included a "violet colored cloth coat, black silk stockings, red and white caps, a blue suit and a green waistcoat." "Carver" chairs, named for John Carver (died 1621), first Governor of Plymouth Colony, are generally simpler than Brewster types. The decorative turnings are confined to positions above the seat.

12. Left: Carver armchair. Probably from Connecticut. 1655–1670. Ash. H. 44″, W. 18⅜″, D. 12⅜″. This unusual chair retains part of an old rush seat. (New Haven Colony Historical Society)

The turned chairs, figures 14, 15, and 16, relate to Brewster chairs in that they have turned spindles below the seat.

The example shown in figure 12 descended from Edith Day (1648–1688), one of the first members of the New Haven Colony. Its purpose is puzzling, since the seat is too deep to accommodate a child and yet too narrow for an adult. Perhaps it was intended to be used by an invalid or someone with a physical deformity.

14. Right: Brewster armchair. New England. 1640–1660. Oak. H. 37¾", W. 24", D. 18¾". The construction of this chair is peculiar, since the stretchers, seat supports, and arms extend through the front and rear posts, and the two turned upper members of the back do not extend through the back posts. Lozenge-shaped patches are evident in the middle of the back posts. (Henry Ford Museum)

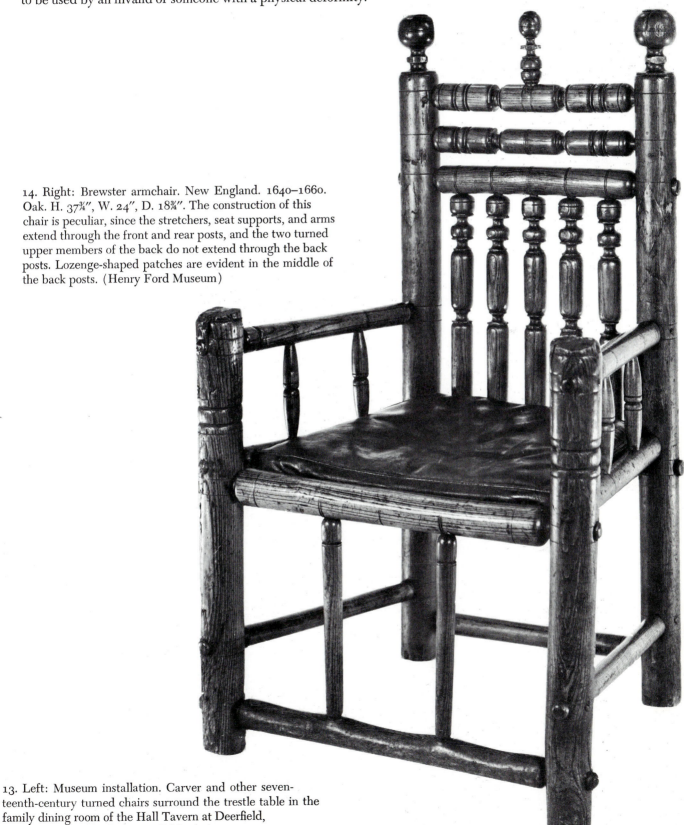

13. Left: Museum installation. Carver and other seventeenth-century turned chairs surround the trestle table in the family dining room of the Hall Tavern at Deerfield, Massachusetts. (Historic Deerfield, Inc.)

15. Left: Brewster armchair, originally owned by the Stryker family of New York. New York. Late seventeenth century. Ash. H. 39½″, W. 24″, D. 17″. The rush is a replacement for an earlier wooden seat. (The Metropolitan Museum of Art)

16. Right: Brewster armchair. Possibly Connecticut. Late seventeenth century. Ash, hickory. H. 41½″, W. 23″, D. 16½″. This turned chair, with a built-in slanting back, has immense front posts which indicate a seventeenth-century date of construction. It retains traces of the original red stain. This example, and figure 15, are the only two known American chairs of this type. (The Connecticut Historical Society)

17. Above: Carver armchair. Virginia. Ca. 1720. Ash arms and legs, oak rails, and juniper spindles. H. 38¾″, W. 20″, D. 17½″. This chair, with a history of early ownership in Suffolk, Virginia, was constructed with an unusual variety of spindles. (The Colonial Williamsburg Foundation)

18. Above: Cromwellian side chair. New England. 1650–1690. Maple, red oak. H. 35³/₁₆″, W. 18⅜″, D. 17⅜″. The English, woolen, Turkey-work upholstery, ca. 1675, is held in place with brass-headed tacks. Turkey-work is needlework embroidery that imitates the design of Turkish carpets. (The Henry Francis du Pont Winterthur Museum)

19. Above: Cromwellian settee. American? 1670–1680. Maple.
H. 46½″, D. 21″, L. 60″. This ball-turned piece is covered
with Turkey work brought from Normandy around 1686 by
Huguenot immigrants. (Essex Institute)

Cromwellian Chairs

During the mid-1600's in England, joint stools were replaced at the dining table in fashionable homes by "back stools," or padded stools with an attached padded back. This new-style seating furniture was soon adopted for use in the colonies where chair seats and backs were stuffed with marsh grass and covered with leather or Turkey work. Maple was the wood most often used in the construction of Colonial Cromwellian chairs, so-called because of their introduction during the English Commonwealth under Sir Oliver Cromwell. The side chair, figure 21, from Crosswick's Creek, now called White Horse, New Jersey, displays elaborate spiral turnings. The recessed seat would have been fitted with a padded cushion, or squab, possibly made by a female member of the Pearson family, the original owners of the piece. Inventories indicate that such chairs were made throughout the last half of the seventeenth century in America. These more comfortable types of seating were enjoyed by the wealthy and fashionable colonists, but were seldom owned by the man of more modest means.

Existing records indicate that in 1691 John Bowles's "Parlour" at Roxbury, Massachusetts, contained "13 Leather chairs," "6 Turkey work chaires" and "4 Stools with: Needle work covers" in addition to several other pieces of furniture. The chairs, following the European custom, were probably placed in rows against the walls.

20. Above: Cromwellian side chair. New England. 1680–1690. Maple, oak. H. 33¼″, W. 18½″, D. 18½″. This leather-upholstered side chair retains traces of the original red paint. (Henry Ford Museum)

21. Right: Cromwellian side chair. New Jersey. Late seventeenth century. Walnut. H. 39⅛″, W. 18⅞″. English chairs similar to this example were often called farthingale chairs because they were constructed with a broad seat to accommodate a lady wearing a farthingale, a series of hoops extending horizontally from the waist. (Philadelphia Museum of Art)

22. Far left, top: Pilgrim turned stool. Suffield, Connecticut. 1700–1735. Maple, ash, oak. H. 10¾", W. 14", D. 13". This piece, with sausage-turned stretchers, descended in the Sikes family. (Mrs. Henry M. Clark)

23. Near left, top: Pilgrim turned stool. Connecticut. 1640–1680. Oak with pine top. H. 14½", W. 21⅛", D. 14½". The "breadboard" top on this stool, found near Guilford, is a replacement. (Wadsworth Atheneum)

24. Left, bottom: Museum installation. The "hall" of a 1684 Essex, Massachusetts, home. This room is furnished in a manner typical of the period, with a long, rude, "joyned" form (bench) before a center dining table. Stools similar to those illustrated on these pages were common in such a dwelling. Their legs, raked for strength, were turned on a lathe. One-board tops were secured to the frame with nails or pegs. After being used for dining, stools were tucked under the table to provide additional space in such crowded dwellings. (Winterthur Museum)

25. Below: Pilgrim turned stool. Connecticut, probably Cheshire. 1700–1735. Pine, maple. H. 20". W. 32", D. 11½". Because of its size, this piece could be used either as a stool or a small table. (Mrs. Henry M. Clark)

Turned Stools

33

26. Left: Pilgrim chair-table. New England. 1675–1700. White oak with pine top. Height of seat: 19½". The top of this piece is a restoration and the original wood pintle hinges are missing. Ancient records from Plymouth, Massachusetts, indicate that in 1633 Will Wright owned "a little chaire table." (The Metropolitan Museum of Art)

27. Right; 27a. Center: Pilgrim chair-table. Massachusetts. 1650–1680. Oak, pine. Height, opened: 56", Diameter of top: 46½". This ancient piece is one of the most aesthetically satisfying and complete examples of this form to have been passed down through the centuries. The drawer under the seat is of the side-runner construction, and the front board is decorated with semicircular carvings. Originally, the chair would have had feet below the stretchers, but they have worn away. (Henry Ford Museum)

Chair-tables

Chair-tables are known to have been used in the American colonies during the 1630's. These space-saving devices were essentially tables that, when not in use for eating purposes, could be converted into chairs by tilting the hinged top backward. This multiple-purpose furniture must have been very popular with the seventeenth-century Pilgrim housewife whose small home provided only limited living space. Many of these chair-tables were fitted originally with a drawer under the seat. Later versions frequently have a bank of drawers extending from the floor to the seat; others are constructed with a storage well topped by a lid which, when closed, can be used for sitting.

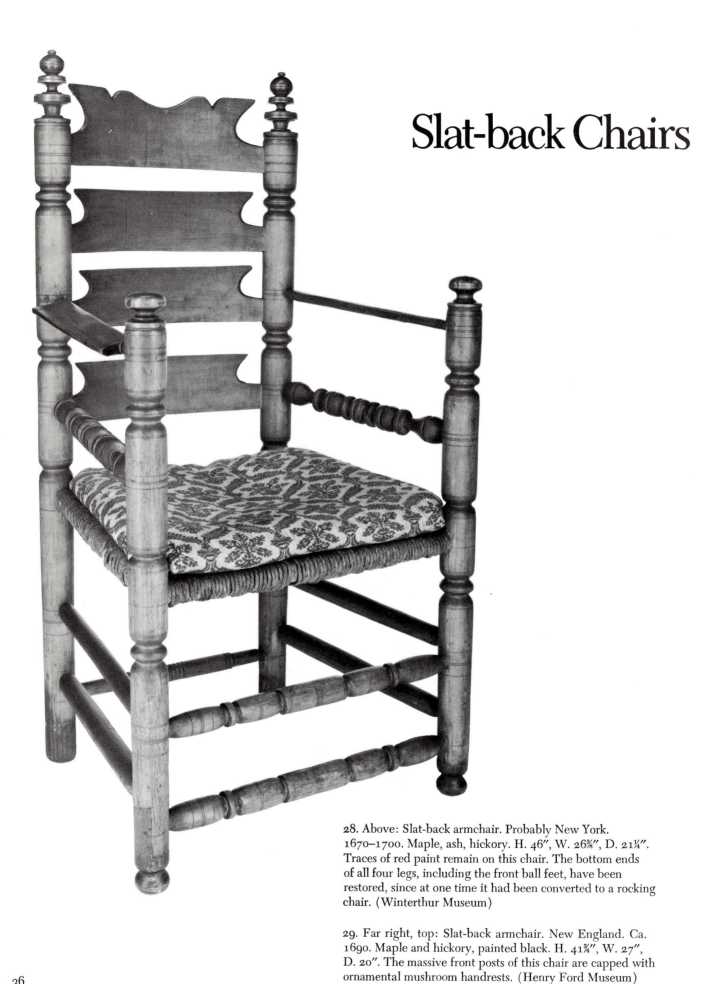

Slat-back Chairs

28. Above: Slat-back armchair. Probably New York. 1670–1700. Maple, ash, hickory. H. 46″, W. 26⅜″, D. 21¼″. Traces of red paint remain on this chair. The bottom ends of all four legs, including the front ball feet, have been restored, since at one time it had been converted to a rocking chair. (Winterthur Museum)

29. Far right, top: Slat-back armchair. New England. Ca. 1690. Maple and hickory, painted black. H. 41¾″, W. 27″, D. 20″. The massive front posts of this chair are capped with ornamental mushroom handrests. (Henry Ford Museum)

The bold handsome form of the winged-slat-back chair, figure 28, is similar to Flemish examples. The massive size of both the turned front and back maple posts indicates a date within the seventeenth century. The use of a turned connecting member under a flat flaring arm is frequent in chairs dating from 1670–1700. The construction mirrors, almost exactly, a chair in the collection of Strangers' Hall, Norwich, England. That example is made of ash and has a board seat replacing the original woven rush.

The sloping arms of the late seventeenth-century New England slat-back armchair, figure 29, are, like the posts and stretchers, simply turned. Constructed from maple and hickory and painted black, the chair has a splint seat. The monumental simplicity of this piece is impressive. The worn side of the lower front stretchers has been turned under. This was a common practice when chairs were repaired and strengthened. More fully developed, in terms of design, is figure 30. The turning of the posts on this chair is more carefully executed, and the back slats are cut in a cyma-curved design.

Misty-eyed romantics, when speaking of Colonial America, often envision an elderly mother-figure sitting in an ancient chair, rocking gently. The fact is, chairs with rockers did not become popular until the opening years of the nineteenth century. Earlier examples are known, but they are infrequent. One such piece is a slat-back armchair illustrated by Luke Vincent Lockwood in his book, *Colonial Furniture in America*. The back posts were originally enlarged to receive rockers set into grooves cut into the bottom of the legs. This method of adapting otherwise stationary chairs was practiced during the late eighteenth and early nineteenth centuries. At the close of the eighteenth century, chairmakers were constructing pieces that included rockers as an integral part of the design. On these examples, the legs were extended and doweled into the rocking member, a method of construction still used today.

30. Above: Slat-back armchair. New England. 1660–1690. Maple, ash, oak. H. 43⅜″, W. 24¾″, D. 23″. All four legs of this chair have been pieced at the bottom where rockers were removed. (Winterthur Museum)

31. Left, top: Slat-back armchair. New England. Seventeenth century. Oak, pine. H. 48″, W. 22¾″, D. 16″. The finials on the back posts of this early chair are similar to those seen on Brewster and Carver types. The wooden seat is a replacement for one woven of either rush or splint. (Essex Institute)

32. Left, bottom: Slat-back armchair. New England. Ca. 1680. Oak. H. 41″, W. 19″. This chair retains traces of the original paint and, therefore, is more desirable than it would be if it had been refinished. (Shelburne Museum, Inc.)

33. Above: Slat-back armchair. Southern Massachusetts or New England. 1660–1690. Maple, ash. H. 40″, W. 22½″, D. 19″. The ring turnings on the front posts match those on the back posts. When related in this manner, they create a unified chair design. (The Art Institute of Chicago)

34. Right: Slat-back armchair. New England. Ca. 1700. Maple, ash. H. 48½″, W. 24″, D. 17″. Turnings decreased in size at the close of the seventeenth century as demonstrated by this chair, one of a pair. (Privately owned)

35. Below: Museum installation. This "hall" was constructed with the beams and floor from a house in Wrentham, Massachusetts, dating 1680. The furnishings, almost entirely seventeenth century, include distinctive slat-back armchairs. (The American Museum, Bath, England)

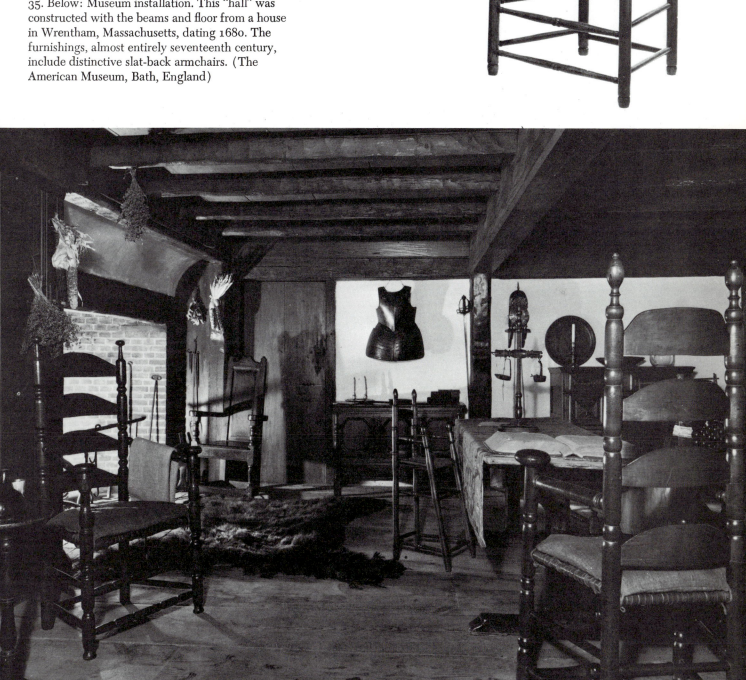

The heavy oak Jacobean-style furniture, so popular under the rule of Oliver Cromwell, was gradually replaced at court and in polite London society when Charles II, restorer of the Stuart monarchy, in 1660 took as his queen the Portuguese princess, Catherine of Braganza. Catherine introduced into the drab English court many innovations and exotic customs. At the close of the Revolution of 1688, the Dutchman, William of Orange, was persuaded to rule with Mary Stuart as his queen. William brought with him countless Dutch and Flemish craftsmen who grafted onto conservative English cabinetmaking a new popular style, which included deeply cut and pierced Flemish scrolls, elaborately carved Spanish feet, and introduced such "India and Chinese curiosities" as the caning of chair seats and backs.

In America, royal officials and other members of the affluent society continued to ape the styles of the parent country. They ordered from abroad clothing and furniture created in the new fashion.

In the Northern colonies, chairmakers borrowed and adapted English designs. Cargo lists indicate that in the South imported furniture was purchased by rich planters eagerly attempting to identify with English society's way. The William and Mary style prevailed over a long period of time. As late as 1734 one Philadelphia shop offered caned chairs "after the best and newest fashion."

36. Left: William and Mary side chair with caned seat and back. New York, or possibly English. Late seventeenth century. Maple, beech. H. 52¾", W. 18", D. 15". Because beech is one of the woods used in the construction of this chair, it is possible that it is of English rather than American origin. In much William and Mary furniture, there is what is considered a "Baroque balance"—the design of the carved front stretcher is identical with the crest rail. (The Metropolitan Museum of Art)

37. Right: A detail from *The Tea-Table*. England. Late seventeenth century. Print. Sold by "Jne. Bowles, Print and Map seller at No. 73 in Cornhill, London." (The British Museum)

CHAPTER 2

FASHIONS FROM ABROAD

1680-1730

William and Mary Chairs

38. Left: William and Mary easy chair. Attributed to John Gaines III. Portsmouth, New Hampshire. 1725–1743. Maple. H. 50½″, W. 29½″, Depth of seat 18″. The easy chair was an innovation during the William and Mary period. This example was constructed with "Spanish feet." (New Hampshire Historical Society)

39. Below: Painting of Captain Johannes Schuyler and his wife, Elizabeth Staats. Attributed to John Watson. American. Early eighteenth century. Oil on canvas. H. 53½″, W. 71″. Mrs. Schuyler sits in an upholstered armchair with her Bible resting on a cushion, a custom frequently practiced in early Colonial America. In 1650 John Osgood bequeathed "to the meeting hous off newbery 18 shillings to Buie a Cushion for the minister to lay his *Book* Vpun." (The New-York Historical Society)

40. Right: William and Mary easy chair. New England. 1700–1725. Maple. H. 51⁹⁄₁₆″, W. 29¾″, D. 34⅛″. The rectangular, obliquely angled back with arched crest and the slightly curved wings indicate an early version of the William and Mary style. (Winterthur Museum)

41. Overleaf: Museum installation. The paneling
from a Connecticut house, ca. 1730, was used for
this room. It is painted green. The oak floor is
painted and stenciled in a geometric pattern similar
to that on a hallway floor in a Hopkinton, New
Hampshire, house. (New Hampshire Historical
Society)

42. Below; 42a. Above: William and Mary daybed. New England, or possibly English. Late seventeenth century or early eighteenth century. Beech. H. 40½″, W. 21½″, L. 60″. "India"-style daybeds with caned backs and seats were usually fitted with a cushion for added comfort. This example, long considered to be of domestic origin, is possibly a "naturalized American," since beech is the predominant wood. (The Metropolitan Museum of Art)

43. Far right: William and Mary "Boston" side chair. Massachusetts. Ca. 1700. Maple. H. 42⅛″, W. 17⅞″, D. 17″. This "spoon-back" Boston chair has square outside stretchers. The ball feet are restorations and the leather upholstery is modern. (Henry Ford Museum)

Chief Justice Samuel Sewall of Massachusetts sent to England for furniture for his daughter Judith in 1719. Among the pieces ordered were "A Duzen of good black Walnut chairs, fine Cane, with a Couch." The couch, like the easy chair, was a concession to comfort developed during this period. These daybeds were designed for sitting during the day and were equipped with cushions and matching pillows to be used against the canted back. Their crest rails and scrolled stretchers were frequently constructed to match chairs intended for use in the same room. Often, the backs on these elaborate daybeds were adjustable and could be lowered with a chain or ratchet.

"Spoon-back" chairs, first made in and around Boston, and called "Boston chairs," found their way to numerous ports of call frequented by ships from that New England seaport. These pieces with S-shaped backs were often painted and upholstered with leather which was more durable and less expensive than cane.

44. Left: William and Mary armchair. American, probably Hudson River Valley. 1690–1700. Maple with old black paint. H. 47½″, W. 25¼″, D. 27″. An elaborately carved stretcher and crest decorate this red moreen upholstered armchair which descended in the Van Cortlandt family of New York. (Sleepy Hollow Restorations)

45. Above: Detail from a painting by James Eights (1798–1882) of the *Northwest and Northeast corners of State and North Pearl Streets, Albany, New York, 1814.* Watercolor on paper. H. 11³⁄₁₆″, W. 15⅜″. This painting illustrates Dutch architecture in seventeenth-century Colonial America. The house of Domine Schaets (foreground) was erected in 1657. The watercolor is signed on the reverse, "Drawn by Jas Eights in 1849 from original sketches made by himself." (Albany Institute of History and Art)

46. Right: Portrait of Helena Sleight (1739–1819), probably from Kingston, New York. Painted by John Vanderlyn or John Vanderlyn II after an original painting by Pieter or Nicholas Vanderlyn. American. Ca. 1856. Oil on canvas. H. 44″, W. 56″. This portrait shows Miss Sleight standing on a geometric-patterned floor in front of a flag or rush-seated chair. Note the wicker basket on the table. Inventories of the seventeenth century often record wicker chairs. The appraisers of the Estate of Captain George Corwin, Salem, Massachusetts (died 1684), prized his "old Wicker Chaire." (Museum of the City of New York)

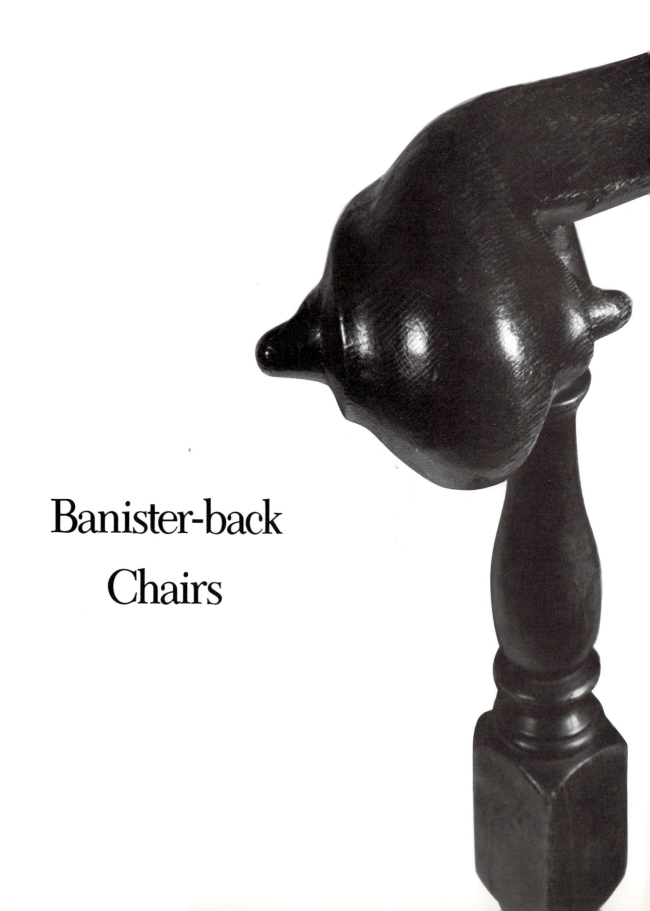

Banister-back
Chairs

47, 47a. Banister-back armchair. New England. Ca. 1700. Maple, oak, ash. H. 48″, W. 30½″, D. 22″. Carved ram's-horn terminals frequently appear on late seventeenth- and early eighteenth-century armchairs. Spanish feet, a common feature in the William and Mary period, were used on this chair. (The Metropolitan Museum of Art)

Banister-back chairs were so named because split banisters (more accurately, *balusters*) were used in the construction of the back. These were made by gluing together two blocks of wood, turning them on a lathe, and then separating the blocks. The banisters generally were mounted with the flat part facing the sitter. In some unusual examples, the rounded portion faces front, and not even a back pad makes them comfortable for the sitter. Banister-back chairs appear to be a simplification of the earlier, tall cane-back chairs, but they were actually produced by a different kind of craftsman.

48. Above: House interior. The decorated ball-footed William and Mary chest is flanked by side chairs which have flat, reeded banisters. (Privately owned)

Joiners generally were responsible for the creation of cane-backs. Banister-backs were produced in the shops of wood turners. Many times the crests of these pieces, pierced by carving, are identical to those found on the tall-back chairs; however, rare indeed is a banister-back with a cane seat; generally rush was used. Banister-backs were usually constructed of maple, with secondary woods of ash, oak, hickory, and pine, and they were painted a dark color. The most prized armchairs have ram's-horn arms like those on figure 47.

It is difficult to associate banister-back chairs with specific craftsmen. In most instances it is even impossible to establish the geographic location of their manufacture. Figure 49, with its small stylish feet and unique crest with molded edge and two carved rosettes topped by an acorn finial, probably is from Connecticut. Made of maple and painted black, it is one of a set of four.

Another kind of banister, and, technically speaking, not a banister-back at all, is that constructed with straight, reeded, vertical slats. The crest of the example on the left of the chest in figure 48 sits on the rear rails and banisters, while that on the right is framed between the rear stiles. The chest of drawers and small box are from a group of furniture made in the Guilford–Saybrook, Connecticut, area.

49. Right: Banister-back side chair, one of a set of four. New England. Ca. 1690. Curly maple, painted black. H. 46½″, W. 18″, D. 18″. Securing cushions with tasseled cords was a practice of the late seventeenth and early eighteenth centuries. This distinctive chair originally had a rush seat. During the late nineteenth century, it was fitted with wooden seat rails to hold a slip-seat. (Henry Ford Museum)

Banister-back chairs were constructed over a span of many years. The elaborate crests and turned stretchers of early examples were simplified in later adaptations. Most desirable are the chairs with banisters that are bold in design, like those shown in figures 50, 51, 52, and 53. The relief-carved crest and the outside stretchers under the seat of the massive maple armchair, figure 50, indicate a construction date before the close of the seventeenth century. Figure 51, with its turned, sloping arms, front posts topped with mushroom finials, plain-shaped crest, and sausage-turned front stretcher, would have been made just a few years later. The pierced crest of figure 52, with its cornucopia-like openings at the sides

50. Above, left: Banister-back armchair. New England. Ca. 1690. Curly maple, painted black. H. 55½", W. 26¾", D. 25". The distinctive crest rail of this robust chair is elaborately scroll carved. Like figure 49, the seat of this chair was altered during the late nineteenth or early twentieth century, and the rush seat was replaced by a slip-seat. (Henry Ford Museum)

51. Above, right: Banister-back armchair. New England. Ca. 1700. Maple, painted brown. H. 48¼", W. 26⅛", D. 17¼". The sloping arms and the sausage-turned front stretcher are typical seventeenth-century features. The chair probably was originally somewhat taller and had a second front stretcher, and the front legs perhaps terminated in ball feet. (Henry Ford Museum)

and the triple tier of spirals in the center, seems to reach back to the earlier English cane-backs for its inspiration. The ring, spool, and disc-turned front stretcher connects the block-and-flattened-ball-turned front legs which terminate in Spanish feet. The turning of the banisters on this piece is unusually intricate. The bulbous-turned front stretcher of figure 53, the baluster-turned side stretchers, and the turned-vase stretcher in the rear add distinction and variety to this crown-crested example. This chair has an additional unusual feature—the mid stretcher is of the same design as the front stretcher. Painted black, it is fitted with a blue-and-white tasseled cushion, typical of the period.

52. Above, left: Banister-back armchair. New England. Ca. 1710. Maple, hickory, and oak, painted black. H. 44⅝″, W. 26¾″, D. 32½″. The crest rail of this banister-back chair is elaborately carved and pierced. The front stretcher, though surprisingly slender, is original. (Henry Ford Museum)

53. Above, right: Banister-back armchair. New York. 1700–1720. Maple and hickory, painted black. H. 49⅞″, W. 22″, D. 16½″. The massive vase-and-ring-turned front and medial stretchers are typical of those found in the Hudson River Valley area. This chair, unlike the others shown on these pages, has five banisters. (Museum of the City of New York)

In the early years of the New England Pilgrim settlements, colonists, ill-prepared to brave harsh winters, spent most of their time, when not in pursuit of fuel or food, huddled about the hearth. Settles, or benches with backs and sometimes hoods, shielded these brave folk from piercing drafts. Settles were occasionally constructed with a bed under the seat to be folded out for sleeping. Elder William Brewster owned two such devices. In America, settles never ceased to be fashionable. At the close of the nineteenth century, built-in inglenooks, or benches, created from the designs of such distinguished Americans as Will H. Bradley, Fra Elbert Hubbard, Gustav Stickley, and Frank Lloyd Wright, were used to fulfill commissions from their affluent patrons. Because settles were made over such a long time-span, they are often difficult to date. Early examples sometimes have turned arm supports, legs, and stretchers of maple or walnut, and are occasionally covered with leather or fabric. Others are constructed of pine and have backs which are built to meet the floor. This method of construction afforded more protection for the sitter. The use of raised panels in figure 55 indicates a date in the second quarter of the eighteenth century.

54. Far left: Settle with hood. Probably New England. Late seventeenth or early eighteenth century. Pine, painted dark red. H. 63½", W. 49", D. 15½". (The Metropolitan Museum of Art)

55. Left: Settle with hood, fielded panels, and lobed armrests. Probably New England. Ca. 1740. Pine. H. 59", W. 84½", D. 22¼". (The Metropolitan Museum of Art)

56. Below: William and Mary settle. Pennsylvania. Ca. 1700. Walnut, with leather upholstery. H. 54", D. 22½", L. 72". (The Metropolitan Museum of Art)

Settles

CHAPTER 3

THE QUEEN ANNE STYLE 1720-1755

Introduction

57. Left: Portrait of Princess Anne before her ascent to the English throne in 1702. Dimensions unavailable. (Current whereabouts unknown)

58. Right: Queen Anne Speaker's Chair. Virginia. Ca. 1753. Walnut, tulipwood, pine. H. 97½″, W. 39⁵⁄₁₆″, D. 26⅜″. A chair, described in a requisition dated 1703 as a "large Armed Chair for the Speaker to sit in, and a cushion stuft with hair Suitable to it," was destined for the Hall at the House of Burgesses. This chair probably replaced the original. (The Colonial Williamsburg Foundation)

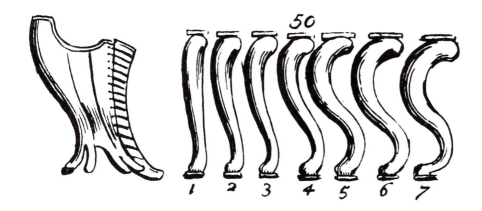

50

1 2 3 4 5 6 7

William and Mary ruled between the years 1689 and 1702. The French Huguenot, Daniel Marot, architect and interior designer, entered William III's service ca. 1685. While working in London in 1702, he published his first collection of furniture designs. A second enlarged edition, published in 1712, introduced design concepts often associated with the Queen Anne style—chairs with cabriole front legs united to stump rear legs by stretchers, and with curvilinear outlines of the back rails enclosing solid central splats.

Princess Anne ascended to the throne in 1702. During her reign, trade with China through the East India Company probably brought to the English market "bended-back" chairs with yoke-shaped top rails. Around 1710, another motif, originating from the same source of inspiration, caught the fancy of Londoners. The cabriole leg with claw-and-ball foot was adapted from Oriental carvings of a dragon's claw grasping a pearl. At first only modestly popular, this form ultimately dominated not only chair construction, but also all furniture-making. Marot's innovative concepts achieved popularity in London toward the end of Queen Anne's twelve-year reign. Only slightly later, the fashion-conscious Colonials demanded furniture in the new style. It was not, however, until about 1720 that these new design elements were familiar enough to be used extensively or with any great skill by American craftsmen. In 1742, the English author and artist, William Hogarth, published *The Analysis of Beauty*. In it, he strongly stated what had essentially become an accomplished fact in furniture-making in Colonial America—that the curved or cabriole leg (so named by nineteenth-century Victorians) had replaced the straight angular designs of the seventeenth century.

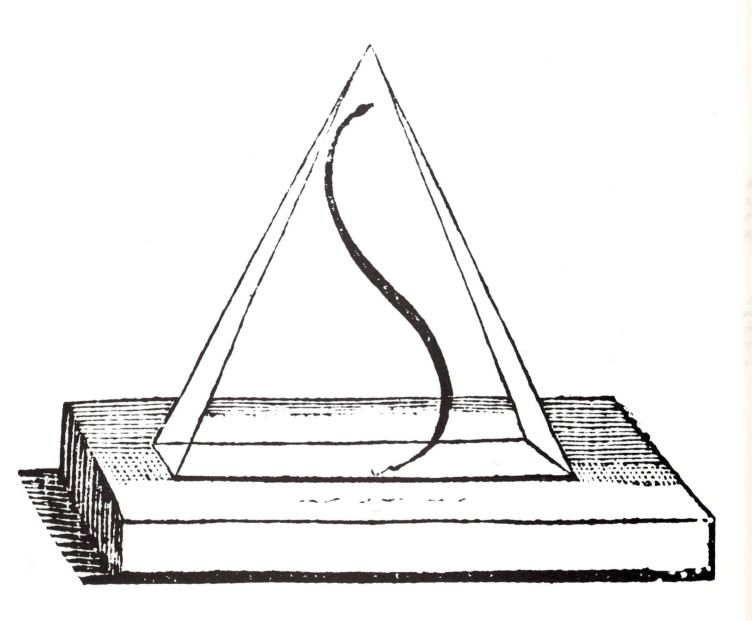

59. Far left; 59a. Above: Line engravings used as illustrations on the title page of William Hogarth's 1742 publication, *The Analysis of Beauty*. Hogarth satirized then-popular fashions and likened a woman's stays to the "line of beauty." (The New York Public Library)

Regional Varieties

60. Above; 60a. Right: Queen Anne side chair. Attributed to an unidentified member of the Southmayd family. Middletown, Connecticut. 1725–1740. Maple, painted black. H. 43¾″, W. 21½″, D. 17″. This and related chairs retain their original embroidered seat covers with stylized flora in shades of rose, green, blue, and brown. (The Metropolitan Museum of Art)

Within the years commonly defined as the Queen Anne period, 1720–1755, furniture-making in the population centers such as Boston, Newport, and New York in the North, and Philadelphia, Charleston, and Annapolis in the South, developed in independent ways which produced subtle variations in the construction of chairs. Cabinetmakers and chairmakers, working in proximity, developed a common vocabulary, enabling students of the American decorative arts to determine readily the origin of a piece of furniture. These regional varieties are perhaps most noticeable when seating pieces from New England and Philadelphia are compared. The legs of New England Queen Anne chairs are almost always braced by block-and-turned stretchers, the front and side rails are mortised into the legs, and the use of square or angular slip-seats is frequent, figure 60a. A pad, or cushioned-pad, foot is commonly used. Chairs originating in Philadelphia more closely echo English fashions of the day. The back leg is "stumped," or oval-shaped in cross section. The front legs dowel into the framed seat, figure 61a. The slipper, drake, trifid, stocking, web, and claw-and-ball foot, based upon the Oriental motif of a dragon hold-

61. Left; 61a. Above: Queen Anne side chair, one of a pair. Philadelphia, Pennsylvania. 1740–1750. Mahogany. H. 41⅝″, W. 21″, D. 17″. Philadelphia chairs of the Queen Anne period frequently were embellished with carved volutes on the back splats and crest rail. (The Metropolitan Museum of Art)

ing a pearl, developed at an early date. The front rails of chairs constructed with balloon seats are sometimes embellished with delicately carved shells. The tenons of side rails on Philadelphia chairs extend through the rear stiles and are secured in place by wooden pegs cut square or octagonal, and driven into round holes prepared to receive them. New York chairs of the Queen Anne period are perhaps more English in design than those from any other Colonial American center. The splats, which are broader and more generous, are sometimes enriched by the application of fine veneer. The seat dimensions and seat construction are also more generous than those of chairs made in other centers. Occasionally New York chairs are constructed with pointed-hoof feet. In England, the Queen Anne period is synonymous with "The Age of Walnut." The socially conscious Colonials preferred furniture constructed from this beautiful material, and requested cabinetmakers to copy the patterns most often ordered by the affluent society of the Mother Country. Other woods, however, were used to great advantage. Cherry and maple were often stained or painted. Later in the period, imported mahogany was sometimes favored over walnut for the construction of the more costly examples.

62. Far left; 62a. Left: Portrait of Francis Brinley (1690–1765). Painted by John Smibert (1688–1751). American. Ca. 1731. Oil on canvas. H. 50″, W. 39¼″. The town seen in the background of this portrait is Boston, Massachusetts, almost a century after its founding. (The Metropolitan Museum of Art)

63. Below: Portrait of James Bowdoin (1676–1747). Painted by Joseph Badger (1708–1765). American. Oil on canvas. H. 51⅛″, W. 40″. Bowdoin sits in an upholstered armchair with cabriole back legs. Oftentimes, chairs shown in early portraits were merely artists' props. (The Detroit Institute of Arts)

Port of Boston

John Smibert, the English artist, arrived in America in 1729, and two years later was commissioned by Colonel Francis Brinley, figure 62, to paint his portrait and that of his wife and child. In Smibert's portrait, Brinley sits in a framed armchair with an upholstered back and seat. The rear legs of the chair are shaped in a cabriole form, an English practice seldom used by American cabinetmakers. Of the wealthy upper class, the Brinleys resided in Datchet House at Roxbury, Massachusetts. Splendid indeed was their "Blue Chamber . . . to the right of the large hall . . . forty-four feet in length and 22 in depth." This room was hung with blue damask and further decorated with "a number of prints" and "5 prs. of paint[ings]."

In 1732, the English engraver, George Vertue, wrote about Smibert being "abroad, in Boston, New England." Vertue described the artist as "a good and ingenious man [who] paints and draws handsomely." Smibert accompanied George Berkeley, Dean of Derry and Bishop of Cloyne, on his "romantic design . . . to go to the West Indies, New York, or Bermudas . . . to lay the foundation of a college for all sorts of Literature on Bermudas" and "to Instruct the European and Indian children in the Christian faith and other necessary educations . . ." Evidently Berkeley considered painting one of the "other necessary educations." In the painting of Dean Berkeley and his wife and family, figure 64, the subjects gather at a table covered with a Turkey-work carpet.

64. Overleaf: *The Bermuda Group*. Painted by John Smibert. American. 1739. Oil on canvas. H. 69½″, W. 93″. John Smibert included his self-portrait. The gentleman in the far left foreground sits in a Queen Anne-style side chair. (Yale University Art Gallery)

65

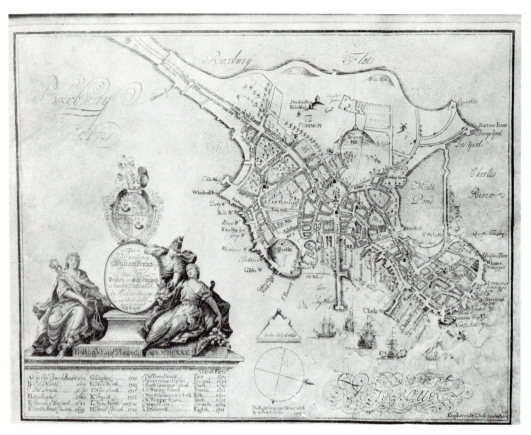

65. Above: Printed map of Boston. Engraved by Thomas
Johnson. Published by William Burgis. 1728. H. 11¾",
W. 15¼". (The Metropolitan Museum of Art)

During the Queen Anne period the bustling town of Boston,
Massachusetts, emerged as the primary seaport in Colonial North
America. Crafty captains sailed New England's tall-masted ships
to ports the world over. "Imbrace the first fair wind and proceed
to Sea and make the best of your way to the windward part of
the Coast of Africa and at your arrival there dispose of your
cargo" instructed one ambitious shipowner. On the return voyage,
slaves were deposited in numerous ports of the South—North
Carolina, South Carolina, Maryland, and Virginia. For the final
run back to New England, holds were filled with barrels of
molasses and sugar for Northern rum distilleries.

There was another kind of commerce. Packet boats made
domestic "runs" between Boston, Salem, Newport, New York,
Philadelphia, and points south. "Clearances of the British Colonies
in America," a manuscript in the collections of the Boston
Atheneum, indicates that in 1744 the sloop *Lydia* left Boston
destined for New York. Part of her cargo constituted "Venture"
furniture. Among other things, she "had board 5 chairs, 8 desks,
1 great chair, 1 cradle, 2 dozen chairs here made." New England
furniture-makers augmented their income considerably by con-
signing lots of furniture such as this to adventuresome captains
who attempted to sell it in foreign ports and invest the money in
cargoes which they hoped to sell in Boston at considerable profit.

66. Above: *A South East View of ye Great Town of Boston in New England in America*. Drawn by William Burgis. Engraved by I. Harris. Published by William Prince. Ca. 1743. H. 27⅜″, W. 56″. This print, which was originally dedicated to Peter Faneuil, Esquire, was sold in Boston. The first state of the print was published in 1723. (Winterthur Museum)

Queen Anne Japanned

Shortly after 1660 the East India Company began importing into England lacquered furniture from Japan and China. Elegant small cabinets fitted with numerous drawers were especially popular and elaborate Baroque gilt or silvered stands were designed by domestic cabinet-makers to display these precious case pieces. A basic ingredient used to achieve the shiny black-and-red finish on these imported treasures was developed from the sap of the lac tree, a species not found either in Europe or in Colonial America. Oriental rulers jealously guarded the export of this precious substance. Consequently, during the late 1680's, London craftsmen, in an effort to satisfy popular demand for the "India" style, shipped furniture to the Orient. Once lacquered, it was returned to England where it was sold for extravagant sums.

The earliest examples of American furniture decorated with japanning were made during the William and Mary period. Tall chests-on-frames, popularly called highboys, looking glasses, and tall-case clocks are the forms most frequently embellished with decorative figures built up of "gesso."

67. Left; 67a. Right: Queen Anne side chair, one of a set of six. Boston, Massachusetts. Ca. 1750. Walnut. H. 39¾", W. 20½", D. 15". This set of chairs was made for the Winthrop–Blanchard family of Boston (the family coat of arms appears on the seat rail). According to tradition, the chairs were shipped to the Orient during the early years of the nineteenth century and decorated there. (The Bayou Bend Collection, The Museum of Fine Arts, Houston)

In urban Colonial cities, "Jappan" furniture commanded large sums of money from wealthy clients who were anxious to duplicate London life. Craftsmen capable of executing this form of decoration were especially well paid, so much so that English decorators, attracted by high wages, emigrated to America. Mr. William Price, in his shop situated "against the West-End of the Town-House" in Boston, offered in the *Boston Gazette* of April 4–11, 1726, "All Sorts of Looking Glasses of the newest Fashion, & Jappan Work, viz. Chest of Drawers, Corner Cupboards, Large & Small Tea Tables, &c. done after the best manner by one late from London." Since japanning was practiced by a relatively small group of artisans, their names can sometimes be associated with specific pieces of furniture. John Pimm of Boston is known to have made a Queen Anne highboy for Commodore Joshua Loring ca. 1740–1750 which was decorated by Thomas Johnson. Gerardus Duyckinck advertised in New York City in 1736 "Looking glasses—frames plain, Japan'd or Flowered." Certainly most Americans practicing this art were aware of the standard guidebook on the subject—*A Treatise of Japaning and Varnishing*, published in 1688 at Oxford, England, by John Stalker and George A. Parker. This book contained twenty-four plates of engravings with stylized animals, birds, insects, human figures, trees, and architecture. In his foreword, Stalker, speaking of his designs in relationship to those of Japanese origin, had this to say—"Perhaps we have helpt them a little in their proportions, where they were lame or defective, and made them more pleasant yet altogether as Antick."

68. Right; 68a. Left: Queen Anne side chair. Boston. Ca. 1750. Walnut. H. 39¾", W. 20½", D. 15". The japanned decoration, though similar to that found on early eighteenth-century pieces, represents a revival of interest in this decorative technique. (Historic Deerfield, Inc.)

Country
Queen Anne

70. Above: *Portrait of a Man in a Brown Coat.*
American. Dated 1755. Oil on canvas. H. 20¼″,
W. 15½″. Colonial portraits very frequently indicate
how furniture was used within the period. The
cabriole front legs on the gentleman's chair appear
to be straightforward, a peculiar arrangement indeed.
(Hirschl & Adler Galleries)

71. Near right: *Portrait of a Woman in a Gold
Gown.* American. Dated 1755. Oil on canvas.
H. 20¼″, W. 15½″. This and figure 70 are from a
group of four mid-eighteenth-century paintings. The
floral festoon that appears to have been painted on the
walls, though unusual, is not without precedent in
an American home of this period. (Hirschl & Adler
Galleries)

69. Above: Queen Anne side chair. New England. Ca. 1730.
Maple. H. 41″, W. 21½″, D. 20⅞″. (Henry Ford Museum)

Queen Anne chairs from New England frequently exhibit similar characteristics in the method of their construction. The backs are deeply scooped or "spooned," an effort to provide more comfort for the sitter, and the rear legs terminate in square raking sections. The legs are almost always united by stretchers running from front to back; the stretchers are joined by a turned medial stretcher tenoned into square blocks. The two back legs are also joined by a turned member. See figures 69 and 72.

72. Right: Queen Anne side chair. Connecticut River Valley. Ca. 1740. Maple, painted black. H. 42″, W. 20½″, D. 19¼″. Of special interest is the unusual modified Spanish foot and incised line decoration on the front legs. (Henry Ford Museum)

73. Above: Queen Anne armchair with Spanish feet. Attributed to a member of the Gaines family (possibly John Gaines II). Ipswich. 1710–1740. Cherry, hard and soft maple. H. 43″, W. 29″, D. 16¾″. Like so many early chairs that were constructed from numerous kinds of woods, this example was originally painted black. (Winterthur Museum)

74. Right: Queen Anne side chair. Perhaps by a member of the Gaines family. Portsmouth, New Hampshire. Ca. 1720. Maple. H. 40½". The ornately carved crest rail and curved front legs with unusual pad feet relate this to chairs known to have originated in the Portsmouth, New Hampshire, area. (Museum of Fine Arts, Boston)

John Gaines III (1704–1743) of Portsmouth, New Hampshire, son of the Ipswich, Massachusetts, turner and chairmaker, John Gaines II (ca. 1677–1750), created seating furniture with a style uniquely his own. His chairs display elements of both the William and Mary and Queen Anne styles. The Spanish feet and boldly turned ball-and-ring front stretchers, as well as the ram's-horn terminals on the arms, belong to the William and Mary period. The solid splats are typical of Queen Anne chairs.

A new form, developed during this era, was the "nursery" chair. It is thought that these pieces, today referred to as slipper chairs, were constructed with their seats close to the floor so that ladies could more comfortably adjust their footwear. Figure 75, simple in form, is an early example of such special-purpose furniture.

75. Above: Queen Anne slipper chair. New England. 1720–1730. Maple. H. 36½", W. 19⅞", D. 19⅝". This provincial example of an unusual form is fitted with a slip-seat. The front legs of more sophisticated examples usually terminate with pad feet. (Henry Ford Museum)

76. Above, left: Queen Anne armchair. New England. 1725–1750. Maple. H. 41⅞″, W. 26¾″, D. 16″. This armchair, similar in form to figure 73, has a simplified top rail and front stretchers. (The Metropolitan Museum of Art)

77. Below, left: Queen Anne armchair. Connecticut. 1730–1750. Walnut. H. 38″, W. 28″, D. 21″. The low slip-seat is upholstered with roller-painted cotton. The plain cabriole front legs terminate in flat, circular pad feet. (Winterthur Museum)

78. Above, right: Needlework picture. By Prudence Punderson (1758–1784). Connecticut. Ca. 1776. H. 8″, W. 7″. The disciple James rests his arm on a transitional William and Mary–Queen Anne-style side chair similar to figure 79. (The Connecticut Historical Society)

79. Below, right: Queen Anne side chair. Massachusetts. 1720–1730. Maple, hickory. H. 42¼″, W. 19⅛″, D. 16″. This chair has two turned stretchers on each side uniting the front and back legs. (Henry Ford Museum)

Transitional country chairs like those shown on these pages were made throughout New England during the early eighteenth century. As varied in form and shape as the personalities of their makers, they represent a true cross-section of the chairmaker's craft. Solid vase-shaped splats are similar in outline to the imported Oriental porcelains so popular in America during the Queen Anne period. Most sophisticated examples were constructed of walnut. In general, the less expensive chairs constructed of maple were the products of country craftsmen who continued to use design elements, such as the Spanish foot, long after they had passed from favor in urban centers.

The needlework picture of James, one of Christ's twelve disciples, is the work of Miss Prudence Punderson of Preston, Connecticut. Unusual in design, it and eleven companion pictures by Miss Punderson are a dazzling display of needlework art.

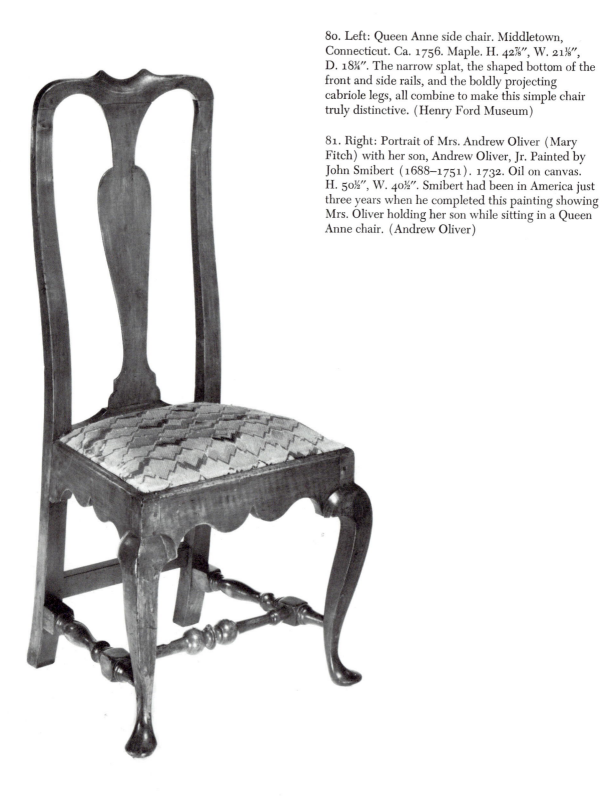

80. Left: Queen Anne side chair. Middletown, Connecticut. Ca. 1756. Maple. H. 42⅞″, W. 21⅛″, D. 18¼″. The narrow splat, the shaped bottom of the front and side rails, and the boldly projecting cabriole legs, all combine to make this simple chair truly distinctive. (Henry Ford Museum)

81. Right: Portrait of Mrs. Andrew Oliver (Mary Fitch) with her son, Andrew Oliver, Jr. Painted by John Smibert (1688–1751). 1732. Oil on canvas. H. 50½″, W. 40½″. Smibert had been in America just three years when he completed this painting showing Mrs. Oliver holding her son while sitting in a Queen Anne chair. (Andrew Oliver)

82. Left; 82a. Above: Queen Anne side chair. Attributed to John Goddard. Newport, Rhode Island. Ca. 1750. Walnut. H. 40⅞″, W. 21¼″, D. 22″. The seat on this side chair retains its original linen undercover. (Henry Ford Museum)

83. Below: Queen Anne daybed. Attributed to Job Townsend. Newport. Ca. 1743. Curly maple. H. 40″, W. 22″, L. 68″. This daybed is one of a group of pieces thought to have been made by Job Townsend for the Eddy family of Warren, Rhode Island. One labeled piece is still in the family's possession. (The Metropolitan Museum of Art)

Queen Anne in Rhode Island

84. Right: Queen Anne side chair. Attributed to Job Townsend. Newport. Ca. 1740. Walnut. H. 41½″, W. 22¾″, D. 20¾″. Though the crest rail is a later replacement, the chair is especially interesting since the back legs are cabriole shaped. Very few American examples are known with this feature. (Henry Ford Museum)

85. Overleaf: *A South West View of Newport.* Drawn by S. King. Engraved by L. Allen. Line engraving issued in 1795. H. 7³⁄₁₆″, L. 14⁵⁄₁₆″. This view of Newport clearly shows three of the city's churches—from left to right: the Second Congregational Church, Trinity Episcopal Church, and the First Congregational Church. (Emmet Collection, The New York Public Library)

Rhode Island furniture of the Queen Anne and Chippendale periods will always be associated with the Goddard–Townsend dynasty of cabinet-makers which for three successive generations worked in the general vicinity of the bustling seaport, Newport. The chairs crafted by numerous members of these two Quaker families in the Queen Anne period show a distinct propensity for the retention of Baroque designs. Job Townsend (1699–1765), John Townsend (1732–1809), the son of Job's brother, Christopher, and John Goddard (1723–1785), Job's son-in-law, were the principal craftsmen whose work has been positively identified. Newport chairs resemble some found in New York in that they have broad splats and relief-carved silhouetted shells on the crest rails. Broad and less naturalistic than the shells on New York chairs, they usually terminate with volutes at the sides. See figure 82a.

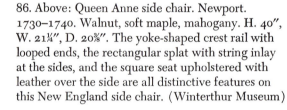

86. Above: Queen Anne side chair. Newport. 1730–1740. Walnut, soft maple, mahogany. H. 40″, W. 21¼″, D. 20⅜″. The yoke-shaped crest rail with looped ends, the rectangular splat with string inlay at the sides, and the square seat upholstered with leather over the side are all distinctive features on this New England side chair. (Winterthur Museum)

87. Left: Queen Anne armchair. Rhode Island. Ca. 1750. Walnut. H. 29″, W. 22″, D. 17″. This rare form is fitted with a horseshoe-shaped slip-seat. (Israel Sack, Inc.)

Most early Rhode Island Queen Anne chairs have broad, shallow, disc-shaped feet. On later pieces, the talons which grasp the ball on chairs with claw-and-ball feet are frequently undercut or pierced. Newport pieces, following the New England practice, are constructed with stretchers uniting the legs. Often these are turned; however, flat members occasionally were used. Figure 86, with its C-scrolls and carvings on the knees, displays the use of such stretchers.

During the William and Mary period the couch, or daybed, was introduced. Figure 83, a Queen Anne example, is constructed of curly maple and thought to be from Job Townsend's shop located on Easton's Point in Newport.

Because of Newport's deep harbor and strategic geographical location, local cabinetmakers, like their Boston contemporaries, were able to sell or consign "Venture" furniture to sea captains for sale in distant ports.

Christopher Champlin, an owner of many vessels which he docked at his Newport wharf, received chairs from the shop of Joseph Vickory to ship on his brig *Betsy*. Stephen and Thomas Goddard, sons of John, also delivered furniture to Champlin's store and warehouse. In 1744, Christopher Townsend sold case pieces to Isaac Stellé for export. Though the city's prosperity was abruptly halted by the Revolution, shortly after the hostilities ceased, cabinetmakers joined in cooperative shipments and the export of chairs increased sharply.

88. Left; 89. Above: Portraits of Mr. and Mrs. Robert Feke. Painted by Robert Feke. Newport. Ca. 1750. Oil on canvas. H. 42″, W. 32″. Robert Feke died before he could complete his self-portrait and the accompanying portrait of his wife. A later owner employed James S. Lincoln to "finish them" about 1878. The chair in which Mrs. Feke sits probably was completed by Lincoln. Mr. Feke's chair, in contrast, is only vaguely outlined and probably remains unaltered. (The Rhode Island Historical Society)

New York's
Queen Anne

90. Above: Queen Anne side chair. New York. Ca. 1740–1760. Walnut. H. 38¾", W. 22", D. 18¼". The Cupid's-bow carving just under the splat is very frequently found on New York chairs. (Henry Ford Museum)

91. Left: Queen Anne side chair. New York. Ca. 1740. Walnut. H. 38½″, W. 20½″, D. 18½″. This side chair, one of a set of eight made for the Apthorp family, has elaborate carvings on the crest rail and knees. The splat is walnut-veneered. The flat stretchers are unusual in New York chairs. (Benjamin Ginsburg)

92. Right: Queen Anne side chair. New York. 1730–1750. Walnut. H. 40⅝″, W. 21¾″, D. 20⅞″. Claw-and-ball feet were used more often and at an earlier date in New York than in New England. (Winterthur Museum)

Queen Anne chairs made in New York, like those from New England and Rhode Island, display construction elements that demonstrate a familiarity with Oriental design concepts. The profile of the splats of the sophisticated urban examples resembles in form a Chinese ginger jar sitting on top of a vase-shaped lower portion. See figures 90 and 91. New York chairs of this period also reflect the geographical position of this seaport area in that they are clearly a combination of designs used in England, New England, and Philadelphia. Frequently, chairs are constructed without stretchers bracing the legs, figure 90, a practice most often encountered in Philadelphia; others, like figure 91, are not only braced, but are further strengthened with a turned stretcher uniting the back legs, a construction practice of craftsmen in the more northern colonies.

93. Above: *A South Prospect of y. Flourishing City of New York in the Province of New York in America.* Line engraving by J. Harris after William Burgis. Issued March 25, 1746. H. 20$\frac{7}{16}$″, L. 70$\frac{10}{16}$″. The detail of this engraving indicates that the shoreline was dotted with the profiles of stepped-end, Dutch-style houses. (Stokes Collection, Prints Division, The New York Public Library)

In the thriving city of New York, the claw-and-ball foot was used early within the Queen Anne period and, closely following the English precedent, the rear legs were shaped at their terminal point into modified pad feet. Decorative carvings in the form of shells, often executed in high relief, add distinction to the crests and knees of the most elegant examples. Further embellishment was sometimes created by piercing the shell on the crest rail as illustrated by figure 91. Another distinctive feature found on chairs made for wealthy patrons of the lower Hudson River was a "Cupid's bow" used at the base of the splat. The seats of New York pieces are generally closer to the floor than those from the other areas discussed. The documentation or attribution of chairs to specific chairmakers is difficult, since time and again numerous fires ravaged this cosmopolitan center, destroying inventories and drawings. The Dutch Colonial period of New York terminated when the English, led by

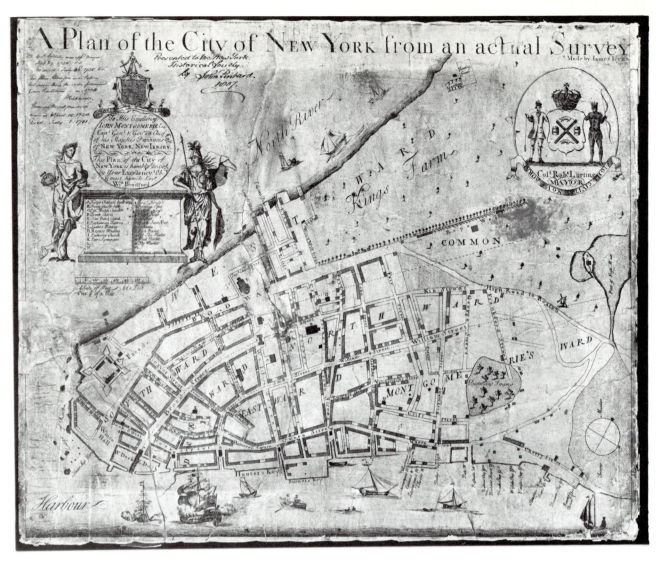

94. Above: *A Plan of the City of New York from an Actual Survey.* Printed and published by William Bradford. 1730. Engraving. H. 18½″, W. 23″. This view shows Broadway running north from Fort Amsterdam. (The New-York Historical Society)

the Duke of York, superseded the rule of Peter Stuyvesant and the Dutch West India Company in 1664. The Dutch populace, however, clung tenaciously to Dutch traditions. Warren Johnson, in 1760, records that "A Dutch Parlour has Alway a bed in it and the man and woman of the House Sleep in it. Their beds are good, for they mind noe other furniture." In 1749, Peter Kalm, the Swedish naturalist, wrote: "The inhabitants of Albany and its environs are almost all Dutchmen. They speak Dutch, have Dutch preachers and the divine service is performed in that language. Their manners are likewise quite Dutch; their dress, however, is like that of the English." Another writer, Mrs. Anne Grant, observed in her memoirs published in 1808 that, forty years earlier in Albany, "Valuable furniture (though perhaps not very well chosen or assorted) was the favourite luxury of these people . . ."

The side chair, figure 92, and armchair, figure 95, both have boldly projecting cabriole legs which terminate in pad feet. The armchair is unusual in that its design is embellished with a turned, button-like decoration applied to the leg just under the seat. Both examples demonstrate craftsmanship beyond that required to produce the sim-

pler, solid-splat, trumpet-turned pieces as illustrated in figure 99. The front legs of these chairs usually terminate in a modified pad-foot. The form was popular in the upper Hudson River area, northern New Jersey, and Long Island throughout most of the eighteenth century and well into the middle of the nineteenth century. Generally painted, usually black, these simple pieces were constructed most often of maple, although hickory, ash, and poplar also were used. The seats were of woven rush or splint made from split saplings which had been soaked in water to soften them enough for weaving. Sometime during the 1830's, Mrs. Isaac Day, figure 98, posed for the artist, Henry Walton, in the village of Ithaca, in the Finger Lakes region of New York. Mr. Walton is known to have solicited commissions while residing for several months in a room at Mr. R. P. Clark's on East Hill. Walton, warmly praised by the local press in 1838, let it be understood that "if sufficient encouragement is given, he intends to locate himself permanently in this village."

Chairs similar to the one in Walton's painting might well have been used in the farmhouse shown on pages 96 and 97.

95. Above: Queen Anne armchair. New York.
1720–1745. Maple. H. 43½″, W. 25¼″, D. 22″. A
nearly identical chair, probably crafted by the same
cabinetmaker, is in the Winterthur collection.
(Henry Ford Museum)

96. Right: Queen Anne side chair. Hudson River Valley, New York. Ca. 1735. Maple, ash. H. 40⅜", W. 19¾", D. 15¼". Countless New York country chairs were constructed with a similar yoke-shaped top rail. (Henry Ford Museum)

97. Left: Queen Anne armchair. Hudson River Valley. Mid-eighteenth century. Cherry, oak, pine. H. 45¾", W. 28¼", D. 21½". The shape of the splat and the bold, vigorous turnings indicate a New York origin, although it is possible that this country chair might have been crafted in Connecticut. (Van Cortlandt Manor, Sleepy Hollow Restorations)

98. Above: Portrait of Mrs. Isaac Day. Painted by Henry Walton. Ithaca, New York. Ca. 1830. Oil on Canvas. H. 31¼″, W. 24¾″. Mrs. Day sits in a form of country Queen Anne armchair which was popular throughout Long Island, northern New Jersey, and upstate New York. (DeWitt Historical Society of Thompson County, New York)

99. Right: Queen Anne armchair. New York. 1735–1750. Maple with ash stretchers. H. 45⅝″, W. 24″, D. 20⅞″. Trumpet-turned legs indicate a New York origin for this chair which retains traces of the original black paint. (Henry Ford Museum)

100. Overleaf: Detail of an overmantel painting. A view of the Martin Van Bergen house built in Leeds, New York, in 1729. Oil on panel. H. 18″, L. 87″. (New York State Historical Association)

The Philadelphia Style

The South East Prospect of The City of Philadelphia By Peter Cooper Painter

Of all the schools of Colonial cabinetmaking, the pieces created in and near Philadelphia most closely follow English designs and methods of construction. So great were the similarities that until recently many American examples made during the Queen Anne and Chippendale periods were mistakenly thought to have been constructed in the homeland. Figure 102 illustrates one construction practice that, when discovered on American chairs, almost without exception indicates a Pennsylvania origin—placing the side rail tenon through a mortise cut into the rear leg. This "bare-faced" tenon is secured on the outside edge of the back leg (not visible in the illustration) by two small "squarish" pegs driven into round holes.

101. Top, left: *South East Prospect of The City of Philadelphia*. Painted by Peter Cooper. American. Ca. 1720. Oil on canvas. H. 20¼″, W.87″. (The Library Company of Philadelphia)

102. Bottom, left: Detail of a Queen Anne side chair. Philadelphia. 1740–1750. Walnut. H. 40½″, W. 21″, D. 20½″. (Henry Ford Museum)

103. Right; 103a. Top right: Queen Anne side chair. Philadelphia. 1740. Walnut. H. 42¾″, W. 14¼″, D. 19¼″. The richly carved top rail is further embellished with punched decoration. The splat has two carved rosettes, and the front cabriole legs are decorated with shells and leaf carving, while the ankles are carved with vertical panels. (Museum of Fine Arts, Boston)

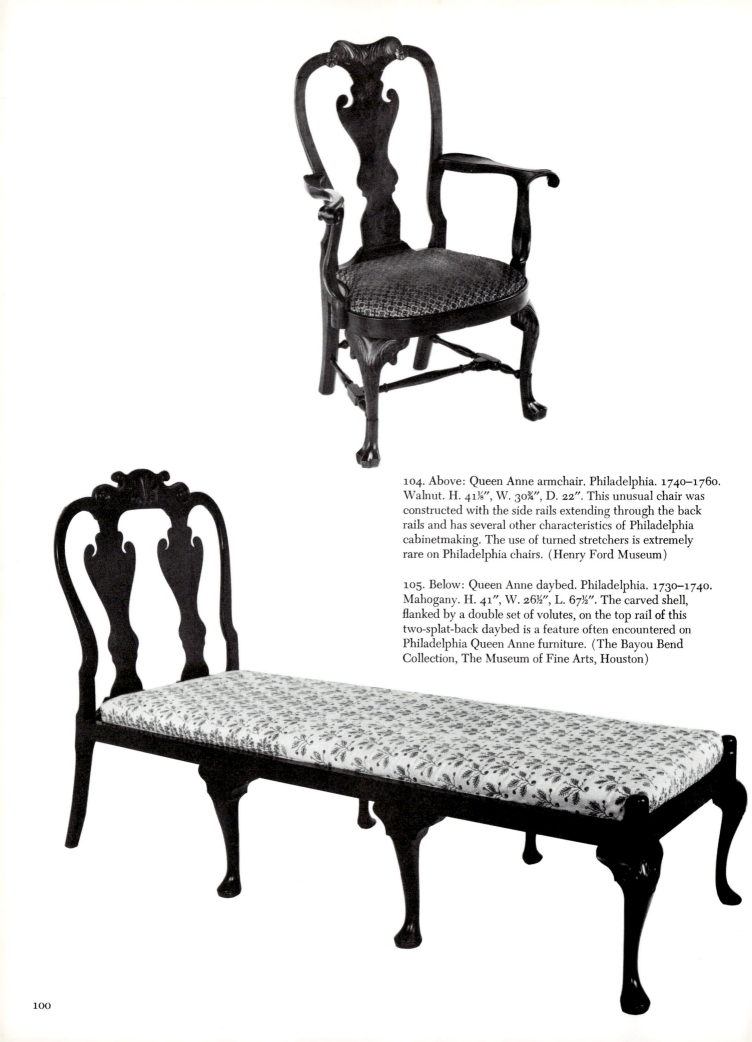

104. Above: Queen Anne armchair. Philadelphia. 1740–1760. Walnut. H. 41⅛″, W. 30¾″, D. 22″. This unusual chair was constructed with the side rails extending through the back rails and has several other characteristics of Philadelphia cabinetmaking. The use of turned stretchers is extremely rare on Philadelphia chairs. (Henry Ford Museum)

105. Below: Queen Anne daybed. Philadelphia. 1730–1740. Mahogany. H. 41″, W. 26½″, L. 67½″. The carved shell, flanked by a double set of volutes, on the top rail of this two-splat-back daybed is a feature often encountered on Philadelphia Queen Anne furniture. (The Bayou Bend Collection, The Museum of Fine Arts, Houston)

It is not surprising that methods of construction mirror European prototypes. During the early eighteenth century, this busy port on the Delaware River was allied, both socially and politically, with the English capital. Such ties are further reflected in chair construction. Seat frames were made from four pieces of wood in a "compass" or balloon (horseshoe-like) design. The legs, unlike Northern examples, dowel into the underside of the seat frame which consequently rests on top of the legs. Back legs are constructed with a pronounced "rake" or flaring, and most often are stumped, that is, round or ovoid in cross section. Front feet are frequently trifid, drake (figure 104), slipper, pad, biscuit, or web, and the fully developed claw-and-ball foot occurs early in the second quarter of the eighteenth century. "Spooned" back splats are shaped to fit the curvature of the human spine and occasionally are veneered, like those found in New York, to show fine, figured graining. The attachment of arms to chairs is very different in this center of furniture-making. See figures 104 and 110. On both, the flat, shaped arm, which terminates in a carved, knuckle-like design, is supported by a subtly carved upright that is attached to the seat. The hoop-type armchair, so popular in England, while not typical of chair construction in this region, does occasionally appear, figure 108. In general, Philadelphia chairs do not have stretchers. However, when stretchers are used, they are unlike the turned examples from other colonies. Flat members unite the legs, much like those of Rhode Island examples. Their pleasing shape adds strength where necessary.

The furniture of Philadelphia, as varied as its population, often produces surprises. The Quaker cabinetmakers, adhering to the tenets of their faith, produced simple, yet extremely beautiful chairs for conservative clients.

106. Above: Queen Anne side chair. Philadelphia. 1740–1750. Mahogany. H. 41″, W. 21″, D. 20″. This fully developed Queen Anne side chair with carved shells at the crest and in the center of the balloon seat was constructed with claw-and-ball feet. (Henry Ford Museum)

107. Below: Queen Anne armchair. English. 1715–1720. Walnut. H. 42¾″, W. 25″, D. 22″. Colonial craftsmen at first slavishly copied the products of London cabinetmakers. The earliest Philadelphia Queen Anne pieces are very similar to English prototypes. (The Art Institute of Chicago)

108. Right: Museum installation of the Vauxhall Room from Vauxhall Gardens, the Greenwich home of Thomas Maskell, built in 1700 in Cumberland County, New Jersey. This room, part of an addition made in 1725, has a large bolection-framed fireplace opening typical of the Queen Anne period. The chairs are distinguished examples of Philadelphia cabinetmaking in the Queen Anne style. (Winterthur Museum)

109. Right: *Kitchen Interior.* Painted by Thomas Hicks. American. Ca. 1865. Oil on canvas. H. 18″, W. 12″. In this painting, a Philadelphia Queen Anne armchair with a broken splat is used to prop the door open. (Department of Arts and Sciences, International Business Machines Corporation)

110. Left: Queen Anne armchair, one of a pair. Philadelphia. 1740–1750. Walnut. H. 41¼″, W. 32¼″, D. 22″. The horseshoe-shaped slip-seat is covered with beige-colored cotton with pink-and-blue painted decoration in the form of butterflies, small flowers, and a large central flower on a heavy stem. This East Indian fabric dates 1725–1775. (Winterthur Museum)

The craftsmanship of William Savery (1721–1788) is, of course, well celebrated. His chair, figure 111, displays an intaglio leaf carved on the knee of a cabriole leg, a design often associated with this distinguished craftsman. His work tends to bridge both the Queen Anne and Chippendale styles, and a labeled side chair at the Raleigh Tavern in Colonial Williamsburg has a Queen Anne vase-shaped splat, flat stretchers, pad feet, and a Chippendale bowed crest. Other examples of his work include a labeled daybed and side chairs, constructed in the Queen Anne style and illustrated in Hornor's *Blue Book, Philadelphia Furniture*. Solomon Fussell, another furniture-maker of more than passing interest, worked in a manner that also bridged the Queen Anne and Chippendale styles. His chair, figure 113, illustrated in Hornor's *Blue Book*, is truly transitional in nature. A top crest embellished with a relief-carved shell and spiraled volute ears occurs on many examples associated exclusively with the Chippendale style. In these chairs, it is easy to observe a distinct change in construction approach by the chairmaker. The front and side rails now become an integral part of the seat frame and are no longer doweled into it.

111. Above: Queen Anne side chair. Attributed to William Savery. Philadelphia. Ca. 1760. Maple. H. 41¾", W. 21½", D. 20¼". Flat, shaped stretchers are sometimes found on chairs originating in Philadelphia and Rhode Island. The carving at the knees and the general profile of the top rail and splat speak strongly for the attribution to William Savery, a Quaker cabinetmaker. (Henry Ford Museum)

112. Detail of *An East Prospect of the City of Philadelphia*. Engraved and published by T. Jefferys. London. Before 1754. H. 18⅜″, W. 34⅞″. In the foreground of this view (which would be the New Jersey shore) is a ferry, loaded with cattle, that appears ready to depart for the city across the river. Among other considerations inherited by Samuel

owel III in 1756 from his grandfather were over
nety houses in the city of Philadelphia. While in
ngland, he was advised by his uncle against the
urchase of furniture, since Philadelphia joiners
ould surely object and it might be "as cheap and as
ell made from English patterns" at home. (Stokes
ollection, The New York Public Library)

107

113. Left: Queen Anne side chair. Made by Solomon Fussell. Philadelphia. Ca. 1748. Walnut. H. 41¾″, W. 21½″, D. 20½″. This and a matching chair were crafted for the distinguished American statesman, Benjamin Franklin. In 1754 Fussell owned "1 pr. old Cheretree Draws Chest of Chest." Fussell also made rush-bottomed chairs. (Henry Ford Museum)

114. Above: Queen Anne side chair. Philadelphia. 1755–1765. Walnut. H. 41¼″, W. 21⅜″, D. 19½″. The pronounced scrolled ears on the top rail are echoed by similar carvings on the splat. The seat is upholstered with early leather. (Henry Ford Museum)

115. Right: Queen Anne armchair. Made by William Savery. Philadelphia. 1750–1770. Walnut. H. 42¾″, W. 30½″, D. 22¼″. The outside edges of the back rails and top crest are decorated with a carved molding. (Henry Ford Museum)

116. Above: Queen Anne corner chair. New England. 1725–1740. Maple. H. 30¼″, W. 28¾″, D. 29⅝″. The block-and-vase-turned legs terminate with pad-and-disc or cushioned-pad feet. Eight sausage-turned stretchers unite the legs. (Winterthur Museum)

Though often associated with American chair-making, the corner chair is not indigenous. The form first appeared in Colonial America at the close of the seventeenth century. Frequently used as desk chairs, these handsome pieces occasionally served other purposes. Figure 119 was designed with a deep, heavy skirt to conceal a commode and is more fully developed than figure 116, the earliest example shown. An even earlier example with Spanish feet and flat, square stretchers around the outside is in the Heritage Foundation Collection at Old Deerfield, Massachusetts. It is essentially William and Mary in style. The Philadelphia chair with slipper feet, figure 117, has a slip-seat made of hard pine. The seat rail is unusual in that it is formed from narrow interlocking strips of wood. The comb-back corner chair, figure 118, is accompanied by an inscription that describes it as a "Large Round about chair with top." The block-and-turned cross stretchers of this chair are distinctively Rhode Island and are found on other types of seating furniture from that area. Occasionally, chairmakers constructed corner chairs with the back leg terminating in a button or ball foot. The three "front" legs in these examples always match. The provenance of corner chairs is easily determined by the same methods used with more frequently encountered pieces. For instance, figures 117 and 119 are from Philadephia, since the arm supports and feet are similar in design to those found on other forms originating in that area.

117. Left: Queen Anne corner chair. Philadelphia. 1740–1750. Walnut. H. 30⅝″, W. 27⅝″, D. 24½″. The arm supports on this distinctive chair are the inverted cabriole type. Carved shells decorate the knees of the front and both side legs. (Winterthur Museum)

Corner Chairs

118. Right: Queen Anne corner chair. Newport. 1735–1750. Walnut and cherry. H. 44½″, W. 30″, D. 27⅜″. Like so many Rhode Island pieces, the legs are braced by a block-and-turned cross stretcher. An inscription on the seat rail indicates that the chair "Belonged to Elizabeth/Wentworth wife of Joseph Haven/Grandmother Thacher's uncle." (Winterthur Museum)

119. Left: Queen Anne corner chair. Probably Philadelphia. 1745–1765. Walnut. H. 32⅝″, W. 27⅝″, D. 27⅞″. The deep skirt with pendant lunettes was designed to conceal a commode. (Winterthur Museum)

120. Above: Queen Anne upholstered armchair, one of a pair. New York. 1730–1750. Walnut. H. 36″, W. 27¾″, D. 19″. This armchair was once owned by the James family of Flushing, New York. Six nearly identical pieces in the Winterthur Museum have a history of ownership associated with the Tibbits family also of that city. These chairs, designed with outward flaring arms, were made to accommodate the wide hoopskirts so popular during this period. The original linen upholstery was so decayed that the crewel appliqué was removed and mounted on a fresh backing of linen. (The Metropolitan Museum of Art)

121. Left: Queen Anne upholstered armchair. Rhode Island, probably Newport. 1740–1750. Walnut, white pine, maple. H. 41⅛″, W. 29¼″, D. 23″. This chair with high, rectangular back and yoke-shaped top has a history of ownership in the Ellis family of Dedham, Massachusetts. (Winterthur Museum)

122. Above: Museum installation. The fireplace and overmantel cupboard with sliding doors and raised panels is from the Providence summer home of the Rhode Island merchant, Metcalf Bowler. Pilasters and raised or fielded paneling flank the cupboard and fireplace opening which is faced with blue-and-white Delft tiles. (The Metropolitan Museum of Art)

Queen Anne Upholstered

123. Above, left: Queen Anne slipper chair. Rhode Island. Ca. 1740. Walnut. H. 38¼", W. 21½", D. 21". Slipper chairs or "back stools" in themselves are rare. In at least one instance, a slipper chair and an upholstered easy chair were designed en suite, figures 196 and 197. (Henry Ford Museum)

124. Above, right: Queen Anne easy chair. Philadelphia. 1740–1750. Maple, beech, mahogany. H. 47", W. 38¾", D. 27⅜". This outstanding chair was constructed with four cabriole legs that terminate with trifid feet; carved shells embellish the knees. (Winterthur Museum)

125. Above: Queen Anne settee. Philadelphia. Ca. 1740. Walnut. H. 48″, D. 22″, L. 58½″. This settee was made for James Logan (1674–1751), Governor of Pennsylvania, and is thought to have been used at Stenton, Logan's country house in Germantown. An inventory completed in 1776 of the estate of William Logan, son of James, includes a "walnut settee" in the parlor of the family house on Second Street. The central front leg, which for years was missing, has been restored, and a retaining edge added to the front seat rail. These restorations are appropriate and desirable in such an important piece. (The Metropolitan Museum of Art)

126. Right: Queen Anne easy chair. New England. 1720–1740. Walnut, maple. H. 45½″, W. 36″, D. 31″. An interesting feature of many New England easy chairs is that the front legs are of walnut and the rear legs of maple. This piece has been upholstered in eighteenth-century crewel worked in a "tree of life" pattern. (Henry Ford Museum)

127. Left; 127a. Above; 127b. Below: Queen Anne
upholstered armchair. New England. 1740–1760. Walnut.
H. 41″, W. 26″, D. 30″. An internal view of this armchair
shows the method of construction used to fasten the rear
legs to the chair frame. The side and back rails are mortised
into the back leg and pinned. The back leg was then nailed
to the upright member. A side view of the chair reveals
raking rear legs which cant back; open, flaring arms; bold,
cushioned-pad feet; and turned stretchers. (Henry Ford
Museum)

128. Left; 128a. Right: Queen Anne easy chair made or upholstered by "Gardner Junr." Newport. 1758. Walnut, maple. H. 46¾", W. 31½". This chair is inscribed on the back of the crest rail: *Gardner Junr/Newport May/1758.* (The Metropolitan Museum of Art)

The first easy chairs were introduced in the William and Mary period. These prototypes had Spanish feet and surviving examples display bold, vigorous turnings. Queen Anne examples are ample in size and certainly comfortable to sit in. The form was instantly popular, and, judging from early inventories, any man wealthy enough to acquire these expensive pieces made a point of doing so. Of course, the fabric a gentleman selected for the upholstery of his easy chair to some extent demonstrated his financial and social status. It is not surprising to discover that fabrics and upholstery materials are extensively advertised in early newspapers. "India Counterpanes" are offered in August, 1716, in the *Boston News-Letter* and "Linens," and "tickings" from Scotland in 1719. Available for sale at Clark and Kilby's warehouse near the Swing-Bridge were "Ticklingburgs, Oznabrigs, Dowlas, Kentings; Russia, Dantzick, Polonia and Pomerania Linnens, York wide, seven Eights, and three Quarter Garlix, Gulick and Bag Hollands, Lawns, Cambricks, . . . check'd Linnens, brown, dyed and,

strip'd Hollands, . . . and other European Goods." This advertisement, inserted in the *Boston Gazette* of August 11–18, 1735, indicates not only that there were "special goods" available for those with the means to purchase them, but also that many of these fabrics have passed out of common use today. Their names either have disappeared or have evolved into modern terms. The easy chair illustrated still retains the original needlework upholstery on the back. Shown in detail is a shepherd driving his flock to pasture. Deer and birds abound in sun-bathed orchards and forests.

A basic difference exists in the design of New England and Philadelphia easy chairs. The former have arms that roll vertically and the cabriole legs almost always are united by block-and-turned stretchers. Philadelphia chairs are more complex, and C-scrolls are incorporated into the design of the arms. The six-legged settee, figure 125, is an example where horizontal rolls are upholstered in the C-scroll shape. As with other forms of seating furniture from this area, the legs are not connected by stretchers.

The 1754 publication of Thomas Chippendale's pattern book, *The Gentleman and Cabinet-Maker's Director,* was an immediate success; so much so, that it was reissued in 1755 and a revised and enlarged edition published in 1762. Chippendale, of Yorkshire origin, was born into a family of carpenters and furniture craftsmen ca. 1718. In 1753, after residing in London for some five years, he married and moved to a rather exclusive district more appropriate to his financial success. He maintained a shop in St. Martin's Lane, and, though he never succeeded in obtaining royal appointment, his furniture designs influenced and altered furniture-making throughout the world during the eighteenth century. His drawings included elements of the Rococo, a contraction of the French term "rocailles et coquilles" or "rock and shell work"; of Chinese designs derived from imported Oriental objects; and of the Gothic style which had never completely disappeared in England. Chippendale used these diverse design sources to create a style of furniture that today bears his name. Writing in his *Director,* Chippendale had this to say:

Upon the whole, I have here given no design but what may be executed with advantage by the hands of a skillful work- man, tho' some of the profession have been diligent enough to represent them (especially those after the Gothic and Chinese manner) as so many specious drawings, impossible to be work'd off by any mechanic whatsoever. I will not scruple to attribute this to malice, ignorance and inability: and I am confident I can convince all Noblemen, Gentlemen, or others, who will honor me with their commands, that every design in the book can be improved, both as to beauty and enrichment, in the execution of it, by Their Most Obedient Servant. THOMAS CHIPPENDALE.

The original subscribers to his publishing effort indicate his position in the community. Not only nobility, but cabinetmakers, upholsterers, carpenters, joiners, carvers, plasterers, and picture-frame makers, through subscription, hoped to derive benefits from exposure to this talented man's design ideas. Chippendale was neither creator nor innovator of the style bearing his name. He was a compiler of current taste. He gathered together the most current designs and styles used by English furniture designers. The influence of his publications is recognized by the naming of some thirty-five years of American furniture-making after this gifted craftsman.

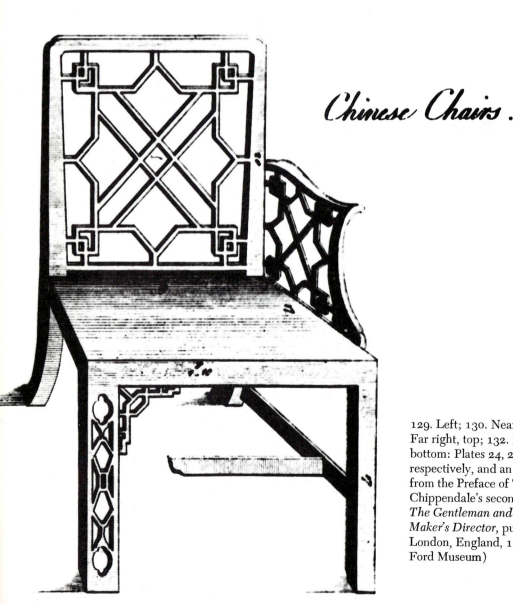

Chinese Chairs.

129. Left; 130. Near right; 131. Far right, top; 132. Far right, bottom: Plates 24, 22, and 20, respectively, and an illustration from the Preface of Thomas Chippendale's second edition of *The Gentleman and Cabinet-Maker's Director,* published in London, England, 1755. (Henry Ford Museum)

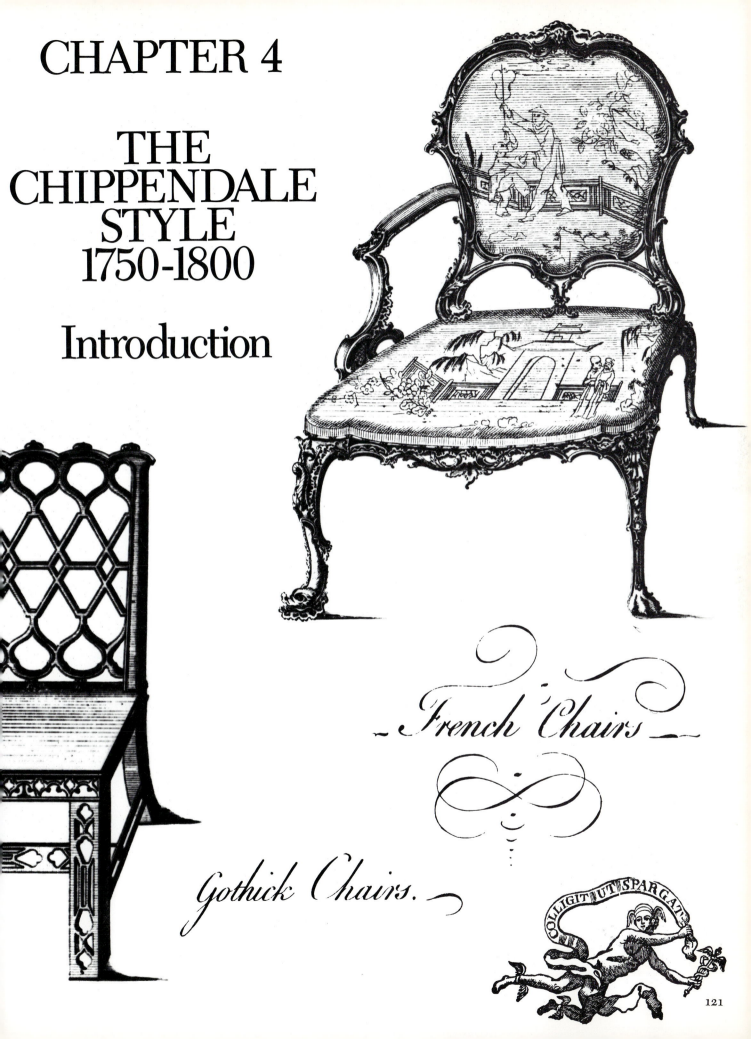

CHAPTER 4

THE CHIPPENDALE STYLE 1750-1800

Introduction

French Chairs

Gothick Chairs.

COLLIGIT UT SPARGAT

133. Above: Chippendale easy chair. Attributed to Benjamin Randolph. Philadelphia. Ca. 1770. Mahogany. H. 45¼", W. 22⅝". This "sample chair" represents the American application of Chippendale's Rococo design. Randolph, in his shop "At the Sign of the Golden Eagle in Chestnut Street," provided "Cabinet and Chairwork, Likewise Carving, Gilding &c, Performed in the Chinese and Modern Tastes." (Philadelphia Museum of Art)

134. Right: Museum installation. The Stamper–Blackwell Parlor from a Philadelphia town house built in 1762. The side chair at the left in the photograph, with carved seat rail and hairy-paw feet, is one of the six sample chairs attributed to Randolph. (Winterthur Museum)

Philadelphia Rococo

The influence of Chippendale's *Director* was far-reaching. Records exist indicating it was sold in Germany and Spain, and a French edition was published in 1762. Introduced in the American colonies, it was extremely influential in Philadelphia, where it inspired a school of cabinet- and chairmaking that developed into the most sophisticated and cohesive movement in the history of American furniture-making.

The 1769 catalogue of the Library Company of Philadelphia lists Chippendale's *Director* of 1762 (third edition) in its collection. The distinguished craftsman, Thomas Affleck (1740–1795), kept a copy of "Shippendale's Design." Benjamin Randolph (working 1760–1778) also was personally inspired by Chippendale's work. The use of Chippendale's name to represent the design movement his work inspired is thought to have originated with the English firm of Wright and Mansfield which, late in the nineteenth century, manufactured furniture modeled on designs taken from his various editions of the *Director*.

135. Left; 135a. Far left: Chippendale side chair. Attributed to Benjamin Randolph. Philadelphia. Ca. 1770. Mahogany. H. 37⅞", W. 21⅞". Randolph incorporated Chippendale's Gothic motifs into the design of the splat on this chair. The leg is finished with an ornately carved "French" foot. Unlike many of his fellow cabinetmakers, Randolph was an ardent patriot, and George and Martha Washington and Thomas Jefferson were his good friends. Randolph closed his shop in November of 1778. The sale of "A Quantity of Carvers and Cabinet-Makers Tools . . . at public vendue" was one of his last transactions as a cabinetmaker. (Philadelphia Museum of Art)

136. Right: Chippendale side chair. Charleston, South Carolina. Ca. 1770. Mahogany. H. 39¼", W. 24½", D. 24". This chair, which is from a suite of exquisitely carved seating pieces of the highest quality, was made for use in the Georgian plantation, Drayton Hall, at Charleston, South Carolina. This design masterpiece is constructed of mahogany throughout, including the corner blocks under the seat. The front legs terminate in hairy-paw feet, a device used in Philadelphia by Benjamin Randolph. (Henry Ford Museum)

137. Below: Chippendale easy chair. Philadelphia. 1775–1785. Mahogany. H. 48″, W. 35″, D. 30⅛″. This chair was constructed with Marlborough legs and block feet. (Henry Ford Museum)

139. Above: Illustration of a "French" chair. Plate 13 from Thomas Chippendale's *The Gentleman and Cabinet-Maker's Director*, Volume 1, 1754 edition. (The Metropolitan Museum of Art)

140. Right: Chippendale upholstered easy chair. Attributed to Benjamin Randolph. Philadelphia. 1760–1775. Mahogany. H. 46½″, W. 39¼″, D. 27¾″. This chair, like the sample chair in figure 133, is attributed to Randolph because of its descent in the Randolph family. (Henry Ford Museum)

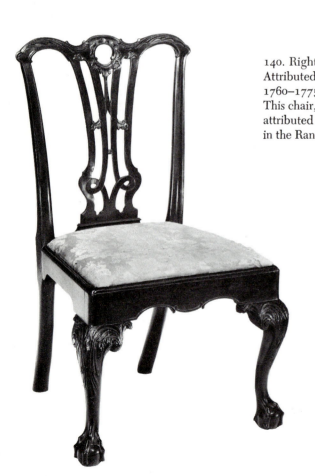

138. Above: Chippendale side chair. Attributed to Benjamin Randolph. Philadelphia. 1760–1775. Mahogany, oak. H. 38½″. (Israel Sack, Inc.)

141. Right: Trade card of Benjamin Randolph. Engraved by I. Smither, Sculpt. Philadelphia. Ca. 1765. H. 9″, W. 7⅛″. (The Library Company of Philadelphia)

Benjⁿ Randolph

Cabinet Maker,

at the Golden Eagle in Chesnut Street

— Between third and fourth Streets, —

PHILADELPHIA,

Makes all Sorts of   Cabinet & Chair work

Likewise Carving, Gilding &c   Perform'd in the Chinese
and Modern   Tastes.

B·R's
Ware
Room

The Scottish-born Thomas Affleck (1740–1795) joined fellow cabinetmakers in Philadelphia in 1763. In 1783 his occupational tax of 250 pounds far exeeded that paid by his contemporaries—Jonathan Gostelowe paid 100; Thomas Tufft, 50; and John Gillingham, 40. Politically, Affleck was a Loyalist and counted among his distinguished clients many with similar sympathetic attitudes toward England. His Loyalist activities were directly responsible for his banishment to Virginia in 1777. He later returned to Philadelphia and received important commissions which included, in 1794, the construction of furniture for Congress Hall. See figures 142 and 144.

142. Above, left: Chippendale armchair. Made by Thomas Affleck. Philadelphia. Ca. 1794. Mahogany. H. 51″, W. 31½″, D. 32″. This chair was made to be used as the Speaker's Chair for the Supreme Court in Philadelphia's Congress Hall. The bead-and-reel carving on the arms and legs is a familiar aspect of Affleck's cabinetmaking. (Henry Ford Museum)

143. Above, center: Chippendale side chair. Attributed to Thomas Affleck. Philadelphia. 1770–1780. Mahogany. H. 35⅝″, W. 23½″, D. 20¾″. Elaborate Gothic, Chinese, and Rococo motifs embellish most of the surface of this distinctive piece. (Henry Ford Museum)

144. Top, right: Chippendale upholstered side chair. Attributed to Thomas Affleck. Philadelphia. Ca. 1775. Mahogany. H. 39″, W. 23″, D. 21″. The channel-molded Marlborough front legs are carved on the outside with Affleck's customary egg-and-dart motif. Affleck made similar chairs for Governor John Penn. (William Rockhill Nelson Gallery of Art)

145. Right: Chippendale armchair. Attributed to Thomas Affleck. Philadelphia. 1760–1780. Mahogany, American white oak. H. 42¾″, W. 28¾″, D. 29¾″. This chair is believed to be from a set originally owned by Governor John Penn and used in his home, Lansdowne. (The Colonial Williamsburg Foundation)

146. Above: Chippendale side chair. Attributed to Thomas Affleck. Philadelphia. 1760–1775. Mahogany. H. 40¼″, W. 21″, D. 15″. The elaborately carved top rails of this and a matching chair are centered with a deep-cut shell, a motif repeated at the ears. (Museum of Fine Arts, Boston)

147. Left: Chippendale side chair. Philadelphia. 1760–1780. Mahogany. H. 41½″, W. 23½″, D. 22¼″. The carved tassel in the center and the gadrooned band at the bottom of the pierced splat are frequently found on New York chairs. (Henry Ford Museum)

148. Near left, top: Chippendale side chair. Philadelphia. 1760–1780. Walnut. H. 41½″, W. 23¾″, D. 20¼″. A large oval medallion centering the top rail is composed from shell-and-leaf designs. A carved molding frames the back stiles and top rail. (Henry Ford Museum)

149. Near left, bottom: Chippendale armchair. Attributed to Thomas Affleck. Philadelphia. Ca. 1770. Mahogany. H. 39¼″, W. 28½″, D. 24″. The Marlborough front legs are carved with geometric and foliage designs similar to those found on Affleck's documented pieces. (Henry Ford Museum)

150. Above: Museum installation. The Chinese Parlor is so named because the furniture and furnishings depict the influence of Chinese design on Western decorative arts. The walls are covered with Chinese wallpaper, ca. 1770, providing an appropriate setting for American Chippendale furniture. Thomas Chippendale was fascinated with Oriental objects and included in his *Director* many drawings for furniture incorporating Eastern motifs. (Winterthur Museum)

151. Right: Chippendale armchair. Made in China. 1770–1790. Teak. H. 37⅞″, W. 24½″, D. 24″. During the eighteenth century, Orientals were adroitly copying imported objects from the Western world. The construction of this chair, with the side rails extending through the back legs, is similar to techniques employed by Philadelphia cabinetmakers. (Henry Ford Museum)

152. Left; 152a. Center: Chippendale side chair. Philadelphia. 1760–1780. Mahogany. H. 41½″, W. 22½″, D. 21½″. (Henry Ford Museum)

153. Far right: Chippendale side chair. Philadelphia. 1760–1770. Mahogany. H. 41¹³⁄₁₆″, W. 24⅜″, D. 22¼″. (Winterthur Museum)

The decoration on the side chairs illustrated on these pages represents some of the most elaborate executed in America during the Chippendale period. Upholstered in French antique silk brocade, ca. 1770, figure 153 is from a set originally made for the Lambert family of Philadelphia. When compared to figure 152, it is obvious that additional carving embellishes the seat rail. The craftsman, by extending the carving over the knee of the leg and onto the skirt and its surrounding base, has concealed the basic form.

154. Overleaf: *The American School.* Painted by Matthew Pratt (1734–1805) in London. American. Dated 1765. Oil on canvas. H. 36″, W. 50¼″. The London studio of Benjamin West (1738–1820) became a mecca for youthful American artists during the mid-eighteenth century. Pratt, in this painting, shows himself and fellow compatriots working with West (far left). Upon his return to Philadelphia in 1768, Pratt was unable to earn a living by painting portraits and supplemented his income by executing signs for local shopkeepers. (The Metropolitan Museum of Art)

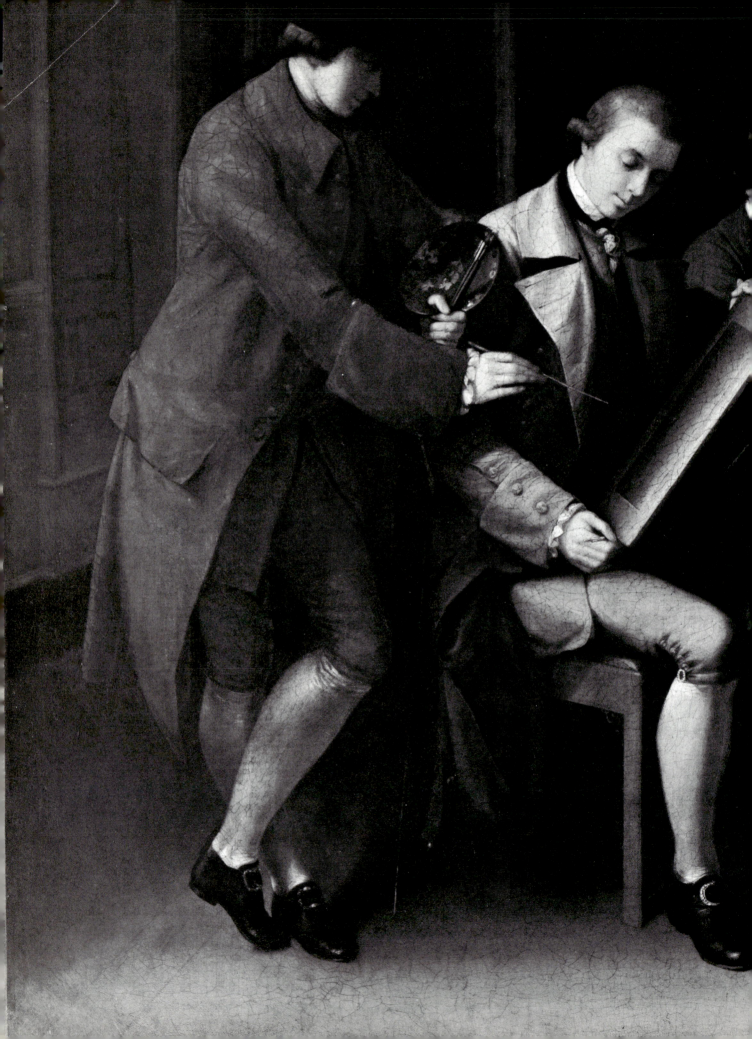

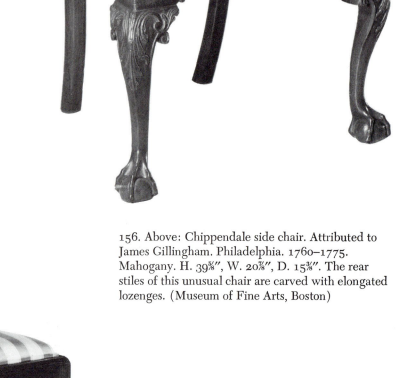

The work of both Philadelphia cabinetmakers, James Gillingham (1736–1781) and Thomas Tufft (active before 1772, died 1788), is documented by chairs retaining their original labels. Gillingham first operated within a partnership formed with Henry Clifton. Dissolving this, he moved to a shop located on Second Street, recorded because its address is included on his label. In 1773 Tufft assumed responsibility for Gillingham's shop. Here he made furniture for Philadelphia's more distinguished families—the Logans of Stenton, the Morrises, and the Powels.

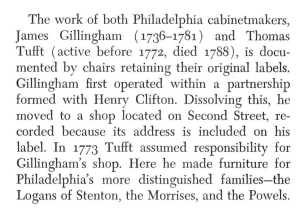

156. Above: Chippendale side chair. Attributed to James Gillingham. Philadelphia. 1760–1775. Mahogany. H. 39⅝″, W. 20⅞″, D. 15⅜″. The rear stiles of this unusual chair are carved with elongated lozenges. (Museum of Fine Arts, Boston)

155. Left: Chippendale side chair. Attributed to Thomas Tufft. Philadelphia. 1770–1785. Mahogany. H. 38½″, W. 23⅝″, D. 21½″. Carved motifs on this piece are identical to those found on labeled chairs by Tufft. The front cabriole legs are decorated with a circular cartouche, leafage, and scrolls which extend down the legs. (Henry Ford Museum)

157. Left: Chippendale side chair. Attributed to
Thomas Tufft. Philadelphia. 1770–1775. Mahogany.
H. 39¼", W. 23¼", D. 21". (Henry Ford Museum)

158. Right; 158a. Lower right: Chippendale side
chair. Made by Thomas Tufft. Philadelphia.
1760–1780. Mahogany, white cedar. H. 37⅞",
W. 23¾", D. 21⅜". Tufft's label on this chair reads:
"MADE and SOLD by/THOMAS TUFFT,/
Cabinet and Chair-Maker, FOUR Doors from the
Corner of/ Walnut – Street in Second/Street,
Philadelphia." (Winterthur Museum)

159. Left: Chippendale side chair. Philadelphia.
1760–1775. Mahogany. H. 40⅝", W. 23⅞", D. 17".
The warm glow of the original finish accents the
craftsman's use of subtle carving to contrast with
flat, plain surfaces. A truly distinctive chair of
superior quality. (Henry Ford Museum)

160. Above: Chippendale armchair. Attributed to John Elliott, Sr. Philadelphia. 1760–1780. Walnut. H. 38¼", W. 29¼", D. 21". This graceful demonstration of Philadelphia cabinetmaking is transitional in nature—the front legs are reminiscent of the Queen Anne period while the splat is pierced, a feature more often encountered on Chippendale style chairs. (Henry Ford Museum)

The craftsman William Savery (1721–1788) worked from about 1740 until his death using design elements of both the Queen Anne and Chippendale styles "At the sign of the Chair, a little below the Market, in Second Street, Philadelphia." His chairs, which many times are unadorned by the customary Rococo carving of the period, probably reflect the preference of a Quaker fulfilling commissions from the large Quaker community. The cabinetmaker to whom the armchair, figure 160, is attributed, John Elliott, Sr. (1713–1791), specialized in the manufacture of looking glasses. In his Philadelphia shop he supplied clients both with imported pieces and those of his own manufacture.

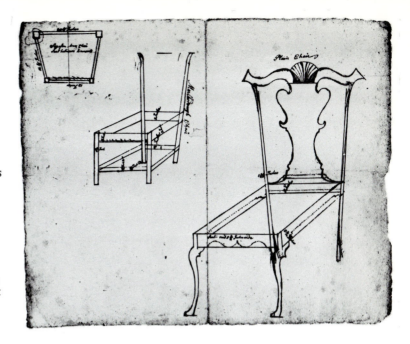

161. Left: Chippendale armchair. Made by William Savery. Philadelphia. 1758. Walnut. H. 40⅜″, W. 29⅞″, D. 21½″. An inscription on the inside of the front apron reads "W S" for William Savery and is dated "1758." The deep apron was constructed to conceal a commode. The unusual rounded arm supports form beautiful C-scrolls with the armrest terminal volutes. (Henry Ford Museum)

162. Left, bottom: Chippendale armchair. Attributed to William Savery. Philadelphia. 1750–1770. Walnut. H. 42¾″, W. 30½″, D. 22¼″. This chair once belonged to Francis Scott Key, the composer of "The Star-Spangled Banner." (Henry Ford Museum)

164. Above: Drawing of Chippendale chairs by Samuel Mickle. American. Ca. 1765. H. 13″, W. 16½″. This drawing, shows three views of chairs and gives detailed measurements of an "Arm Chair," a "Marlborough Chair," and a "Plain Chair." (Philadelphia Museum of Art)

163. Near left: Transitional Chippendale side chair, one of a pair bearing the original paper label of William Savery. Philadelphia. 1750–1760. Walnut, red pine. H. 39″, W. 21″, D. 20¼″. The intaglio leaf carving on the knees of this chair frequently appears on pieces from Savery's shop. (The Colonial Williamsburg Foundation)

165. Right: Chippendale side chair. Philadelphia. 1760–1780. Mahogany. H. 38¼″, W. 21¼″, D. 17½″. The pierced splat on this Marlborough-legged chair is centered by a Gothic motif similar to those found in Chippendale's *Director.* (Henry Ford Museum)

166. Top: Chippendale sofa. Made by John Linton. Philadelphia. 1775–1780. Mahogany. H. 36¼″, D. 33½″, L. 79¾″. (Winterthur Museum)

167. Bottom: Chippendale sofa. Made by Thomas Affleck. Philadelphia. 1763–1766. Mahogany. H. 40″, D. 28″, L. 96″. (Mr. and Mrs. Samuel Chew)

John Linton, the South Carolina upholsterer, moved to Philadelphia where, in 1780, he is recorded as an "upholder." Since his name is chalked into the frame of the camel-back sofa, figure 166, one of a pair, it seems certain that it originated in his shop.

Probably the most impressive and important American Chippendale sofa known, figure 167, was made by Thomas Affleck for Governor John Penn. This Marlborough-legged piece was purchased by Chief Justice Benjamin Chew in the late eighteenth century when Penn returned to England. The gadrooned edge of the skirt and the Chippendale Gothic carving on the legs remain unequaled in the American decorative arts.

Splendor in New York

168. Far left: Museum installation, including a self-portrait by Charles Willson Peale in which Peale is seen sitting in a Windsor armchair. The transitional Queen Anne–Chippendale side chair with pierced splat is one of a set of six. (The Bayou Bend Collection, The Museum of Fine Arts, Houston)

169. Above: Transitional Chippendale side chair. New York. Ca. 1745. Walnut. H. 41½″, W. 22½″, D. 22″. New York chairmakers adopted the claw-and-ball foot before 1750. This side chair was made for Robert and Margaret Livingston who were married in 1742, and the splat is carved with their initials—"R M L." (The Bayou Bend Collection, The Museum of Fine Arts, Houston)

171. Right: Chippendale two-chair-back settee. Attributed to Gilbert Ash. New York. 1750–1770. Mahogany. H. 38½", D. 26¼", W. 58½". American Chippendale chair-back settees are a rare form. Settees, like humans, could not be expected to last forever. ". . . The Steeple of Trinity-Church in this City was struck with the lightning . . . Mr. Callow's House in Wall-Street . . . sustained little or no damage. It came down the Chimney, and run along the brass nails that was in a Settee near the Hearth, blackening the Heads of all of them; it then entered the Settee, shivered it to pieces, and took its course thro' the Hearth . . ." The seat frame of this example is carved with a band of gadrooning and the arms terminate in bird's-head carvings, both devices used in New York. This unusual form was made en suite with six side chairs and two armchairs. (Henry Ford Museum)

170. Left: Chippendale side chair. New York. 1760–1770. Mahogany. H. 38¼", W. 22½", D. 21¼". Fully developed New York Chippendale chairs are nearly as opulent as Rococo examples originating in Philadelphia. A chair signed and dated "1756" by Gilbert Ash (active 1748–1763) has ears that are carved with leafage. On the knee of the illustrated chair is a carved ruffled shell which overlaps the seat rail. (Henry Ford Museum)

172. Right: Portrait of Colonel Marinus Willett (1740–1830). Painted by Ralph Earl (1751–1801). American. Ca. 1791. Oil on canvas. H. 91¼", W. 56". The New York City cabinetmaker, Marinus Willett, in 1773, "removed his Vendue store to the house lately occupied by Weldron & Cornell next door to Abraham Lott's Esq. Treas." (The Metropolitan Museum of Art)

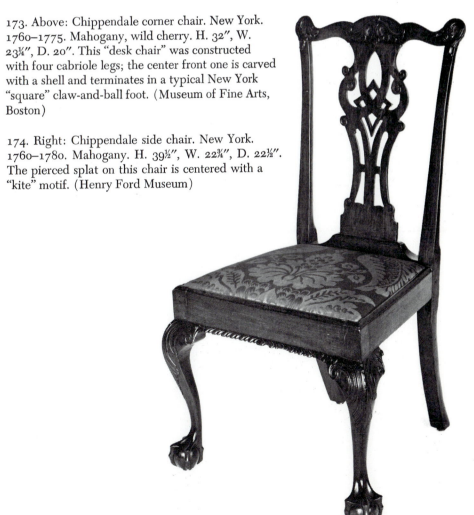

173. Above: Chippendale corner chair. New York. 1760–1775. Mahogany, wild cherry. H. 32″, W. 23¼″, D. 20″. This "desk chair" was constructed with four cabriole legs; the center front one is carved with a shell and terminates in a typical New York "square" claw-and-ball foot. (Museum of Fine Arts, Boston)

174. Right: Chippendale side chair. New York. 1760–1780. Mahogany. H. 39½″, W. 22¾″, D. 22½″. The pierced splat on this chair is centered with a "kite" motif. (Henry Ford Museum)

177. Top: Museum installation. The great central hall from Stephen Van Rensselaer's magnificent Georgian house was decorated with hand-painted paper in yellow and shades of gray and white. (The Metropolitan Museum of Art)

178. Below: Chippendale side chair. New York. 1760–1780. Mahogany. H. 38¼″, W. 23¾″, D. 22″. The knees on this chair are decorated with carved acanthus leaves, and the front legs terminate in a squared claw-and-ball foot. Carved tassels were popular motifs in the overall design of New York Chippendale chair splats. (Henry Ford Museum)

175. Left: *Portrait of an Unidentified Gentleman*. Painted by John Mare (1739–ca. 1795). America. 1767. Oil on canvas. H. 48½″, W. 38½″. Mare's subject stands with his hand resting on a carved mahogany New York chair. His gray suit with gold buttons is an effective contrast to the crimson damask drapery and tassel fringe. (The Metropolitan Museum of Art)

176. Above: Chippendale side chair. New York. Ca. 1770. Mahogany, red oak. H. 38¾″, W. 24″, D. 18″. This chair, which is upholstered in yellow wool damask, is from the Verplanck house. (The Metropolitan Museum of Art)

179. Left; 179a. Far left: Chippendale side chair. New York. 1775. Mahogany. H. 38⅛", W. 23¼", D. 20¼". The splat of this chair is pierced with Gothic designs. The Marlborough legs are decorated with unusual beading. A similar walnut chair with cabriole legs and claw-and-ball feet was owned by the Thompson family of Brooklyn. (Henry Ford Museum)

180. Right: Chippendale easy chair. New York. 1760–1775. Mahogany. H. 46", W. 36⅛", D. 31½". New York upholstered easy chairs are usually massive and comfortable. The knees of the cabriole front legs are carved with opened acanthus leaves and the feet are typical of claw-and-ball carvings from the area. (Winterthur Museum)

181. Above, left: Chippendale side chair. Salem, Massachusetts. 1750–1780. Mahogany. H. 37¼″, W. 23¼″, D. 21″. An infant school of cabinetmaking during the Queen Anne period, Salem grew into a fully developed center by the mid-eighteenth century. Clinging tenaciously to older construction concepts, the creator of this mahogany chair chose to use supporting stretchers uniting the legs. (Henry Ford Museum)

182. Left: Chippendale side chair. Attributed to Sewall Short (1735–1773). Newburyport, Massachusetts. 1760–1780. Mahogany. H. 38⅝″, W. 22″, D. 21¼″. The serpentine crest rail of this chair is centered by carved leafage on a punched ground, and the front cabriole legs terminate in flattened claw-and-ball feet. Both are characteristics of Sewall Short's work. Like countless New England chairs, the rear legs are square, chamfered, and canted. (Henry Ford Museum)

183. Above: Chippendale side chair. Boston. Ca. 1770. Walnut. H. 36⅛″, W. 22⅞″, D. 23⅞″. Hairy-paw claw-and-ball feet appear only occasionally in New England chairmaking. (Henry Ford Museum)

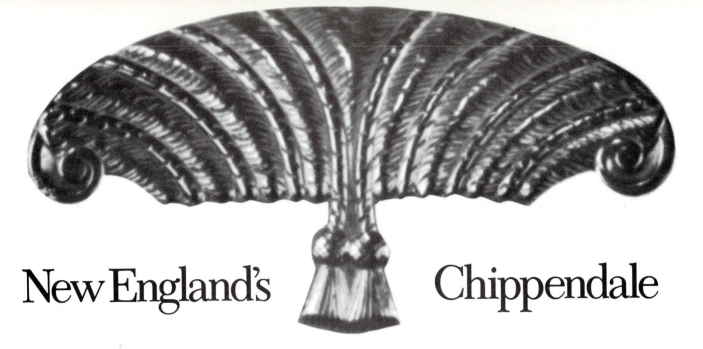

New England's Chippendale

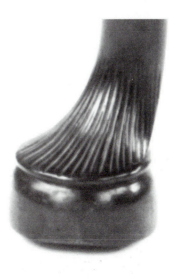

184. Left; 184a. Top; 184b. Bottom: Chippendale side chair. Salem. 1760–1780. Mahogany. H. 38″, W. 20″, D. 23″. The cabriole front legs of this chair terminate in shell-carved, cushioned-pad feet. Rich shell and floral decorations embellish the knees. The distinctive top rail is carved with tassels which extend onto the splat. (Henry Ford Museum)

185. Overleaf: The Reverend Jedidiah Morse family. Painted by Samuel F. B. Morse (1791–1872). American. 1810. Watercolor drawing. H. 19″. W. 23″. This painting is said to be the first picture Morse ever painted. It is interesting that in 1810 a conservative New England family like the Morses still lived with a Chippendale table and chairs. (Smithsonian Institution)

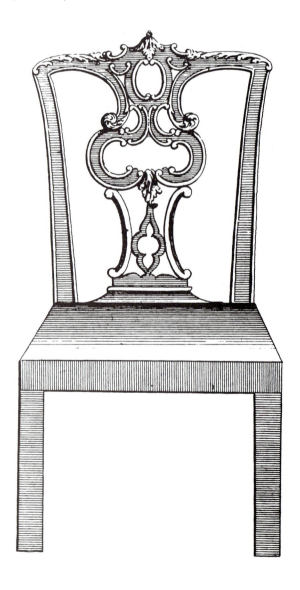

187. Above: Chippendale settee. Massachusetts. Ca. 1770. Mahogany. H. 40½″, D. 26″, L. 75″. This settee and eight matching chairs descended in the Forbes family of Worcester, Massachusetts. (The Bayou Bend Collection, The Museum of Fine Arts, Houston)

186. Above: Chippendale side chair. Probably Boston. 1770–1780. Mahogany. H. 38¾″, W. 22″, D. 22″. This Marlborough-legged chair belonged to the Quincy family of Massachusetts. A rope carving extends down the outside of the stiles and front legs. (Winterthur Museum)

188. Right: Drawing for a "parlour" chair. Plate 9, taken from *The Cabinet and Chair-Maker's Real Friend and Companion,* published by Robert Manwaring. 1756. London, England. Manwaring, an English designer and cabinetmaker, claimed that cabinetmakers could obtain from his book "full and plain Instructions, how he is to begin and finish with Strength and Beauty, all the Designs that are advanced in this Work." (Henry Ford Museum)

189. Left: Chippendale side chair. Massachusetts.
1760–1780. Mahogany. H. 36¼″, W. 21¼″, D. 18¾″.
An unusual feature of this New England chair is that
it is constructed without stretchers. (Museum of
Fine Arts, Boston)

190. Left: Chippendale side chair, one of a pair. New
England. 1765–1770. Mahogany. H. 38⅝″, W. 23½″, D. 17″.
Increasing trade with the West Indies during the
Chippendale period provided ample mahogany for American
furniture-makers. At this time, it was chosen for the
construction of America's finest pieces—a function once filled
by native walnut. The back splat and top rail on this richly
ornamented chair are almost identical to Manwaring's design,
figure 188. (The Metropolitan Museum of Art)

191. Above: Chippendale armchair. Massachusetts. Ca.
1760–1770. Mahogany. H. 38″, W. 24½″, D. 20½″. The
subtle design of this armchair, from a set of four side chairs
and two armchairs, is transitional in nature. (David
Stockwell, Inc.)

155

192. Far left: Portrait of Colonel William Taylor (1764–1841). Painted by Ralph Earl. American. 1790. Oil on canvas. H. 48½″, W. 38″. Earl painted Colonel Taylor sitting in a roundabout or corner chair which is, if American, unusual. The upholstered seat is brass-tacked and the unadorned front cabriole leg contrasts with the square legs in the rear. Obviously not of the latest fashion, it demonstrates how fine furniture was treasured over a long period of time. (Albright–Knox Art Gallery)

193. Left: Chippendale corner chair. Massachusetts. Ca. 1760. Mahogany. H. 31⅛″, W. 30½″, D. 28½″. Corner chairs were often used at a desk. The cabriole front leg of this example has acanthus-leaf carving at the knee and terminates with a claw-and-ball foot. The three rear legs are also cabriole, but they are finished with cushioned-pad feet. Originally this solid splat chair had X-cross stretchers. (Henry Ford Museum)

194. Right: Chippendale. "closestool." New England. Ca. 1770. Mahogany. H. 30¾″, W. 32½″, D. 25½″. The splats of this chair reflect elements of the Gothic taste as introduced by Thomas Chippendale in his *Director*. The deep skirt is scalloped and, as with all commode chairs, the slip-seat can be easily removed. (Henry Ford Museum)

195. Below: Chippendale slipper chair. Rhode Island. 1750–1760. Walnut. H. 36″, W. 22¾″, D. 22″. The lacelike splat and boldly scalloped top rail with jutting carved ears on either side on this and a matching chair at the Van Cortlandt Manor in Tarrytown, New York, are unusual elements on what is otherwise a straightforward Rhode Island example. (Winterthur Museum)

196. Near right, top: Chippendale slipper chair. Newport. 1750–1765. Mahogany. H. 39″, W. 21½″. Although geographically close, surprising differences exist between furniture created in the shops of Newport and of Massachusetts craftsmen. Even more striking is the similarity between Rhode Island furniture and that made in Philadelphia where pieces constructed with flat serpentine stretchers frequently appear. The stretchers on this and the matching easy chair, figure 197, are of the block-and-turned variety. (Parke–Bernet Galleries)

197. Near right, bottom: Chippendale easy chair. Newport. 1750–1765. Mahogany. H. 48½″, W. 31½″. The slipper chair, figure 196, and this easy chair are the only known examples of such Rhode Island forms made en suite. (Parke–Bernet Galleries)

198. Left, bottom: Chippendale corner chair. Newport. 1760–1770. Mahogany. H. 30½″, W. 30″, Height of seat rail 16½″. Design elements incorporating interlacing scrolls were popular in Newport. This corner chair illustrates the Newport cabinetmakers' preference for the Queen Anne design which they used well into the Chippendale period. This chair is one of a pair originally owned by John Brown and that name is inscribed on the frame. (Norman Herreshoff)

199. Below; 199a. Left: Chippendale easy chair. Rhode Island. 1750–1767. Mahogany. H. 49½″, W. 32¼″. Sidney Breese (1709–1767), original owner of this distinguished Newport easy chair, was a New Yorker. Carved shells decorate the knees of the front cabriole legs finished with claw-and-ball feet. (The Preservation Society of Newport County)

200. Right, bottom: Chippendale "lady's chair." Rhode Island. 1740–1760. Walnut. H. 35½″, W. 20¼″, D. 13¼″. Ladies' chairs, or slipper chairs, were purposely constructed with their seats some twelve to fifteen inches from the floor. Queen Anne examples usually have tall upholstered backs; those from the Chippendale period are seldom upholstered and consequently are lightweight and more movable. (Norman Herreshoff)

In Rhode Island

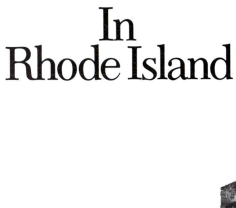

203. Above: Printed paper label from a breakfast table made by John Townsend. (Winterthur Museum)

201. Above: Chippendale easy chair. Perhaps made by John Townsend (1732–1809). Newport. 1770–1780. Mahogany, cherry. H. 47⅞″, W. 35½″. The Marlborough legs of this easy chair are stop-fluted. (Joseph K. Ott)

202. Near right; 202a. Right, center; 202b. Far right: Chippendale side chair. Attributed to John Townsend. Newport. Ca. 1780. Walnut. H. 37″, W. 20⅞″, D. 19½″. Because few documented pieces have been traced to other craftsmen, Rhode Island furniture constructed with carved stop-fluting as a predominant feature of its design is generally considered to have been created in the shops of the Goddards and Townsends. The cross-hatching on the top rail and upper part of the splat is another feature often encountered on these pieces. Simplified, less sophisticated versions of this chair are found in the Hartford, Connecticut, area. The similarity of details on furniture from these two neighboring regions increases during the Federal period. (Henry Ford Museum)

Northern Variations

204. Left: Chippendale armchair. Attributed to Eliphalet Chapin. Hartford County, Connecticut. 1760–1770. Cherry. H. 40¼″, W. 23″, D. 18″. Cherry chairs with splats similar to this example are sometimes attributed to the East Windsor and Hartford furniture-maker Aaron Chapin (1753–1838). Frequently his chairs, like Philadelphia examples of the period, are constructed with the side rails extending through the rear legs. Serving his apprenticeship with his more distinguished second cousin, Eliphalet Chapin, he worked in the Connecticut River area from 1783 until 1838. (The Connecticut Historical Society)

205. Above, left: Chippendale side chair. Hartford, Connecticut. 1765–1785. Cherry. H. 37⅞″, W. 20″, D. 15″. The top rail of this side chair is decorated with a crude cross-hatching that approximates the carvings on Newport chairs from the shops of Townsends and Goddards. See figure 202. (The Connecticut Historical Society)

206. Above, right: Chippendale side chair. Possibly by Aaron Chapin. Connecticut. 1775–1795. Cherry. H. 38″, W. 21″, D. 19½″. (Winterthur Museum)

207. Above: Needlework picture. Created by Prudence Punderson (1758–1784). Preston, Connecticut. Eighteenth century. H. 12½″, W. 16½″. In this splendid embroidered self-portrait, called a mortality picture because it represents birth, life, and death, Miss Punderson sits in a Chippendale chair, her sewing equipment and pewter inkstand are on a Chippendale table. (The Connecticut Historical Society)

208. Below: Chippendale daybed. Attributed to Eliphalet Chapin. Connecticut. Ca. 1770. Cherry. H. 41¼″, D. 24¾″, L. 72″. This daybed, like so much Connecticut furniture associated with the Chapin school of cabinetmaking, is constructed in the Philadelphia manner. The side rails tenon through the back posts, and the seat rail is decorated with carved gadrooning. Eliphalet Chapin, while avoiding a marriage of necessity, spent five years in Philadelphia. His exposure to the sophisticated cabinetmaking techniques of that city was demonstrated by the seating pieces he constructed upon his return to the East Windsor area in 1771. (Wadsworth Atheneum)

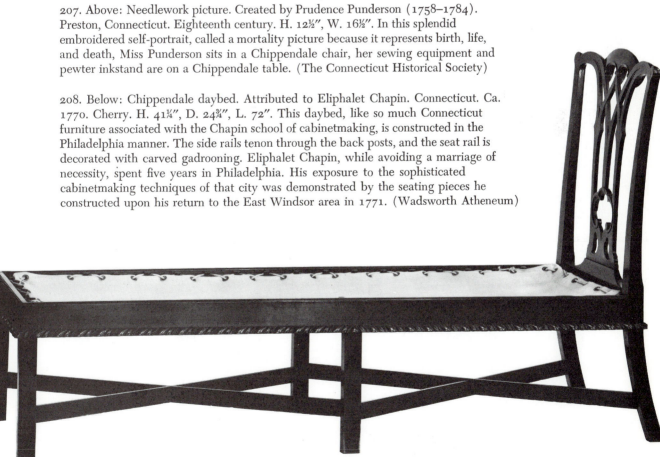

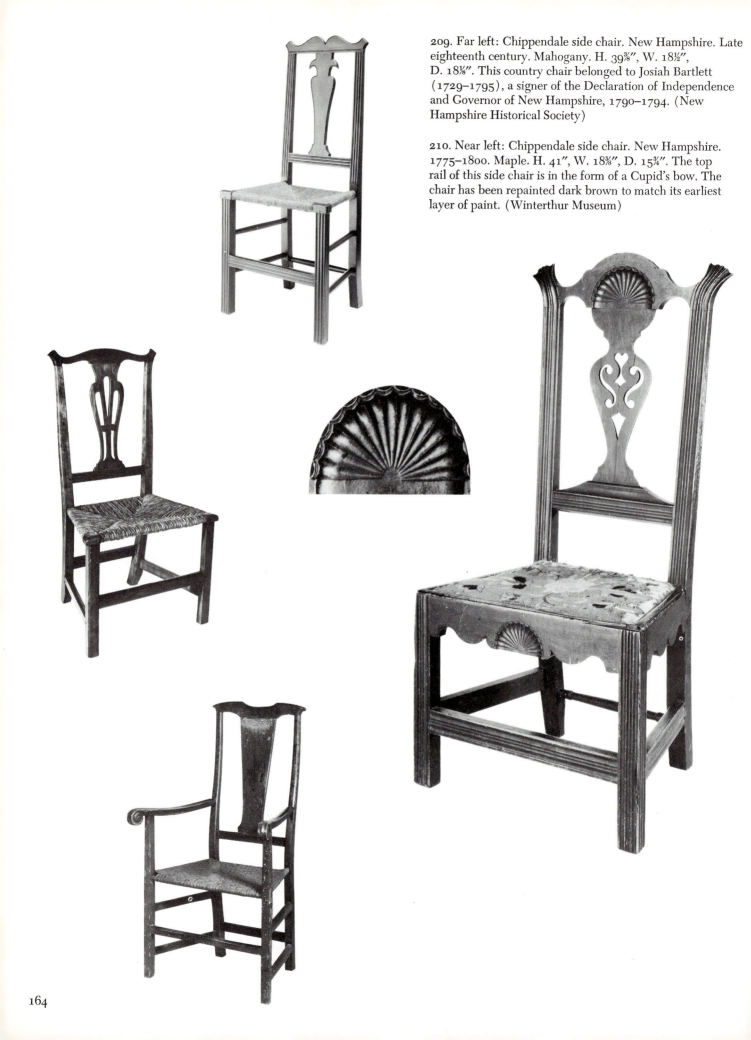

209. Far left: Chippendale side chair. New Hampshire. Late eighteenth century. Mahogany. H. 39⅜″, W. 18½″, D. 18⅛″. This country chair belonged to Josiah Bartlett (1729–1795), a signer of the Declaration of Independence and Governor of New Hampshire, 1790–1794. (New Hampshire Historical Society)

210. Near left: Chippendale side chair. New Hampshire. 1775–1800. Maple. H. 41″, W. 18⅜″, D. 15¾″. The top rail of this side chair is in the form of a Cupid's bow. The chair has been repainted dark brown to match its earliest layer of paint. (Winterthur Museum)

211. Left, bottom: Chippendale armchair. New England. 1780–1800. Maple. H. 44¼″, W. 26″, D. 15¾″. New England country chairs often display elements of design associated with imported objects from the Orient. A coat of black paint conceals the earlier Indian-red finish on this rush-seated chair. (Henry Ford Museum)

212. Center, left (chair); 212a. Center, left (detail): Chippendale side chair. Probably New Hampshire. 1775–1790. Maple. H. 45″, W. 21¾″, D. 16¾″. This side chair is painted a bluish green. The seat rail and top rail are carved with a depressed fan and the splat is pierced with S-scrolls. Stylistically, it relates to the Dunlap school of furniture-making centered in Chester and Salisbury, New Hampshire, in the late eighteenth century. (Winterthur Museum)

213. Below: *A Lady With Her Pets.* Painted by Rufus Hathaway. Massachusetts. 1790. Oil on canvas. H. 34½″, W. 32″. (The Metropolitan Museum of Art)

Major John Dunlap (1746–1792) is perhaps the best known craftsman of the Dunlap dynasty of furniture-makers from New Hampshire. With his cabinetmaking relatives, he created a unique style of country furniture using the familiar Chippendale vocabulary. They constructed maple chairs during the late eighteenth and early nineteenth centuries. Other forms made by these gifted craftsmen include highboys, lowboys, and chest-on-chests, and a paneled room-end with a richly carved corner cupboard which is now part of the Winterthur collections.

Country chairs, when compared with those manufactured in the sophisticated shops of the more urban centers of Boston, Salem, and Portsmouth, can almost be classified as folk art. True folk artists often painted in a style archaic to their time. Dr. Rufus Hathaway (1770–1822) of Duxbury, Massachusetts, painting in flat linear patterns, created a design masterpiece, figure 213.

214. Above: *Mrs. Sylvanus Bourne* (Mercy Gorham). Painted by John Singleton Copley (1738–1815). American. 1766. Oil on canvas. H. 50¼″, W. 40″. Mrs. Bourne (1695–1782) sits in an elegant open armchair of ample proportions while having her portrait painted by the American prodigy, John Singleton Copley. During the eighteenth century, the upholsterer's trade developed into a specialized art. John Simpkins in his "shop the North Side of the Mill-Bridge" advertised in the *Boston Gazette* on June 17, 1765, "Crimson, green and yellow Harrateens, Chaneys, Linceys . . . &cs . . . any sort of Upholsterer's Work done in the best Manner, at the lowest Rates." (The Metropolitan Museum of Art)

Chippendale
Upholstered

215. Above: Chippendale easy chair. Newport. 1765–1780. Walnut, maple. H. 47¼″, W. 35¼″, D. 30½″. (Winterthur Museum)

216. Top, right: Portrait of Mrs. Nicholas Salisbury. Painted by Christian Gullager (1759–1826). American. Eighteenth century. Oil on canvas. H. 35¹⁵⁄₁₆″, W. 28¾″. Mrs. Salisbury sits in a very fine damask-covered easy chair. (Worcester Art Museum)

217. Right: Portrait of Miss Mary Warner. Painted by John Singleton Copley. American. 1767. Oil on canvas. H. 48⅛″, W. 40″. Miss Warner plays with a bird perched on a string tied to one of the arms of an upholstered armchair. (Toledo Museum of Art)

219. Left: Chippendale easy chair. Massachusetts. Ca. 1760. Mahogany, maple, white pine. H. 47¼", W. 27", D. 30". Countless American chairs were upholstered in wool worked in a flamestitch pattern. Flamestitch originally developed during the William and Mary period in Italy where it was known as "bargello work." (Henry Ford Museum)

218. Left: Chippendale settee. New England. 1750–1775. Mahogany, curly maple. H. 36¾", D. 22½", L. 58½". Like most New England upholstered easy chairs of the Chippendale period, this diminutive settee was constructed with mahogany front legs and curly-maple back legs. The design of this piece is second to none. (The Metropolitan Museum of Art)

220. Right; 220a. Center: Chippendale open armchair. Massachusetts. Ca. 1750. Mahogany. H. 42¾", W. 31⅞", D. 23". As noted earlier, New England Queen Anne chairs were almost always braced by stretchers. This construction practice continued into the Chippendale period when the seats of upholstered open armchairs were built close to the floor and ample in breadth. This example is richly carved and has arm terminals in the form of a bird's head and wing. It is upholstered in scarlet damask. A similar fabric was imported from London by the Boston firm of Hunt and Torrey in 1760. (Henry Ford Museum)

221. Above: *The Squire's Tea*. Painted by Benjamin Wilson. English. Eighteenth century. Oil on canvas. H. 25″, W. 30⅜″. The chairs in this interior were fitted with slipcovers. (Toledo Museum of Art)

222. Right: Chippendale sofa. Connecticut. 1760–1805. Mahogany, cherry, pine, poplar. H. 40¾″, L. 92⅝″. A scratched pinwheel motif is on the inner frame of the back of this piece. (The Connecticut Historical Society)

223. Right, top: Chippendale sofa. Newport. 1770–1780. Mahogany. H. 39½″, D. 30¼″, L. 98¼″. Rhode Island sofas are extremely rare. This example was part of the original furnishings in the John Brown house and has descended in the family of the original owner. The stop-fluted legs are typical Rhode Island features. (Norman Herreshoff)

224. Below, right: Portrait of Colonel Benjamin Tallmadge and his son, William Smith Tallmadge. Painted by Ralph Earl. American. 1790. Oil on canvas. H. 70⅛″, W. 55″. Earl's subjects are placed in an interior enriched by an ingrain carpet. Wearing the Badge of the Order of the Cincinnati, Tallmadge sits in a "nailed" chair with a fringe. Few indeed are the examples that survive with such fringe intact. Boston shopowner, Elizabeth Murray, offered "fringes" through a local advertisement in 1751. (The Litchfield Historical Society)

225. Overleaf: Family portrait. Painted by Ralph E. W. Earl (1788–1838). American. 1804. Oil on canvas. H. 46½″, W. 63½″. The sofa on which the man and his family sit is finished with brass-nailed fringe. The artist achieved a sense of unity by adorning the draperies with fringe also. Since Earl was a "matter-of-fact" painter, the house was probably furnished in this manner. (National Gallery of Art)

226. Above: Installation in the John Quincy Adams State Drawing Room. George Washington owned "2 doz. strong, neat and plain but fashionable Table chairs" which are thought to have been pretzel-back chairs similar to the one shown in this illustration. (The United States Department of State)

227. Right, top: Chippendale side chair. Probably Massachusetts. 1775–1800. Maple, birch. H. 40⅝″, W. 20⅝″, D. 17½″. (Winterthur Museum)

228. Below: Chippendale side chair. Attributed to Daniel Trotter. Philadelphia. 1775–1800. Mahogany. H. 38″, W. 22½″, D. 18¼″. (Henry Ford Museum)

Elegant Chippendale ladder-back chairs with serpentine slats, often pierced, were frequently included in the furnishings of late Colonial homes, especially in Philadelphia, where the form seems to have been most popular. "Pretzel-back," "ribbon-back," and "pierced ladder-back" chairs are known to have been made by both Ephraim Haines (1775–ca. 1811) and Daniel Trotter (1747–1800). Commissioned by the famous Philadelphian, Stephen Girard, Trotter followed English models and constructed chairs with a pierced splat in parallel curves, centered with a carving of feathers in a medallion. The mahogany armchair with pretzel-back, figure 229, is fitted to receive a commode. Like most Philadelphia chairs of this period, the side rails mortise through the rear stiles, a practice originating in the Queen Anne period.

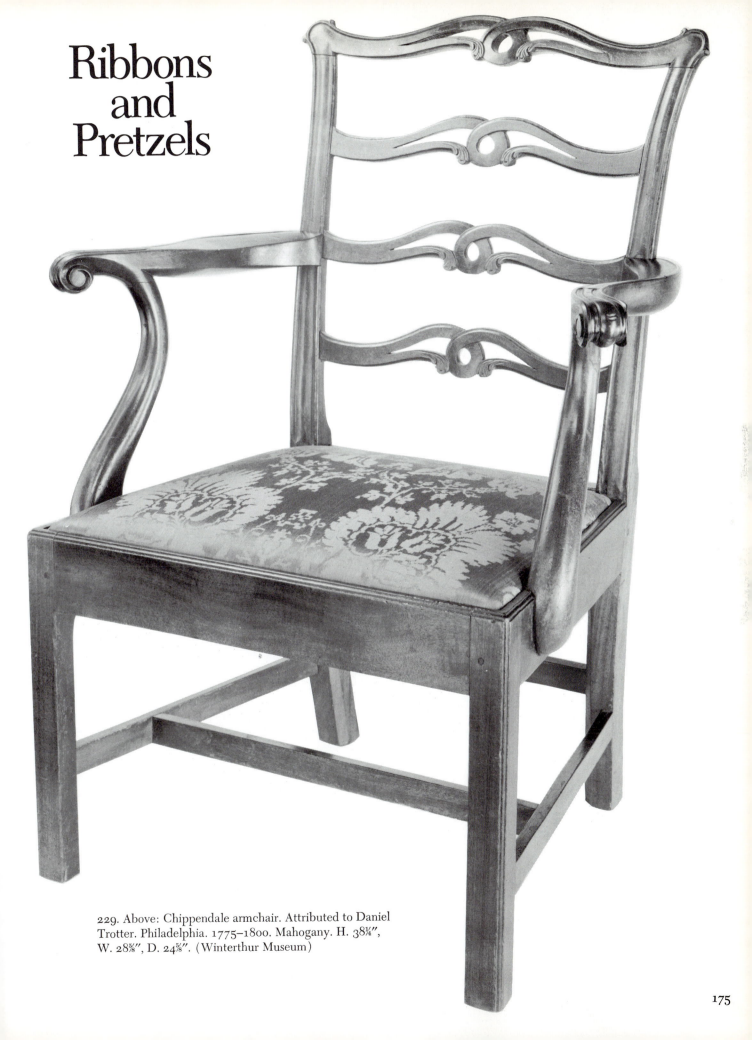

Ribbons and Pretzels

229. Above: Chippendale armchair. Attributed to Daniel Trotter. Philadelphia. 1775–1800. Mahogany. H. 38¼″, W. 28⅝″, D. 24⅝″. (Winterthur Museum)

230. Left: Chippendale bed rest. Connecticut. 1770–1800. Maple. H. 19″, W. 16⅝″, D. 22½″. This adjustable bed rest with pierced splats is unique. (Henry Ford Museum)

231. Right: Chippendale side chair. Possibly made by William Porter. Massachusetts. 1790. Mahogany, maple. H. 37¼″, W. 21¼″, D. 18¼″. This chair bears the brand of "W. Porter" on the bottom of the back seat rail. It was originally constructed without corner blocks and is upholstered over the seat and adorned with brass tacks. (Winterthur Museum)

232. Right, top: Chippendale side chair. Connecticut. 1775–1800. Cherry. H. 39″, W. 20½″, D. 16¼″. The slip-seat on this simple country chair retains its original needlepoint upholstery. (The Connecticut Historical Society)

233. Far right: Chippendale side chair. New Hampshire. 1780. Mahogany. H. 38½″, W. 21⅛″, D. 19¾″. The unpierced serpentine ladders on this chair are a simplified version of the pretzel-back. (Henry Ford Museum)

Rural approximations of city furniture are often unusual and beautiful. Their simple, flowing lines do not need the embellishment of rich carvings. Sturdy in nature, the chairs shown on these pages were the prized possessions of country gentlemen of the eighteenth century.

234. Above: Museum installation. Half-timbered frame houses, built in a style reminiscent of the homeland, were the first homes of German settlers in Pennsylvania. During the middle eighteenth century, these structures were frequently replaced by fieldstone farmhouses with furniture made from walnut, a durable wood that fulfilled the Teutonic desire for strength. The Baroque-style stucco-and-beamed-ceilinged room is from a house in Wernersville, Pennsylvania, built in 1755. It is furnished with Germanic-inspired American forms—the *schrank* or wardrobe, the sawbuck or trestle table, and the plank chairs. (Winterthur Museum)

235. Right, top: Slat-back armchair. Pennsylvania. Ca. 1730. Maple. H. 47″. This six-slat ladderback has many stylistic similarities to slat-backs created in the Delaware River Valley.

The large vase-and-ring-turned front stretcher, the ball feet on the front legs, and the shaped arms are all features that are encountered on "river chairs." (Museum of Fine Arts, Boston)

236. Near right: Chippendale style armchair. Pennsylvania. 1725–1775. Walnut. H. 44¼″, W. 26⅞″, D. 19¼″. This chair represents a rural Germanic interpretation of the Chippendale style. (Winterthur Museum)

237. Far right: Wainscot armchair. Pennsylvania. Ca. 1700. Walnut. H. 40½″. Wainscot chairs with solid wood seats were made well into the eighteenth century in Pennsylvania. This example, which was constructed with raised panels, is fitted with a padded cushion and probably was intended to be used as a commode chair. (Philadelphia Museum of Art)

From Germany

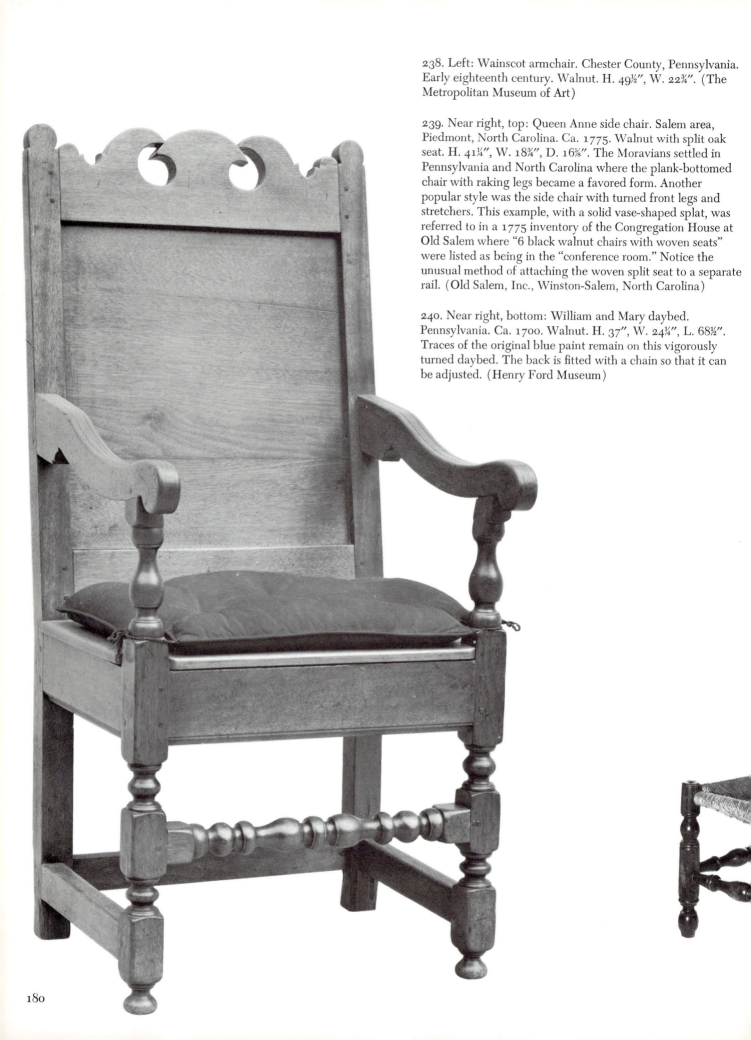

238. Left: Wainscot armchair. Chester County, Pennsylvania. Early eighteenth century. Walnut. H. 49½″, W. 22¾″. (The Metropolitan Museum of Art)

239. Near right, top: Queen Anne side chair. Salem area, Piedmont, North Carolina. Ca. 1775. Walnut with split oak seat. H. 41¼″, W. 18¾″, D. 16⅝″. The Moravians settled in Pennsylvania and North Carolina where the plank-bottomed chair with raking legs became a favored form. Another popular style was the side chair with turned front legs and stretchers. This example, with a solid vase-shaped splat, was referred to in a 1775 inventory of the Congregation House at Old Salem where "6 black walnut chairs with woven seats" were listed as being in the "conference room." Notice the unusual method of attaching the woven split seat to a separate rail. (Old Salem, Inc., Winston-Salem, North Carolina)

240. Near right, bottom: William and Mary daybed. Pennsylvania. Ca. 1700. Walnut. H. 37″, W. 24¼″, L. 68½″. Traces of the original blue paint remain on this vigorously turned daybed. The back is fitted with a chain so that it can be adjusted. (Henry Ford Museum)

241. Top: Museum installation. The Innkeeper's Quarters in the Salem Tavern are furnished with plank-bottomed chairs. Through the open doorway one can see Moravian slat-backs around the kitchen table. (Salem Tavern, Old Salem, Inc., Winston-Salem, North Carolina)

242. Above: Plank-bottomed chair. Pennsylvania. 1770. Walnut, white oak. H. 31¼″, W. 16¼″. The heart-shaped pierced back is carved with incised figures of a leaping stag, the initials "I H A," and is dated. Traces of brownish-red paint over an undercoat of yellow remain. (Winterthur Museum)

243. Below: "Monastery chair." Northern New England or Canada. Eighteenth century. Maple. H. 35″, W. 17″, D. 14½″. Monastery chairs were popular wherever French immigrants settled. This example, which retains traces of the original paint, was found in Vermont. (Shelburne Museum, Inc.)

244. Right: Louis XVI armchair. Louisiana. Ca. 1790. Cherry. H. 39½″, W. 23⅜″, D. 24½″. Because fruitwood was popular with provincial cabinet-makers in France, they continued to use it after they had emigrated to America. (Felix H. Kuntz)

From France

245. Right: Exterior of the Louis Bolduc house built at St. Genevieve, Missouri. Ca. 1785. This dwelling is typical of eighteenth-century French-Colonial architecture found in the middle Mississippi River Valley. (Missouri Historical Society)

246. Right: Large common living room of the Bolduc house. French Provincial furniture created in America resulted from a combination of diverse styles, making the origin of these pieces difficult to determine. Numerous maple chairs with salamander slats, like the early eighteenth-century armchair before the fireplace, were discovered in northern New England and, until recently, were always considered American. The child's chair with two salamander slats is possibly Canadian and of the seventeenth century, since the armposts are capped by mushroom-turned handrests, and the arms, which tie the back posts to the front posts, slope downward in front. (Missouri Historical Society)

247. Right: Hallway of the Bolduc house. This corridor, furnished both with Canadian and domestic pieces, divides the house into two rooms. (Missouri Historical Society)

248. Below; 249. Bottom: Portraits of young ladies painted by Anna Maria Von Phul. St. Louis, Missouri. 1818. Watercolor on paper. 248: H. 9⅞", W. 7¾". 249: H. 8½", W. 6⅜". Anna Maria Von Phul executed numerous drawings and watercolors which record St. Louis life during the early nineteenth century. The Directoire settee in figure 248 indicates that local cabinetmakers were well aware of the current Eastern fashions. (Missouri Historical Society)

250. Right: Salamander slat-back armchair. Found in Maine. 1780–1800. Maple. H. 45⅝", W. 21¾", D. 16¼". This chair was originally painted Indian red, a finish sometimes made from a buttermilk base. (Henry Ford Museum)

251. Below: Slat-back side chair. Missouri. Ca. 1800. Hickory, ash. H. 33", W. 18", D. 13". This Creole side chair retains the original finish. (Missouri Historical Society)

252. Portrait of Mrs. Cochran. Painted by Baroness Hyde De Newville (ca. 1779–1849). American. Detail of watercolor. H. 7¼″, W. 13⅜″. The French had occupied the Mississippi Valley almost one hundred years when the Baroness Anne-Marguerite-Henriette Hyde De Newville, a French amateur artist, accompanied her husband into exile in America. Her portrait of an eighty-four-year-old widow shows the venerable lady sitting in a crude slat-back chair. (The New-York Historical Society)

From Spain

253. Left: Church of Santo Tomas built at Las Trampas, New Mexico. Ca. 1760. Looking through the weathered front gate of this ancient adobe structure, one can sense the stark beauty of Spanish-Colonial architecture in the Southwest. (New Mexico State Tourist Bureau)

254. Left: Spanish-Colonial armchair. Probably made in California. Late eighteenth century. Pine with leather back and seat. H. 44″, W. 24″, D. 15″. (Index of American Design)

255. Above: Spanish-Colonial chair-table. Southwestern United States. 1830–1850. Pine. Height of table 25″. Diameter of table 33″. In their quest for gold, Spanish profiteers first entered the Southwest around 1540. In time, rude adobe settlements dotted the ever-expanding trade routes. The first furniture was mostly Hispanic in form. Gradually the task of furniture-making was assumed by native Indians who incorporated carved motifs into their designs. The painted chair-table is an odd mixture of both Indian and Spanish concepts. (Index of American Design)

256. Below: Empire-style side chair. Probably New Mexico. Ca. 1835. Pine. H. 31″, W. 15″, D. 15″. Trade along the Santa Fe Trail began in 1821. By the early 1830's native carpenters had adapted and simplified the American Empire style to create furniture that was distinctly their own. (Mrs. Cornelia G. Thompson, Loan to the Museum of New Mexico)

257. Above: Empire-style armchair. Probably New Mexico. Ca. 1835. Pine. H. 29½″, W. 21″, D. 16″. Native yellow pine was most often used for the construction of Southwestern furniture. This nineteenth-century armchair was fashioned using the standard mortise-and-tenon technique. (Museum of New Mexico)

258. Near right: Slat-back side chair. Northern New Mexico. 1800–1850. Pine. H. 31¼″, W. 15″, D. 14″. The decoration on this side chair was cut with a chisel. Note that the seat rails and rungs extend through the legs. (Historical Society of New Mexico)

259. Far right: Spanish-Colonial armchair. New Mexico. Late eighteenth century. Pine. H. 38″, W. 21″, D. 15″. Large chairs of this general form were called "Priest" chairs since they were made to be used in the sanctuary of a church. (Museum of New Mexico)

260. Above: Detail of a portrait of William Denning and his family. Painted by William Williams. American. Ca. 1772. Oil on canvas. H. 34½", W. 51". Mr. Denning is seated in a blue Windsor chair. The infant city of New York is visible in the background. (Denning Harvey)

The Windsor chair, for most contemporary Americans, remains unequaled in its preeminence as a symbol of America's past. To the uninitiated in the study of furniture, it would indeed be a surprise to discover that these simple forms, while often associated with Colonial leaders, reach back to fifteenth-century Gothic England for their origin. At St. Cross Hospital in Winchester is an ancient chair which in design is a prototype for later sixteenth-, seventeenth-, and eighteenth-century European adaptations. These adaptations, in turn, were the models that inspired Colonial craftsmen in America.

The English Windsor, while immensely popular, never achieved the degree of respectability that American ones enjoyed. Even though formal mahogany Windsor chairs were made by London chairmakers, Thomas Chippendale, in his *The Gentleman and Cabinet-Maker's Director*, 1754, did not include a single plate illustrating this then popular form. Its general use by the simple country folk was well established at the close of the seventeenth century, however, and a London advertisement of 1730—"All sorts of Windsor Garden Chairs, of all sizes painted green or in the wood"—demonstrates an urban English acceptance of the form that was to prevail.

261. Above: Detail of *The Signing of the Declaration of Independence*. From an engraving after a painting by Robert Edge Pine. H. 18", W. 24". Benjamin Franklin sits in

262. Above: Detail of a portrait of Elizabeth Fenimore Cooper. By Mr. Freeman. New York. Ca. 1816. Watercolor. H. 17½″, W. 21½″. Mrs. Cooper, the mother of the famous novelist, James Fenimore Cooper, furnished her home with numerous loop-back Windsor chairs. (New York State Historical Association)

a bow-back Windsor armchair while observing Congress in the final act of signing the Declaration of Independence from England. (Henry Ford Museum)

In America the situation was quite different. The Windsor was the universal chair of the eighteenth century. Even the most eminent and prosperous chose to live with Windsor chairs. Thomas Jefferson, while struggling with his first draft of the Declaration of Independence in late June, 1776, sat in a writing-arm Windsor. Franklin and other members of the Continental Congress, when voting to secede from the parent country on July 4, 1776, sat on Windsors in Independence Hall. General George Washington seated guests on the East portico at Mount Vernon in thirty Windsor chairs. The Windsor, in its more formal form, shared company with Queen Anne and Chippendale furniture of the most luxurious design.

There are essentially seven basic varieties of Windsor chair design—the comb, fan, bow, arch, loop, rod, and low-back. Evidence indicates that in Philadephia, the birthplace of the American Windsor, these forms were made and shipped to other colonies along the Eastern seaboard, where they served as models for local chairmakers. These craftsmen, from diverse backgrounds, adapted, refined, and embellished the basic designs and developed countless variants of the Windsor.

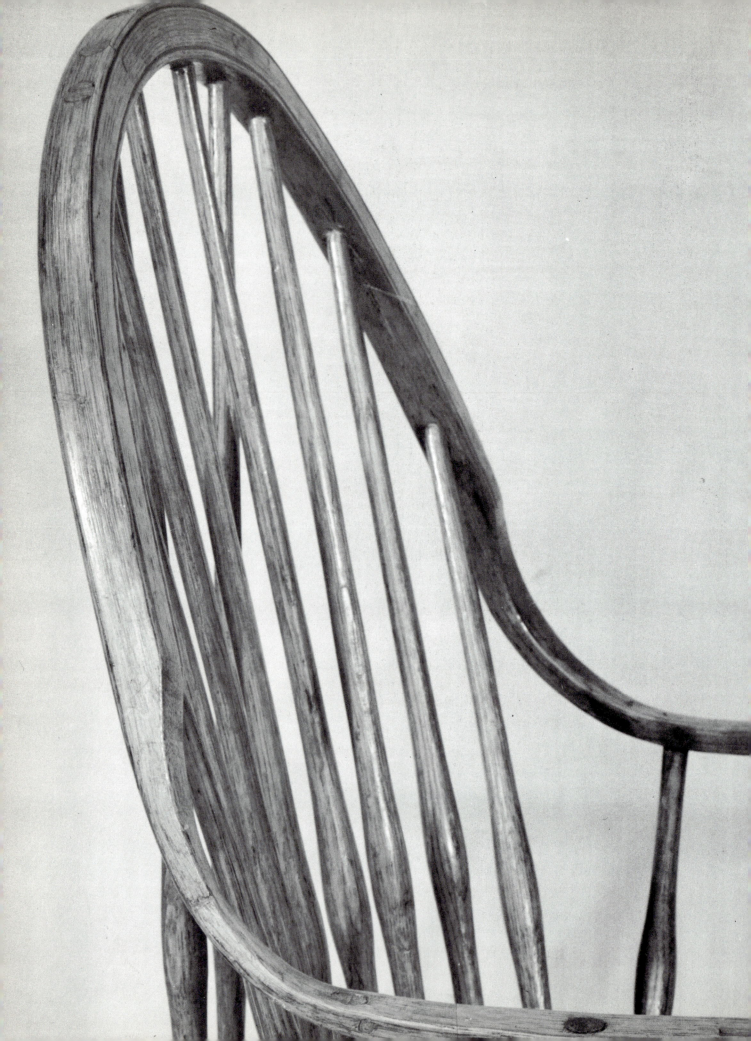

264. Above: Needlework cushion. Made by Martha Washington for use on a Windsor chair. Wool yarn on canvas with silk fringe. W. 18¾″, D. 15½″. This is one of twelve shell-patterned cushions worked by Mrs. Washington over a period of thirty-six years. (The Mount Vernon Ladies' Association of the Union)

"'Brass Nail finish'd around," the braced arch-back upholstered Windsor, figures 263 and 263a, with its original embossed, black leather-covered seat, bears the stamp "EB:Tracy." Connecticut cabinetmaker, Colonel Ebenezer Tracy (1744–1803), so titled for his service in the American Revolution, chose to paint red the undersurface of the seat of this vigorous chair. Since Windsors were intentionally constructed with both seasoned and green woods of several kinds, each chosen for its unique qualities, they were almost always painted—generally black, green, red, or yellow. Chairs with bamboo-turned legs, though often considered to date from the late eighteenth century, were described in a Philadelphia journal of 1763.

In this chair, the bracing device—the two extra spindles that slant from the tapered tailpiece of the seat to the bowed back—gives additional support to an otherwise frequently unsturdy form.

An English visitor to Mount Vernon made note of "yellow bottom Windsor chairs" in the Little Parlor. These chairs were fitted with needlework cushions, figure 264, made by Martha Washington in a tent-stitch shell pattern worked in brown on a yellow ground. Washington's executors listed ten such Windsors in this room.

263. Above; 263a. Far left: Continuous-arm Windsor armchair. Made by Ebenezer Tracy. Lisbon, Connecticut. Ca. 1790. Chestnut, hickory, maple, and oak with original black, embossed-leather upholstery. Height of back 37¼″. (Los Angeles County Museum)

193

265. Left: Bow-back Windsor armchair. New England. 1775–1800. Pine, hickory, maple. H. 36¼", W. 25¾", D. 20". The painted gilt decoration on the legs of this bow-back Windsor armchair is typical of late nineteenth-century coachwork. Few Windsors retain their original finish. The painted gold stars and scrolls and grained seat centered by a sponged diamond are probably later embellishments also. (Henry Ford Museum)

A Boston Gentleman, clothed in a stylish manner typical of the late eighteenth century, appears to be satisfied with himself and his position in life. His rather self-conscious pose and demeanor would seem to indicate that this was a man who meticulously selected the furnishings he wished to live with. The bow-back Windsor in which he sits is more similar in form to those made in Connecticut than those sold by Massachusetts chairmakers, since its back has only seven spindles instead of the nine associated with chairs from the Boston area. The bow-back armchair, figure 265, was especially popular in New England. This example, with its painted decoration, saddled seat, splayed legs, and slightly raked back, is comfortable and elegant. The triple bow-back settee, figure 267, has arms that terminate in knuckle carvings. It demonstrates an excellence of construction and design that places it above most others. Like the armchair illustrated left, the seat is shaped and the legs generously splayed.

266. Left: Portrait of *A Boston Gentleman* sitting in a bow-back Windsor. Painted by Christian Gullager (1759–1826). American. Oil on canvas. H. 71¼″, W. 54″. (Corcoran Gallery of Art)

267. Below: Windsor settee. Massachusetts or Connecticut. 1775–1800. Oak, hickory, maple. H. 38⅛″, D. 22½″, L. 98½″. The New England bow-back Windsor settee is topped by three interlocking combs. It is one of the most distinctive examples of this form known. (Winterthur Museum)

The fan-back Windsor derives its name from the flaring, fanlike outline of the back. Figure 268 illustrates a common example of this type of chair. More sought after are those chairs constructed with nine spindles at the back. Most highly prized is the fan-back that can boast eleven spindles. The fan-back, shown left, is typical of those from New England in that the vase-turned legs are tapered at the bottom. The rather prominent pommel at the center of the carefully shaped saddle seat is pleasingly distinctive. These chairs, as with most Windsors, were made in sets of four or more and were frequently accompanied by matching armchairs.

268. Left: Fan-back Windsor side chair. Rhode Island. 1770–1800. Maple, hickory, pine. H. 40″, W. 14½″, D. 15¼″. Numerous "green chairs" were made in the Providence area and often offered for sale by the dozen during the last years of the eighteenth century. (Mr. and Mrs. Joseph K. Ott)

269. Above: Loop-back Windsor side chair. Philadelphia. 1775–1800. Yellow poplar, maple. H. 37″, W. 16½″, D. 16¼″. George and Martha Washington lived with many Windsor chairs at Mount Vernon. (The Mount Vernon Ladies' Association of the Union)

271. Overleaf: *Country Wedding; Bishop White Officiating.* Painted by John Lewis Krimmel (1787–1821). Philadelphia. Ca. 1819. Oil on canvas. H. 16¾″, W. 22½″. (Pennsylvania Academy of the Fine Arts)

Loop-back side chairs, figure 269, were probably the most common pieces of seating equipment in Colonial America. This, and twenty-six matching "ovel" chairs, were purchased from the Philadelphia Windsor chairmakers, Gilbert and Robert Gaw, in 1796 by George Washington and used at Mount Vernon after his retirement as President of the United States. Evidence indicates that Washington also owned a Windsor riding vehicle—a chair-like affair attached to a platform mounted on two large wagon wheels with springs. Figure 271, an early nineteenth-century painting by John Lewis Krimmel of Bishop White officiating at a country wedding demonstrates the use of a fan-back and a loop-back Windsor chair in an interior far more simple than that enjoyed by the Washingtons. Worthy of note is the impressive scrolled-bonnet tall case clock in the left corner behind the door.

270. Below: Museum installation. The Commons Room at Winterthur is furnished with Windsor chairs of many styles, including a loop-back, a low-back, and a fan-back. (Winterthur Museum)

272. Above: Low-back Windsor bench. Possibly Milford, Connecticut. 1750–1810. Pine, maple, ash. H. 24″, L. 78″. The construction of this piece indicates that it probably never had a top rail or comb. (Taylor Family)

The writing-arm Windsor chair, generally with a comb-back, seems, like so many other forms, to have originated in Philadelphia. A resident of that city, writing in the spring of 1763, recorded his order for two such chairs from "... Richmonde on Sassafras Street, a joiner of much repute who has come out from the Motherland." Later, this same writer, perhaps sitting, quill and sander in hand, in one of the newly acquired chairs, reported, "... Chairs arrived, am so pleased, shall not take them to country."

The footstool, figure 273, clearly demonstrates the method by which most legs were fastened to the body of Windsor chairs. Holes were drilled through the seat; the leg tenon, split at the top, inserted; and a wedge, driven from the upper side of the seat, forced the tenon. A blind joint was occasionally used. Essentially the same procedure was followed in that method of construction. The hole when drilled was not allowed to penetrate through the top of the seat. The spreading wedge was partially inserted before the leg was driven into position. The wedge, forced by pressure from the solid top of the drilled hole, spreads the leg to form the joint.

273. Right: Windsor footstool. New England. 1775–1800. Pine, maple. H. 10¾″, W. 13″, D. 9⅞″. Footstools like this example were called "crickets" during the nineteenth century. (Henry Ford Museum)

274. Above: Comb-back Windsor writing-arm chair. New England. 1760–1790. Maple, hickory, white pine, butternut. H. 46⅛″, W. 35⅞″, D. 31 1/16″. Shallow, dovetailed, sliding drawers are fitted below the writing-arm surface and the shaped saddle seat. (Winterthur Museum)

276. Above; 277. Right: Portraits of the Marquis and Mrs. Calmes IV. Painted by G. Frymeier. Kentucky. 1806. Oil on canvas. 276: H. 29″, W. 24″. 277: H. 27½″, W. 22″. (Chicago Historical Society)

The Pennsylvania armchair, figure 275, is similar to that in which Mrs. Calmes sat while her portrait was painted by G. Frymeier in 1806. Her husband, Marquis Calmes (1755–1839), also painted by Frymeier, participated as a captain in American military engagements during the Revolutionary War. Elevated in rank, he served as a brigadier general during the War of 1812. The legs of Philadelphia armchairs are often deeply splayed or raked and terminate with blunt-arrow feet. The serpentine arms of this distinctive chair are tenoned into the rear stiles which extend from the seat to the crest rail.

275. Left: Braced fan-back Windsor armchair. Pennsylvania. 1750–1780. Tulipwood, maple, hickory, oak. H. 40⅜″, W. 26″, D. 23¼″. Many Philadelphia Windsors are constructed with blunt-arrow feet. (The Art Institute of Chicago)

278. Left: Windsor settee. Rhode Island. 1750–1800. Maple, pine, hickory, painted green. H. 42½″, D. 20″, L. 37″. The design of this unusual form is greatly enhanced by the sensitive dishing of the seat. (Henry Ford Museum)

279. Right: Continuous-arm Windsor high chair. New England. 1765–1780. Maple, pine, hickory, birch. H. 37¼″, W. 19⅜″, D. 19″. (Winterthur Museum)

The Rhode Island Windsor settee, figure 278, and the arched-high-back or continuous-arm bow-back high chair from New England, figure 279, are impressive both for their rarity of form and for their beautiful design. The shaped double-saddled seat of the settee is divided by a thumbnail-like carving over the center front leg. The high chair, with its boldly shaped seat and vigorously turned arm supports, back spindles, powerful raking legs, and bulbous medial stretcher, is a masterpiece of construction. Both the settee and chair are pieces from a large group of furniture constructed with Windsor-type turned members that was made with a special purpose or function in mind. Other forms include simple country tables with breadboard tops and turned Windsor bases, candlestands, footstools or "crickets," and spinning wheels. In countless eighteenth- and nineteenth-century newspaper advertisements, country chairmakers offered their rural clients "fancy chairs, Windsors and Spinning Wheels in the finest, up to date manner . . . both painted, stained or in the natural."

280. Left: Drawing of a "stick chair" by Thomas
Jefferson. 1800. H. 1⁵⁄₁₆″. Jefferson intended to use
this chair in his Virginia home, Monticello.
(Massachusetts Historical Society)

281. Above: Windsor bench. New England.
1810–1820. Pine, maple, hickory, painted black.
H. 36⅛″, D. 19″, L. 83″. The design of the back
and arms on this piece is often called "birdcage."
(Henry Ford Museum)

282. Below: Low-back, writing-arm Windsor. Made by T. C. Hayward. Charlestown, Massachusetts. 1770–1800. Maple, pine, ash. H. 33½″, W. 38⅛″, D. 30″. (Henry Ford Museum)

Rod-back Windsor chairs, from the collector's point of view, are much less desirable than the somewhat earlier, more boldly turned versions illustrated on the previous pages. The simplification of turning on the arms and back of the New England settee, figure 281, is topped with a birdcage-like decorative device which accounts for the naming of seating furniture made in this general form. The writing-arm chair from Charlestown, Massachusetts, is branded "T. C. Hayward" for Thomas Cotton Hayward. Note the "bamboo" turnings on the legs and stretchers of both the settee and chair.

Thomas Jefferson included a drawing of a Windsor side chair, figure 280, in a letter to his business agent, George Jefferson, written from Monticello on July 19, 1800. Originally Jefferson had ordered from Philadelphia, "half a dozen . . . stick chairs" and those delivered were not the style he desired. In 1801 Jefferson was billed for "4 Dozen of Arm Chairs Black and Gold for the President of the United States—$192."

283. Near right: *Schoolmaster and Boys.* Possibly Pennsylvania. Ca. 1815. Watercolor on paper. H. 13⅞", W. 11½". Youths were instructed from *The New England Primer* in Colonial times. In this nineteenth-century watercolor, the two young men learn the Ten Commandments from a schoolmaster who sits in a simple country Windsor chair. (Abby Aldrich Rockefeller Folk Art Collection)

284. Center, right: Portrait of Theodore Dwight (1764–1846). Painted by Ezra Ames (1768–1836). New York. Nineteenth century. Oil on canvas. H. 46½", W. 36". The noted author, editor, and lawyer Theodore Dwight amused himself by writing poetry. In this painting he is shown, quill in hand, sitting in a comb-back Windsor armchair. (Vose Galleries)

285. Far right, top: Portrait of Edward Hicks. Painted by Thomas Hicks. Pennsylvania. 1838. Oil on canvas. H. 27", W. 22". (The Colonial Williamsburg Foundation)

286. Far right, bottom: Portrait of William Whetcroft. Painted by Charles Willson Peale (1741–1827). American. Eighteenth century. Oil on canvas. H. 38", W. 28". The "sins of man" are frequently recorded in the annals of America's past—bowling on the green in seventeenth-century New Amsterdam, golf in 1729, cards and billiards in 1750. It was indeed a wicked world that permitted horse racing. In 1751, a silver trophy was awarded to Lewis Morris, Jr., for the performance given by his horse Old Tenor. The silversmith (goldsmith), besides providing hollow and flatware for dining purposes, often crafted special commission pieces such as this trophy. The eighteenth-century Baltimore silversmith, William Whetcroft (died 1789), sits, holding a cane, in a Windsor armchair. The landscape seen through the open window might be either of Baltimore or of Annapolis, since Whetcroft is known to have worked in both cities. (Yale University Art Gallery)

CHAPTER 7

THE HEPPLEWHITE AND SHERATON STYLES 1785-1815

Easy Chair

287. Right; 288. Below: Designs from George Hepplewhite's *The Cabinet-Maker and Upholsterer's Guide*. Published in London. 1788. (Henry Ford Museum)

289. Far right, top; 290. Far right, center; 291. Far right, bottom: "Backs for Parlour Chairs" from Thomas Sheraton's *Cabinet-Maker and Upholsterer's Drawing Book*, published in London. 1791–1794. (Henry Ford Museum)

Introduction

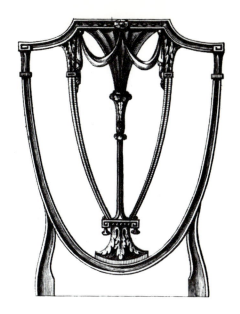

The American Federal style, 1790–1810, is based upon design concepts and drawings published in George Hepplewhite's *The Cabinet-Maker and Upholsterer's Guide,* 1788, and Thomas Sheraton's *Cabinet-Maker and Upholsterer's Drawing Book* of 1791–1794. These Englishmen were, in turn, further refining the designs of Robert Adam (1728–1792). During the period immediately following the 1760's, Adam selected motifs from the Renaissance and ancient past, altered them to suit his own personal taste, and incorporated them into the decorative schemes he was completing for wealthy patrons. Adam's design concepts for furniture were first adapted for wide use in Hepplewhite's *Guide* of 1788. "Chairs in general are made of mahogany, with the bars and frame sunk in a hollow, or rising in a round projection, with a band or lift on the inner and outer edges. Many of these designs are enriched with ornaments proper to be carved in mahogany." Numerous Hepplewhite plates indicate a preference for fine inlay. Though not exclusively, he emphasized tapering legs, square in section, for seating furniture. Specific about chair proportions, he wrote, "The general dimension and proportion of chairs are as follow: Width in front 20 inches, depth of the seat 17 inches, height of the seat frame 17 inches; total height about 3 feet 1 inch. Other dimensions are frequently adapted according to the size of the room, or pleasure of the purchaser." George Hepplewhite, the obscure cabinetmaker of London's Cripplegate, died before success was within his grasp. In fact, his wife Alice published his manuscript some two years after his death in 1786.

The journeyman, Thomas Sheraton, born in Stockton-on-Tees, moved to London in 1790, where he taught drawing and wrote books on design theory. Although he did not have a workshop of his own, he toured London's cabinetmaking shops, where he found inspiration for the illustrations to be used in his *Drawing Book,* including "A Display of the present Taste of Household Furniture; containing also useful Remarks on the manufacturing Part of difficult Pieces. To which are added, some Cornices drawn at large; the Method shewn of Gaging, Working, Contracting, and Enlarging of any Kind; together with two Methods of representing a Drawing-Room." Sheraton favored square backs and recommended the use of turned and reeded legs. Only two shield-back chairs were shown. Speaking of chairmaking in his *Cabinet Dictionary* of 1803, he defined it as "a branch, generally confined to itself; as those who professedly work at it seldom engage to make cabinet furniture."

Furniture crafted in the Hepplewhite and Sheraton styles dominated the American furniture market from 1790 to 1810. Just after the dawn of the new century, however, French influence became apparent. This influence expanded later in the century, and furniture design became an archaeological pursuit.

292. Left: Portrait of Mrs. Thomas Willing Francis (Dorothy Willing). Painted by Gilbert Stuart (1755–1828). American. Ca. 1815. Oil on canvas. H. 29″, W. 24″. Mrs. Francis sits in a carved and gilded "French" armchair. (Privately owned)

293. Below: Federal armchair in the Louis XVI style. Philadelphia. Ca. 1790. Ash, with gesso and gilding. H. 35¼″, W. 24¼″, D. 22½″. (Philadelphia Museum of Art)

294. Right: Detail of *View of the Philadelphia Exchange*. By "W. Strickland, Architect and pinx." American. 1835. Wash drawing, H. 3⅞″. John King, a manufacturer of gold leaf, maintained his shop near the old Philadelphia Exchange. The sign of his establishment can be seen just to the left of the exchange. (The New York Public Library)

Because of a close affiliation with France at the close of the eighteenth century, French-styled furniture was popular with American political leaders. Thomas Jefferson, among other prominent statesmen, favored glided pieces. Edward Burd of Philadelphia originally owned the Louis XVI-style open armchair, figure 293. It is from a set of twelve chairs and a sofa which was originally painted white and decorated with gold. Sheets of gold leaf, manufactured specifically for use on such seating pieces, might have been purchased from the shop of John King, figure 294.

Federal Philadelphia

295. Right: Federal side chair. Philadelphia. Ca. 1790. Mahogany. H. 37½″, W. 21½″, D. 18¾″. This piece is from a set of six consisting of two armchairs and four side chairs. Note the delicate fluted and carved leg terminating in a rounded foot. (Ginsburg & Levy, Inc.)

296. Below: Federal sofa in the Louis XVI style. Philadelphia. Ca. 1790. Ash, with gesso and gilding. H. 37″, D. 26″, L. 73½″. This sofa and twelve matching armchairs, figure 293, are from the famous "Marie Antoinette Suite" that belonged to Edward Burd in the eighteenth century, and then to his son Edward Shippen Burd of Philadelphia. (Philadelphia Museum of Art)

297. Left: Federal "cabriole" armchair. Philadelphia. Ca. 1800. Ash. H. 36½", W. 20½", D. 21¼". This piece is painted white and gilded. Applied and gilded trailing-leaf decoration embellishes much of the surface. (Winterthur Museum)

298. Below: Federal armchair. Philadelphia. Ca. 1790. Mahogany. H. 37½", W. 21½", D. 19". Carved swags and tasseled bowknots decorate the crest rail of this and other pieces from the set. (Ginsburg & Levy, Inc.)

299. Right: Federal settee. Philadelphia. Ca. 1800. Mahogany. H. 36½″, D. 23½″, L. 75″. This piece of seating furniture is from a suite that includes four armchairs and four side chairs. (The White House)

300. Below: Museum installation. The design of the cabriole chairs shown in this room interior is quite similar to that of the White House settee. George Hepplewhite was most specific when he stated, "Chairs with stuffed backs are called cabriole chairs." (Winterthur Museum)

301. Above: Design from James Gibbs's eighteenth-century *Book of Architecture*. Design books were the direct source of inspiration for many American craftsmen and architects, who relied upon these manuals. This particular elevation probably served as the model for James Hoban when he planned "The President's House" (White House). It also was freely used by numerous Philadelphia architects during the late eighteenth and early nineteenth centuries. (Library of Congress).

302. Right: Federal side chair. Philadelphia. Ca. 1795. Beech. H. 38¾", D. 19". This painted and decorated Philadelphia side chair is one from a large suite ordered by Elias Hasket Derby for his Salem, Massachusetts, home. Its design mirrors English chairs of a slightly earlier date. (Museum of Fine Arts, Boston)

303. Above: Printed paper label from a small mahogany chest or cabinet made by Henry Connelly. Philadelphia. 1808–1818. Engraved by J. Draper. (Winterthur Museum)

304. Above, right: Federal side chair. Attributed to Henry Connelly. Philadelphia. 1790–1800. Mahogany. H. 34½″, W. 20½″, D. 19″½. Much Philadelphia furniture of this period is constructed with a "D-shape" seat rail as seen in this example. (Ginsburg & Levy, Inc.)

305. Left: Federal sofa. Attributed to Henry Connelly. Philadelphia. 1790–1800. Dimensions unavailable. This piece is constructed with turned and reeded legs ending with a cylindrical, tapering spade-foot. (Private Collection)

306. Above: Federal armchair. Attributed to Henry Connelly. Philadelphia. 1790–1800. Mahogany. H. 34½″, W. 20½″, D. 19½″. This, with figure 304, is from a set of chairs numbering six, one armchair and five side chairs. Connelly worked at 16 Chestnut Street until 1802 when he moved to 44 Spruce Street. (Ginsburg & Levy, Inc.)

307. Above, right: Portrait of Henry Connelly. Painted by Thomas Sully. American. Nineteenth century. Oil on canvas. H. 36″, W. 30″. (Mr. and Mrs. Harry C. Groome, Jr.)

308. Right: Federal side chair. Attributed to Henry Connelly. Philadelphia. Ca. 1800. Mahogany. H. 37″, W. 20¼″, D. 19¼″. This chair, one of a pair, was constructed with a "racket" back. (Henry Ford Museum)

310. Above: Federal settee. Made by Ephraim Haines. Philadelphia. 1807. Ebony. H. 36″, D. 25½″, L. 72″. The original bill for this settee and accompanying chair, figure 313, dated November 21, 1807, was rendered by Haines to Stephen Girard. Haines is known to have made many pieces for Girard over a period of several years. (Girard College)

The work of the Philadelphia cabinetmakers Henry Connelly (1770–1826) and Ephraim Haines (after 1775–1811) has always been difficult to distinguish. Both of these craftsmen worked in Philadelphia during the early nineteenth century in a style that was similar. Connelly, however, used a turned, crisp spade foot, while Haines preferred a bulbous, pointed terminal. Haines, originally apprenticed to Daniel Trotter, became his partner in 1799. In 1811 he opened a lumberyard which specialized in the sale of fine-grade mahogany. Connelly, in his later years, made furniture in the Empire style. After Haines opened his lumber business, commissions from the prominent Philadelphia educator Stephen Girard went to Connelly, who created for this distinguished citizen a large sideboard on carved animal-paw feet.

309. Left: Federal armchair. Attributed to Henry Connelly. Philadelphia. 1804. Mahogany. H. 33½″, W. 20¼″, D. 20″. The seat of this chair is caned. Originally a thin pad would have probably been used to protect the fragile caning. (Ginsburg & Levy, Inc.)

311. Right: Federal armchair. Made by Henry Connelly. Philadelphia. Ca. 1800. Mahogany. H. 34⅜″, W. 22¼″, D. 22¾″. The urn-and-drapery design so popular in Philadelphia was borrowed from Sheraton. It appeared later in the Philadelphia *Book of Prices*, 1795. (Henry Ford Museum)

312. Right: Federal armchair. Made by Ephraim Haines. Philadelphia. Ca. 1800. Mahogany. H. 34⅝″, W. 22½″, D. 21½″. The turned motifs incorporated into the design of the back on this chair are similar to those shown in Plate 36 of Sheraton's 1792 *Drawing Book*. (Henry Ford Museum)

313. Above: Federal side chair. Made by Ephraim Haines. Philadelphia. 1807. Ebony. H. 35½″, W. 20″, D. 17¾″. Girard's original suite of furniture consisted of a settee, a pair of armchairs, and ten side chairs, and was made for use in his "front parlor." (Girard College)

314. Above, left: Printed paper label of William Camp. Baltimore, Maryland. Late eighteenth century? The label was engraved by James Akin. Camp was a Baltimore cabinetmaker and upholsterer. Many of the pieces which are illustrated on his label were taken from Sheraton's *Drawing Book*. Several of the illustrations on the label of Joseph B. Barry, a Philadelphia craftsman, are also from the same source. (The Baltimore Museum of Art)

315. Above, right: Federal armchair. Baltimore. 1800–1810. Mahogany. H. 38", W. 23", D. 20". The design of this chair is very similar to contemporary examples crafted in New York cabinetmaking shops. (Henry Ford Museum)

316. Left, bottom: *View of Baltimore from the Northwest.*
American. Ca. 1800. Watercolor. H. 12¾″, W. 15⁹⁄₁₆″. The
unknown artist viewed the city of Baltimore from an
elevation above the northern limits of town. The twin-steeple
church is the First Presbyterian Church founded in 1763,
and to the right is the courthouse with its tall spire and
weather vane and arched underpinning where Calvert Street
threaded northward. This underpassage in the courthouse
was cut through in 1786. (Maryland Historical Society)

317. Above: Federal side chair. Possibly by Warwick Price.
Baltimore. Ca. 1800. Tulipwood. H. 37¾″, W. 20⅜″, D. 20″.
The inlay on the upper portions of the splats in the shield-
back and around the seat rails of this chair is similar to that
executed in the shop of Warwick Price at the "foot of High
Street Old Town Baltimore." (Winterthur Museum)

318. Right: Federal side chair. Baltimore. Ca. 1795.
Mahogany. H. 37″, W. 21″, D. 19″. Maryland's large
mid-eighteenth-century Tidewater plantations were
predominantly furnished with English exports. At the close
of the Colonial period, however, Baltimore emerged as an
important center of cabinetmaking where both rich carving
and fine inlay were skillfully executed. The production of
painted and "fancy decorated furniture" was equally
important in that infant cosmopolitan center. The elegantly
carved "draped icicle" splat of this chair is decorated with a
pendant of carved bellflowers. The motif is repeated on the
legs. (The Baltimore Museum of Art)

319. Right; 319a. Center: Federal side chair. Baltimore. Ca. 1800. Mahogany. H. 39¾″, W. 21″, D. 20½″. The plumed splat of this Hepplewhite shield-back side chair is superbly carved. The ample seat is accentuated by a serpentine front rail and by the use of slender tapering legs. (Henry Ford Museum)

320. Left: Federal side chair. Attributed to John Shaw. Annapolis, Maryland. 1785–1795. Mahogany. H. 34″, W. 20″, D. 19″. Annapolis rivaled Baltimore as a center of cabinetmaking. Particularly distinctive is the furniture created by the Scottish-American craftsman, John Shaw (1745–1829). Because this side chair is identical to a labeled example, it is attributed to him. It is believed to be part of a set originally owned by Robert Bowie, Governor-elect of Maryland in 1803. Shaw also made furniture for Maryland's House of Delegates and is especially known for inlaid case pieces. (The Metropolitan Museum of Art)

321. Above: Museum installation. Baltimore drawing room. The furniture in this interior is mostly of Maryland origin. The painted corner tables with marble tops, the cylindrical fall desk-and-bookcase and the chairs before it demonstrate that craftsmen from this area could compete on an equal basis with their Northern contemporaries. (Winterthur Museum)

322. Below: Federal side chair. Baltimore. 1800. Walnut with maple inlay. H. 36¼″, W. 20″, D. 20½″. The bellflower was a popular Federal motif. The central petal of bellflower inlay on Baltimore pieces is almost always longer than the side petals. (Henry Ford Museum)

New York Federal

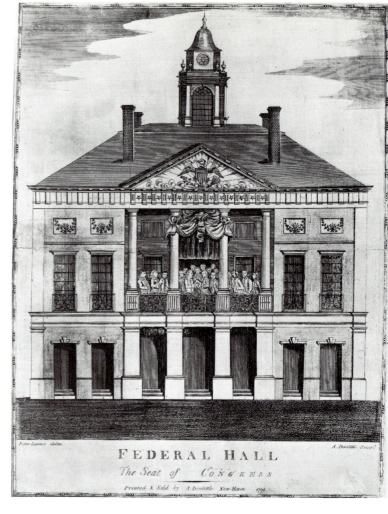

323. Left: Federal side chair. New York. 1788–1795. Mahogany. H. 37″, W. 22½″, D. 20″. This side chair, which matches an armchair in the collection of The New-York Historical Society, is said to have been used at the inauguration of President Washington on April 30, 1789. Both Sheraton and Hepplewhite motifs are incorporated into the design of this piece. (New York State History Collection, Albany; photograph courtesy Ginsburg & Levy, Inc.)

324. Above: *View of Federal Hall, the Seat of Congress.* Printed and sold by Amos Doolittle. New Haven, Connecticut. 1790. Engraving. H. 16⁹⁄₁₆″, W. 12¹³⁄₁₆″. The inauguration of George Washington as first President of the United States took place on the second-story porch of this building. (Stokes Collection, The New York Public Library)

325. Right: Federal side chair. New York. 1790–1805. Mahogany. H. 37½″, W. 19½″, D. 17″. This chair was traditionally used in Federal Hall, where primary meetings were held in an attempt to organize a national government. Federal Hall, originally built in 1699 and reconstructed in 1788–1789 under the direction of the French architect and engineer, Major Pierre Charles L'Enfant, for Washington's inauguration, was used as a meetinghouse for the newly formed Congress. A year later it was razed to provide space for the construction of the United States Custom House. Washington pledged his oath on the draped balcony of this historic building so that the multitudes might observe the important event. The chair is constructed in the fashionable Louis XVI style. (Museum of the City of New York)

326. Below: Museum installation. The Sheraton-style mahogany armchairs and side chairs are probably part of the furniture bought in 1813 for the recently completed New York City Hall. The desk-with-cupboard has cast-iron Egyptian heads crowning the tops of the heavy, reeded legs. Perhaps the designer intended the heads to be gilded in imitation of French ormolu. (Art Commission of the City of New York)

327. Left: Federal armchair. New York. Ca. 1800. Mahogany. H. 36", W. 34¾", D. 20". The carving of the drapery and plumes on the splat of this Sheraton armchair is duplicated in inlay on the side chair, figure 330. (Henry Ford Museum)

328. Right: Federal side chair. New York. 1790–1800. Mahogany, ash. H. 36", W. 21¾", D. 19½". This chair, one of a pair, has front legs that are square, tapered, and slightly flared; the back legs are square, tapered, and canted. (Henry Ford Museum)

329. Top, left: Federal side chair. New York. Ca. 1800. Mahogany with satinwood inlay. H. 36″, W. 21¾″, D. 18½″. Contemporary records indicate that icicle-shaped splats were called "urn" splats. The top rail, the splats, and the front legs of this very sophisticated chair are delicately inlaid with satinwood bellflowers and other fanciful motifs. (Museum of Fine Arts, Boston)

330. Top, right: Federal side chair. New York. 1790–1800. Mahogany with satinwood inlay. H. 36″, W. 21¾″, D. 18½″. The inlaid stars, plumes, and drapery on the back and the legs of this chair are most skillfully executed. The seat is upholstered over the rail and a double row of brass-headed nails secures the fabric. (Museum of Fine Arts, Boston)

331. Right: Federal armchair. New York. Ca. 1800. Mahogany, white oak, tulipwood. H. 35⅛″, W. 22⅜″, D. 21⅛″. This chair has many features that are associated with the cabinetmaking shops of New York. The pierced "urn" splats, the outward curving arms with carved rosettes, and the slightly splayed legs are common expressions of this metropolitan school of cabinetmaking. This piece is from a suite of two armchairs, ten matching side chairs, and a sofa, all owned by Victor Marie du Pont, a resident of New York City. The form is described in the 1802 publication, *The New York Book of Prices for Cabinet and Chair Work*, where it is listed as "a square back chair, no. 11 With three small urn splatts, sweep stay and top rail, with a brake in ditto . . ." (Winterthur Museum)

332. Above; 332a. Left: Federal sofa. New York. Ca. 1800. Mahogany. H. 43″, L. 75¼″. Sofas of this general form have often been attributed to the New York City furniture-makers, Slover and Taylor, working together from 1802 to 1805. Since so many of these pieces have appeared around Albany, it is believed that they were also constructed in that area. Adam DeGrushe, advertising in the Albany *Gazette* in 1799, informed the local inhabitants that he stuffed and covered sofas. He also sold curtains, venetian blinds, and paper hangings. (Albany Institute of History and Art)

333. Left: Federal armchair. New York. 1790–1800. Mahogany, satinwood, beech, spruce, ash, black ash. H. 35⅝″, W. 24½″, D. 21¾″. This spade-footed armchair, one of a pair, is either of New York City or Albany manufacture. An unusual feature is the construction of the rear legs which turn and flare outward. (Winterthur Museum)

334. Right: Museum installation. The Albany overmantel mirror is complemented by a pair of side chairs from the New York shop of Duncan Phyfe. (Winterthur Museum)

335. Top: Federal sofa. Attributed to Duncan Phyfe (1768–1854). New York City. 1800–1810. Mahogany. H. 38½", D. 29", L. 80". The top rail of this three-chair-back sofa is carved with thunderbolts, sheaves of wheat, and tied bowknots. The sensitive handling of the incurved arms is typical of the innovative design concepts that Phyfe and his craftsmen mastered so completely. (Henry Ford Museum)

336. Above: Paper label from a mahogany worktable with marble top, made by Duncan Phyfe. On this label, Phyfe lists his address as 33 and 35 Partition Street where he worked from 1811 to 1816. Few pieces survive that bear Phyfe's original label. (Winterthur Museum)

337. Left: Federal easy chair. New York. 1805–1815. Mahogany. H. 36½", W. 30½", D. 31½". Chairs of this style are called "Fauteuils." A similar chair was illustrated in Sheraton's *Cabinet Dictionary*, Plate 8, No. 2. (Winterthur Museum)

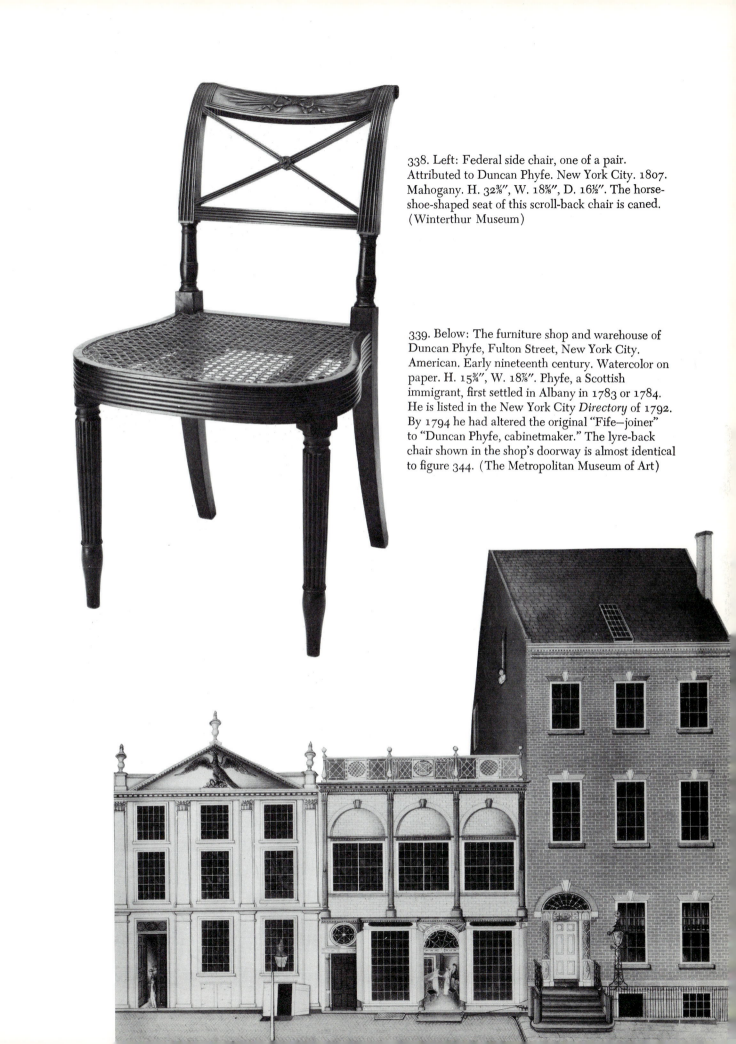

338. Left: Federal side chair, one of a pair. Attributed to Duncan Phyfe. New York City. 1807. Mahogany. H. 32⅜″, W. 18⅜″, D. 16½″. The horse-shoe-shaped seat of this scroll-back chair is caned. (Winterthur Museum)

339. Below: The furniture shop and warehouse of Duncan Phyfe, Fulton Street, New York City. American. Early nineteenth century. Watercolor on paper. H. 15¾″, W. 18⅞″. Phyfe, a Scottish immigrant, first settled in Albany in 1783 or 1784. He is listed in the New York City *Directory* of 1792. By 1794 he had altered the original "Fife—joiner" to "Duncan Phyfe, cabinetmaker." The lyre-back chair shown in the shop's doorway is almost identical to figure 344. (The Metropolitan Museum of Art)

342. Above: Federal armchair. Attributed to Duncan Phyfe. New York City. Ca. 1810. Mahogany. H. 32¾″, W. 20⅞″, D. 17¾″. The front legs of this superbly designed chair terminate with brass hairy-paw feet. Thomas Pearshall was a wealthy merchant and shipowner who lived at 43 Wall Street from 1791 to 1818. This chair, from a large set, was probably made for use in that house. (The Metropolitan Museum of Art)

340. Left: Federal armchair. Attributed to Duncan Phyfe. New York City. Ca. 1810. Mahogany. H. 32½″, W. 19½″, D. 17¼″. This armchair was crafted with a "medallion" splat. The legs terminate with hairy-paw "dog" feet. (Ginsburg & Levy, Inc.)

341. Left: Federal settee. Attributed to Duncan Phyfe. New York City. Ca. 1820. Mahogany. H. 34″, D. 23¼″, L. 76¼″. This three-chair-back caned settee is decorated with carving both on the top rail and on the tops of the arms. The legs are the "Grecian-cross" type. Chairs with Grecian-cross fronts are nearly always of New York manufacture and are inevitably attributed to Duncan Phyfe, though numerous other chair-makers must have used the form. (Museum of Fine Arts, Boston)

343. Above: Federal side chair. New York. 1810–1815. Mahogany, soft maple, beech, white pine. H. 33½″, W. 18″, D. 23⅜″. The axis of the Grecian-cross design, which appears on the front of the settee, figure 341, has been changed, and on this chair and figure 342, it appears on the sides. (Winterthur Museum)

344. Above: Federal side chair. New York. 1800–1820. Mahogany. H. 32½″, W. 16″, D. 18½″. The design of this scroll-back side chair includes a lyre. Most, if not all, New York cabinetmakers produced chairs similar to this example. (Winterthur Museum)

345. Top, right: Sketch attributed to Duncan Phyfe. New York City. 1815–1816. This sketch of a lyre-back chair probably accompanied a letter from Phyfe to Charles N. Bancker of Philadelphia. The notations "Cane bottoms—$22," "Cushions—$3," and "Stuffed—$23" are written at the top. (Winterthur Museum)

346. Bottom, left: Federal armchair. Attributed to Duncan Phyfe. New York City. Ca. 1815. Mahogany. H. 33″, W. 19¼″, D. 20½″. Phyfe did not retire from the cabinetmaking business until 1840. During his long period of furniture-manufacturing, his craftsmen produced much of New York's most fashionable furniture. Brass tubes form the strings of most lyres used as a banister for scroll-back chairs of the Federal period. (Henry Ford Museum)

347. Near left: Federal armchair. Attributed to Duncan Phyfe. New York City. 1800–1810. Mahogany. H. 32⅞″. Six side chairs constructed to match this armchair are branded on the underside of the back rail with the owner's name—E. Brinckerhoff. Members of the Brinckerhoff family lived both in Albany and in New York during the early nineteenth century. (Albany Institute of History and Art)

348. Below: Museum installation. Duncan Phyfe Alcove. The sideboard, as well as numerous other pieces of Phyfe furniture in this interior, were included in Nancy McClelland's 1939 pioneering work, *Duncan Phyfe and the English Regency 1795–1830*. The pair of card tables bear the paper label of the New York cabinetmaker, Michael Allison. (Henry Ford Museum)

349. Left: Federal window seat. Believed to have been made by Duncan Phyfe. New York City. Ca. 1810. Mahogany. H. 29″, D. 14¼″, L. 42″. The convex shape of the leafy carved legs on this window seat is accented by the use of small brass animal-form feet. (The Metropolitan Museum of Art)

350. Bottom, left: Federal window seat. Attributed to Duncan Phyfe. New York City. 1810–1815. Mahogany. H. 29″, D. 16⅛″, L. 36¾″. The feet of this Sheraton-style window seat are finished with square brass caps and casters which enable it to be moved easily. (Henry Ford Museum)

351. Right: *Girl With Dove.* Painted by Cephas Thompson (1775–1856). American. Ca. 1810. Oil on wood. H. 29⅞″, W. 24⅞″. The Massachusetts painter sat his winsome subject on a window seat which is upholstered with blue fabric held to the frame by brass tacks. (Abby Aldrich Rockefeller Folk Art Collection)

352. Below: Federal couch. Made by Duncan Phyfe. New York City. 1820–1830. Mahogany. H. 32″, D. 25¾″, L. 85½″. The front rail of this Greco-Roman sofa is carved with draperies, tassels, and stylized oblong floral rosettes which often appear on Phyfe's pieces. (Henry Ford Museum)

353. Far left: Portrait of Samuel McIntire. Painted by Benjamin Blyth. American. 1746–1747. Pastel. H. 14", W. 9¾". This is the only known portrait of Samuel McIntire (1757–1811) who was one of New England's most gifted architect-craftsmen. The impressive Pingree and Peirce–Nichols houses in Salem, Massachusetts, are monuments to the designer's talents. Often commissioned by Elias Hasket Derby and other leading citizens to decorate pieces of furniture, he developed a vocabulary of carved motifs which, when discovered on furniture, is immediately identifiable. (Essex Institute)

354. Near left: Elevation for the Elias Hasket Derby mansion, Essex Street, Salem. By Samuel McIntire. American. 1795. Ink on paper. (Essex Institute)

355. Above; 355a. Right: Federal side chair. Carving attributed to Samuel McIntire. Salem. 1796–1800. Mahogany. H. 39⅜", W. 21", D. 21". A completely original chair discovered still in the possession of a descendant of Elias Hasket Derby, the Salem merchant prince, suggested that the stuffed back of the chair above, figure 355, was a later addition. Once the inaccurate upholstery was removed and the carved back restored, figure 355a, this chair again resembled Plate No. 8 in Hepplewhite's 1794 edition of the *Guide*. McIntire charged Derby £4:40 on February 17, 1798, "To carving 8 chairs at 10/6 each." (Winterthur Museum)

McIntire in Salem

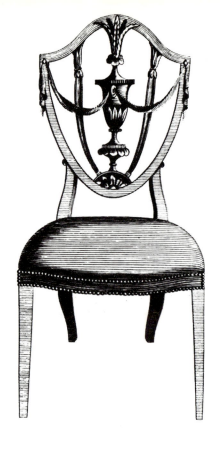

356. Left: Plate 2 from Hepplewhite's *Guide*. Published by I. & J. Taylor. London. 1787. This illustration served as a prototype for McIntire's chair, figure 357. The *Guide* was especially popular with American chairmakers. (The New York Public Library)

357. Left: Federal side chair. Carved by Samuel McIntire. Salem. 1795. Mahogany. H. 38⅜″, W. 21¼″, D. 21½″. Among the Derby family heirlooms were four chairs differing from this example only in that the front legs were decorated with carved grapes and grape leaves in a pendant design. (Henry Ford Museum)

358. Above: Federal armchair. Attributed to Samuel McIntire. Salem. 1785–1790. Mahogany. H. 38¼″. The design of the back of this chair is similar to that found on examples from Rhode Island. The carved basket of fruit at the bottom of the splat has come to be recognized as a McIntire device. (Museum of Fine Arts, Boston)

359. Below: Federal side chair. Made by Joseph Waters and carved by Samuel McIntire. Salem. 1805. Mahogany. H. 39″, W. 22″. (Philadelphia Museum of Art)

360. Right: Federal side chair. Carving attributed to Samuel McIntire. Salem. Ca. 1790. Mahogany, ebony. H. 39⅛″, W. 22″, D. 18⅜″. Ebony appliqués enrich the spade feet of this distinctive chair. It appears to complete a set of six chairs that belonged to Derby's daughter, Elizabeth Derby West. (Winterthur Museum)

361. Below, right: Federal side chair. Attributed to Benjamin Frothingham; carving attributed to Samuel McIntire. Massachusetts. 1790–1800. Mahogany. H. 37½″, W. 21″, D. 20″. Although McIntire frequently executed carving for other furniture-makers there are no known pieces made by him. (Henry Ford Museum)

362. Above, left: Chamber horse. Possibly English. Ca. 1800. Mahogany, leather. H. 37″, W. 29″, D. 20″. This unusual exercising device was originally owned by Elias Hasket Derby and is listed in his inventory as "one riding chair" located in the chamber entry and valued at $10.00. (Essex Institute)

363. Above, right; 363a. Right: Design for a chamber horse by Thomas Sheraton. Plate 22 in the *Drawing Book*. London, England. 1793. (Henry Ford Museum)

365. Below; 366. Right: Pair of Federal armchairs. Carved by Samuel McIntire. Salem. 1810. Mahogany. H. 32½″, W. 21″, D. 18″. These armchairs were made for the Adam Parlor of the Peirce–Nichols house in Salem and were part of the wedding furniture of Sarah Peirce Nichols. The design was taken from Plate 33 of Sheraton's *Drawing Book*. (Philadelphia Museum of Art)

364. Above: Plate 33, design for a chair from Thomas Sheraton's *Drawing Book*. London, England. 1793. (Henry Ford Museum)

367. Left: Federal side chair. Carved by Samuel McIntire or his son, Samuel Field McIntire. Salem. 1800–1810. Mahogany. H. 36″, W. 16″, D. 16″. Unlike his New York contemporaries, McIntire did not often use carved animalistic forms such as the eagle on this piece. The punched groundwork and the leaf device on the arcaded back are familiar evidences of his craftsmanship. (Essex Institute)

368. Right: Federal side chair. Attributed to Samuel McIntire. Salem. 1790–1800. Mahogany. H. 38″, W. 22″, D. 20″. Baskets of fruit and flowers, many times with trailing leaves or vines, clusters of grapes, and sheaves of wheat, were all decorative devices used by McIntire. McIntire's patron, Jerathmael Peirce, remoldeled his Salem house at 80 Federal Street for the marriage of his daughter Sarah to George Nichols. At that time, he commissioned McIntire to carve a set of chairs, two sofas, and four window seats, which were used in the commodious East Parlor. McIntire seems to have preferred to work with mahogany. This chair is constructed from that imported wood. It has an arcaded back and the carved top rail is centered by a basket of fruit. The leather-upholstered seat is secured by brass nails. (Henry Ford Museum)

369. Above: Federal sofa. Carving attributed to Samuel McIntire. Salem. 1800–1810. Mahogany. H. 34⅝″, D. 27½″, L. 74¼″. The star-punched background on the top crest of this sofa with free-standing arms appears in the work of several Salem craftsmen. The other carved motifs, however, indicate the hand of the master carver, McIntire. (The Bayou Bend Collection, The Museum of Fine Arts, Houston)

370. Above: Federal window seat. Carving attributed to Samuel McIntire. Salem. 1795–1800. Mahogany, birch, pine, ebony. H. 27¹⁵/₁₆″, D. 17¼″, L. 51⁷/₁₆″. Window benches were not often carved on the back side since they were almost never intended to be free-standing. The front of this McIntire example is richly decorated and the legs terminate in spade feet. (Winterthur Museum)

371. Above: Federal sofa. Carving attributed to Samuel McIntire. Salem. 1795–1800. Mahogany. H. 37¾″, D. 29″, L. 90). The drapery, floating on a punched-snowflake or star pattern which centers the top rail, and the carved rosettes on the front of the armrests are typical of McIntire's work. (Henry Ford Museum)

372. Below; 372a. Left: Federal sofa. Carving attributed to Samuel McIntire. Salem. 1795–1800. Mahogany. H. 39¼″, D. 36½″, L. 88¾″. This sofa is one of the most elaborate to be associated with the McIntire name. The relief-carved basket of fruit on the molded top rail, the carved rosettes at the arms, and the pendant grapevine and acanthus carvings on the arms and legs are unsurpassed in design and execution. (Winterthur Museum)

373. Left: Federal side chair. Attributed to William Fiske. Boston. Ca. 1800. Mahogany with satinwood inlay, birch. H. 38¼″, W. 21⅝″, D. 17 11/16″. An identical chair, now in the Museum of Fine Arts, Boston, is known to be the work of William Fiske, a cabinetmaker who moved to Roxbury, Massachusetts, from Salem in 1800. (Winterthur Museum)

374. Below: Federal side chair. Attributed to John Seymour. Boston. 1790–1800. Curly, bird's-eye maple, birch, with bands of mahogany. H. 35⅛″. Tradition places this chair in the home of John Hancock, a signer of the Declaration of Independence. The chair is one of a set of four. Dark bands of inlay are used to accent the seat rail, front legs, and back. (Museum of Fine Arts, Boston)

375. Above: Federal side chair. Attributed to John Seymour. Boston. Ca. 1800. Mahogany, satinwood. H. 36¼″. A much-celebrated set of mahogany dining chairs with satinwood inlay was given to Susannah Lord by her father and mother, General and Mrs. John Lord, as a wedding gift when she married Judge William Allen Hayes in Berwick, Maine, on June 2, 1811. Mrs. Hayes's chairs were nearly identical to this example. (Museum of Fine Arts, Boston)

248

376. Left: Federal side chair. Attributed to John Seymour. Boston. Ca. 1800. Mahogany. H. 36″, W. 28½″, D. 16″. Scroll-back Sheraton-style chairs with veneered tablets are often ascribed to Seymour's shop. (The Metropolitan Museum of Art)

377. Below, left: Paper label from a tambour desk made by John Seymour & Son. To date, examples of Seymour seating pieces remain undocumented either by label or bill. (Winterthur Museum)

Boston and the Seymours

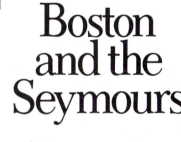

The furniture from the cabinetmaking shop of John Seymour (ca. 1738–1818) and his son Thomas (1771–1848) dominated Boston and its environs. Seymour, already an accomplished craftsman, arrived in Portland, Maine, from England in 1785. Around 1794 he moved to Creek Lane, Boston. The Seymours were masters of the craft of inlaying, and much of their finest work is found on secretaries and other case pieces. Thomas opened his Boston Furniture Warehouse in 1804 and at various times worked in conjunction with James Cogswell, Stephen Badlam, and the painter and decorator, John Penniman.

378. Above: Federal side chair. Attributed to John Seymour & Son. Boston. Ca. 1800. Mahogany, with satinwood and ebony inlay. H. 34½″, W. 19½″, D. 16½″. This pillow and lattice-back Sheraton-style piece is from a set of six side chairs and two armchairs. (Henry Ford Museum)

379. Left: Federal double-chair-back settee. Attributed to John and/or Thomas Seymour. Boston. Ca. 1805. Mahogany, with figured veneer. H. 33½″, D. 18⅜″, L. 40″. This settee was constructed with reeded, roll arms and tablets on the crest rail. (Winterthur Museum)

380. Left: Federal side chair. Attributed to John and/or Thomas Seymour. Boston. Ca. 1805. Mahogany, with satinwood inlay. H. 34⅛″, W. 19″, D. 21″. This side chair is virtually identical to the double-chair-back settee above. The veneered panel on the legs, however, is shorter. (Henry Ford Museum)

382. Right: Federal five-chair-back settee. Attributed to John and/or Thomas Seymour. Boston. Ca. 1805. Mahogany, with figured birch inlay. H. 42½″, D. 22¼″, L. 81″. In contrast to the double-chair-back settee, figure 379, the arms of this unusual piece are outward flaring and the legs are without inlay. (Winterthur Museum)

381. Above: Museum installation. The stairhall of Montmorenci is furnished with three pieces of seating furniture attributable to the Seymour shop. The contrasting shades of light and dark wood are complimented by a vibrant green droguet, a French leaf-and-fruit-patterned silk fabric. Montmorenci was built at Sahocco Springs, near Warrenton, North Carolina, about 1822 by General William Williams. (Winterthur Museum)

383. Below; 383a. Right: Martha Washington armchair. Made by Stephen Badlam. Dorchester Lower Mills, Massachusetts. Ca. 1795. Mahogany. H. 40¾", W. 25⅛", D. 30¾". During the American Revolution, "Captain Stephen Badlam" was considered by his superior, General Lee of New York, "a man of great merit in his way." He later attained the rank of major. Badlam (1751–1815) made this "lolling chair" and signed it with a die or stamp, "S. Badlam." This form of chair was more popular in New England than in any other region. (Winterthur Museum; photographs courtesy Ginsburg & Levy, Inc.)

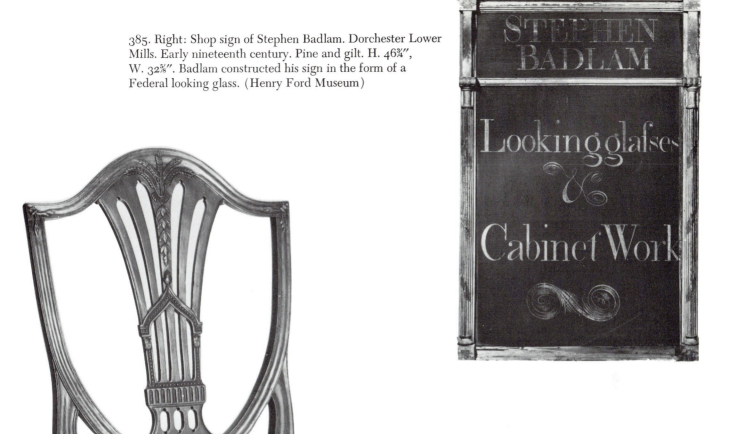

385. Right: Shop sign of Stephen Badlam. Dorchester Lower Mills. Early nineteenth century. Pine and gilt. H. 46¾", W. 32⅜". Badlam constructed his sign in the form of a Federal looking glass. (Henry Ford Museum)

384. Above; 384a. Right: Federal side chair. Made by Stephen Badlam. Dorchester Lower Mills. Ca. 1795. Mahogany. H. 38⅛", W. 21⅜", D. 21½". The cuff or ankle on the front leg of this signed chair is a feature frequently used by Badlam. (Winterthur Museum; photographs courtesy Ginsburg & Levy, Inc.)

386. Below: Federal armchair. Salem. 1800. Mahogany. H. 37″, W. 28½″, D. 18½″. Birdlike carvings serve as terminals on the arms of this rare Salem chair. Upholstered over the seat and richly carved, it is unadorned by inlay. (Henry Ford Museum)

387. Right: Federal side chair. Massachusetts. 1790. Mahogany, with satinwood inlay. H. 38″, W. 21½″, D. 18⅝″. (Henry Ford Museum)

388. Near right: Federal armchair. Massachusetts. 1790–1800. Mahogany. H. 38⅜″, W. 21⅜″, W. 20¾″. Curved splats meet at a carved medallion on this and six matching side chairs. (Henry Ford Museum)

389. Far right: *The Dinner Party*. Painted by Henry Sargent. American. Ca. 1810. Oil on canvas. H. 59½″, W. 48″. A youthful Gloucester, Massachusetts, artist, Henry Sargent (1770–1845) journeyed to London in 1793 to study with Benjamin West. In addition to his artistic endeavors, Sargent became active politically upon his return to the Boston area in 1797. He was elected an honorary member of the National Academy in 1840. This early nineteenth-century painting portrays a bachelors' gathering with two servants in attendance. (Museum of Fine Arts, Boston)

390. Left: Museum installation. 390a. Above: Federal, curved chair-back settee. Probably Portsmouth, New Hampshire, though possibly Boston. Ca. 1800. Mahogany, maple, white pine. H. 34¼″, D. 31½″, L. 84½″. Plate 26 of Hepplewhite's *Cabinet-Maker and Upholsterer's Guide* provided the inspiration for the design of this unique American settee. (Winterthur Museum)

392. Near right: Federal open armchair. Portsmouth. 1790–1800. Mahogany, with satinwood inlay. H. 47½″, W. 25″, D. 20″. Large, elegant armchairs with turned Sheraton-style legs and armposts forming a continuous arm were popular appointments in Portsmouth mansions during the early years of the nineteenth century. (The Metropolitan Museum of Art)

391. Below; 391a. Far right: Federal sofa. Portsmouth. Ca. 1800. Mahogany, with birch and maple. H. 30½″, D. 25¾″, L. 80⅜″. This sofa is similar to several other known examples, including one that originally belonged to William Simes (1773–1824) of Portsmouth. (Ginsburg & Levy, Inc.)

Working in the Federal style, Portsmouth, New Hampshire, cabinetmakers demonstrated a fondness for using contrasting veneers of light and dark woods to create decorative effects. The sofa (figure 391, and the detail, figure 391a) is constructed of mahogany and veneered with figured birch and maple. Carved leaves further embellish the free-standing front posts. Daniel Webster, the distinguished orator, owned a sofa similar to this. The Hepplewhite "Bar back Sofa," figure 390, was made to fit an alcove at the bottom of a spiral staircase in the Haymarket Square home of John Pierce in Portsmouth. The elegant inlay designs on the shield-backs of this settee are similar to the motifs executed by carvers of Salem chairs.

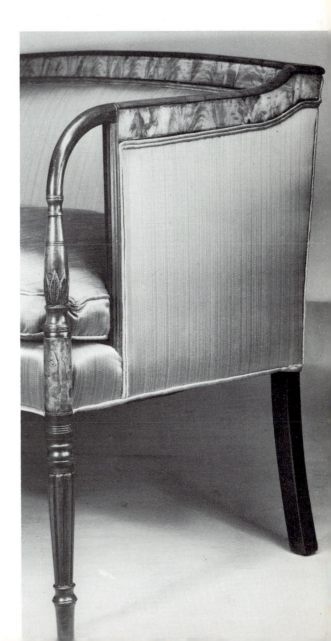

Portsmouth, New Hampshire

393. Left: *The Sargent Family*. Painted by an unidentified American artist. Ca. 1800. Oil on canvas. H. 38″, W. 50¼″. The shape of the backs on the Hepplewhite side chairs in this painting is identical to that found on the Pierce settee, figure 390. The bonneted mistress of the house, surrounded by her infant children, rests in an upholstered open-arm chair similar to New Hampshire examples. (National Galley of Art)

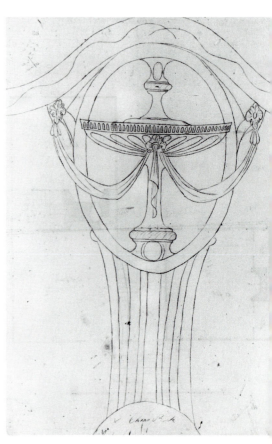

In Rhode Island

394. Near left, top; 394a. Far left: Federal side chair. Providence, Rhode Island. 1790–1800. Mahogany. H. 39½″, W. 22½″, D. 18¾″. Hepplewhite shield-back chairs which incorporated a carved, Greek, footed drinking cup (kylix) were popular in New England. The motif, one of Robert Adam's favorites, is used in the splat of this chair. (Museum of Fine Arts, Boston)

395. Near left, bottom: Drawing of a chair back by Samuel McIntire. American. Late eighteenth century. McIntire used this design when he created a chair that is now in the Karolik Collection at the Museum of Fine Arts, Boston. (Essex Institute)

396. Right; 396a. Below: Federal side chair. Attributed to John Goddard. Newport. 1790–1800. Mahogany. H. 40″, W. 22″, D. 21¼″. Both this chair and figure 394 were constructed with serpentine seats and tapering legs similar to a design in *The London Chair-Makers' and Carvers' Book of Prices for Workmanship* published in 1802. (Henry Ford Museum)

397. Left: A meeting notice for the Providence Association of Mechanics and Manufacturers. Published in the Providence *Gazette*. October 12, 1822. (Rhode Island Historical Society)

398. Below: Federal side chair. Made by John Townsend. Newport. 1800. Mahogany. H. 38½″, W. 21¼″, D. 17¾″. A paper label attached to the inner frame of the back rail states that this chair was "Made by John Townsend Newport 1800." An identical chair is in the collection of Mr. and Mrs. Joseph K. Ott. (Winterthur Museum)

399. Right: Federal side chair. Probably made by Thomas Howard, Jr. Providence. Ca. 1790. Satinwood and ebony inlay. H. 27″, W. 22″. This truncated shield-back side chair has previously been associated with the New York shop of Elbert Anderson. The inlay is almost identical to that on a Hepplewhite armchair with truncated shield-back which family tradition indicates was created in the Providence shop of Thomas Howard, Jr., on South Main Street. (The Metropolitan Museum of Art)

400. Below: Painting of Miss Helen Townsend's room, Newport. Painted by Mary Buffum. Ca. 1887. American. Watercolor on paper. H. 8½″, W. 11¼″. The chairs in this late nineteenth-century interior are, from left to right: A country chair from Yorkshire, England, ca. 1780; a Chippendale mahogany side chair, probably Newport, ca. 1760; an upholstered mahogany armchair, probably Newport, 1780; and a mahogany Hepplewhite armchair, probably Newport, 1790–1810. Some of the other furnishings in the room are from the Queen Anne and Chippendale period, and their inclusion clearly demonstrates that even though a piece was outmoded in terms of style, it was not always discarded. (Newport Historical Society)

401. Above, left: Federal easy chair. New England, possibly
Connecticut. 1790–1800. Cherry, white pine, mahogany.
H. 44⅝″, W. 30¼″, D. 27¼″. The predominant use of
cherrywood for the construction of this Hepplewhite easy
chair appears to indicate a Connecticut origin. The use of a
slip-seat and an exposed seat rail are unique features on
American easy chairs of this period. (Winterthur Museum)

402. Above, right: Federal armchair. Attributed to Samuel
Kneeland and Lemuel Adams. Hartford, Connecticut.
Ca. 1793. Cherry. H. 38¼″, W. 22⅛″. This chair is from a set
Kneeland and Adams made for the Connecticut State
House. (Ginsburg & Levy, Inc.)

403. Right: Federal armchair. Connecticut River Valley.
Ca. 1795. Cherry. H. 39¾″, W. 23¾″. The top rail of this
"necessity" chair is centered with a carved, raised design.
(Museum of Fine Arts, Boston)

404. Right: Federal side chair. Connecticut.
Ca. 1795. Mahogany, cherry, maple, white pine.
H. 40″, W. 21¼″, D. 18½″. This three-lobed
Hepplewhite side chair was owned by James Dana
(1735–1812), minister of the Wallingford,
Connecticut, Congregational Church from 1758 to
1789. (Winterthur Museum)

In Connecticut

405. Above: Engraved label of Kneeland and
Adams. Hartford. Dated 1793. This label, which is
from the top drawer in a chest of drawers, advises
the reader that the firm has "Constantly on hand,
Mahogany Furniture, of the first quality; best
warranted Clocks and Time-Pieces; elegant Looking
Glasses, of their own manufacturing; Cabinet Work
of every kind may be had on very short notice,
warranted equal to any made in America."
(Winterthur Museum)

406. Right: Federal armchair. Made by Lemuel
Adams for the Connecticut State House. Hartford.
Before 1796. Cherry. H. 40½″, W. 22½″, D. 18½″.
Lemuel Adams provided cherry chairs, desks, and
miscellaneous furniture for use in the Connecticut
State House and was paid £105/6 in 1796. (The
Connecticut Historical Society)

407. Above: Federal armchair. Attributed to Samuel McIntire. Salem. 1795. Mahogany. H. 38″, W. 22⅛″, D. 19½″. The superb carving, excellent proportions, and graceful sweep of the arms on this Sheraton-style chair, one of a pair from the Derby house, Peabody, Massachusetts, are noteworthy. (Museum of Fine Arts, Boston)

408. Right, top: Federal armchair. Made by George Bright. Boston. 1797. Mahogany. H. 31″, W. 23⅞″, D. 21¼″. Bright, a Boston cabinetmaker working about 1750–1805, "reckoned a very honest Man and an extradorinary good Workman," and "esteemed the neatest workman in town," manufactured thirty bergère-type chairs for the Boston State House. He billed the State of Massachusetts $8.00 for each of these in 1797. (Henry Ford Museum)

Federal
Upholstered

409. Right: Federal reclining chair. New England. 1790–1810. Mahogany, maple, birch. H. 50½″, W. 24½″, Depth with back down 46″. This reclining chair has ratchets under the seat and between the seat rail, and armrests which enable it to be adjusted to several positions. (Winterthur Museum)

410. Right: Federal square-shaped easy chair. New York. 1800–1810. Mahogany. H. 47¼″, W. 32½″, D. 18″. The frames of late eighteenth-century and early nineteenth-century upholstered chairs are lighter and thinner than those of the earlier periods. (Winterthur Museum)

411. Left: Federal open-arm chair. Probably Rhode Island. Ca. 1795. Mahogany, with light wood inlay. H. 35¾″, W. 21¾″, D. 21⅞″. The back of this upholstered chair terminates with a serpentine crest. The sides are cyma reversa curved and the broad, shield-shaped seat is upholstered over the seat rail. (Winterthur Museum)

412. Left: Federal open-arm chair. Massachusetts. 1790–1800. Mahogany, pine, maple. H. 41¾″, W. 25⅝″, D. 30½″. The construction of the outward flaring back legs of this Hepplewhite "Martha Washington" open-arm chair imparts a sense of stability and rugged support. (Henry Ford Museum)

413. Above: Federal cabriole sofa. Baltimore. 1790–1800. Mahogany, satinwood, tulipwood. H. 38¼″, D. 26″, L. 77″. The partially upholstered, veneered seat rail and exposed mahogany top rail, as well as the inlaid bellflowers on the front legs, indicate a Baltimore origin. (Winterthur Museum)

414. Top: Federal square sofa. Probably
Massachusetts. 1795–1805. Mahogany, birch, white
pine. H. 36⅜″, D. 24¼″, L. 78″. The "crane neck'd
elbows" on the arms of this New England sofa are
outlined with carved reeding. The design for the
sofa is adapted from Hepplewhite's *Guide,* Plate 25.
(Winterthur Museum)

415. Right: Federal open-arm chair. Massachusetts.
1790–1800. Mahogany. H. 42″, W. 26¼″, D. 25″.
With the possible exception of Connecticut
craftsmen, mahogany was the favorite wood of
chairmakers during the Federal period. (Henry Ford
Museum)

416. Above: Federal Martha Washington armchair. Salem.
Ca. 1805. Mahogany. H. 42⅝″, W. 22⅜″, D. 26¼″. This
distinctive Hepplewhite lolling chair is one of a pair. It may
have been originally part of a suite that included a sofa,
now in the Museum of Fine Arts, Boston, Massachusetts.
Identical arms and supports are illustrated in Plate 6, No. 3,
of *The London Chair-Makers' and Carvers' Book of Prices
for Workmanship*, 1802. (Winterthur Museum)

417. Left: Federal armchair. Northeastern
Massachusetts or Portsmouth, New Hampshire.
Ca. 1800. Mahogany, bird's-eye maple. H. 33¼″,
W. 25¼″, D. 25¼″. Bird's-eye maple veneered panels
behind the armposts and on top of the front legs
of this chair are elegant additions further refined by
the use of a tiny hairline banding. (Henry Ford
Museum)

418. Left: Federal easy chair. Boston area. Ca. 1790. Mahogany. H. 46¼", Width at the arms 36". Easy chairs from the Boston area often display exciting design concepts. This fine example is ample in size and yet its curvaceous outline is most delicate. The front legs are inlaid in a pointed arch or Gothic motif. The legs are united by stretchers, a feature reminiscent of the early eighteenth century. Similar chair-backs are shown in Hepplewhite's *Guide*, Plate 15. (Museum of Fine Arts, Boston)

419. Below: Federal sofa. New York. 1795–1800. Mahogany. H. 39½", D. 29", L. 82". The front legs of this Hepplewhite cabriole sofa are reeded and terminate with spade feet. Carved rosettes unite the curvilinear arms to the back. (Henry Ford Museum)

Painted and decorated furniture was found in even the earliest Pilgrim homes. At the close of the seventeenth century, japanning and various other decorating methods were particularly popular. This predilection for brightly painted furniture was again revived during the close of the eighteenth century. At this time, the infant city of Baltimore emerged as a cultural center. Consequently, a school of cabinetmaking peculiar to that region developed. The Russian-born artist, Pavel Petrovitch Svinin (1787/88–1839), writing about this community during the first years of the nineteenth century, found it "one of the fairest cities of North America." In the older centers of furniture-making, this revival of interest in painted furniture was widespread—particularly in New York and New England.

420. Above: Federal side chair. New York City or Albany, New York. 1800–1810. Birch and cherry, painted and decorated. H. 35¼", W. 18¾", D. 19¾". (Winterthur Museum)

421. Right: Federal side chair. Attributed to John Seymour. Boston. Ca. 1800. Maple and birch, painted and decorated. H. 36", W. 19⅜", D. 15½". A nineteenth-century label pasted on the inside rail of this chair states, "Made by John Seymour for the Hon. Nathaniel Silsbee about 1790 when he built his house." The construction of the back is similar to design No. 1, Plate 36, of Sheraton's *Drawing Book* of 1791–1794. (Nina Fletcher Little)

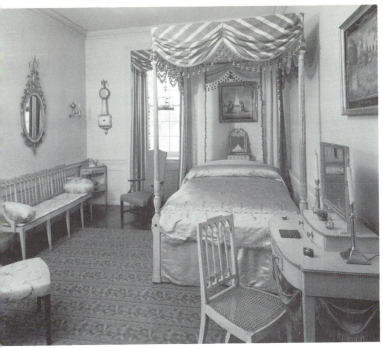

422. Above: Museum installation. The Gold and White Room at Winterthur is furnished with several Federal pieces, including a bed, a four-chair-back settee, a washstand, and a dressing table and chair that have been painted white and decorated with gold. (Winterthur Museum)

Painted Federal

423. Above: Federal side chair. Massachusetts. Late eighteenth or early nineteenth century. Maple, painted and decorated. H. 35″, W. 19″, D. 17″. Robert Cowan (1768–1846) possibly painted and decorated this chair, a simplified version of the Elias Hasket Derby painted oval-back Hepplewhite chairs made in Philadelphia for his Salem mansion. Cowan is known to have executed ornamental painting in 1791 for Derby. (Historic Deerfield, Inc.)

424. Left: Portrait of Gideon Roberts. Painted by Ralph Earl. American. Late eighteenth century. Oil on canvas. Dimensions unavailable. The Bristol, Connecticut, clockmaker, Gideon Roberts, sat in a Sheraton-style side chair while the artist "fixed his likeness." (Photograph courtesy Wickersham Gallery)

Decorated Federal furniture can be best analyzed when separated into two distinct categories—elegant, expensive pieces painted by craftsmen who considered themselves masters, and simple, country articles executed by "ornamental decorators" who were working for a less affluent class and were not above advertising in rural newspapers that they were "experienced . . . inexpensive and good." Increased trade with the "East" created a renewed interest in objects Oriental in nature. In the New England seaports, chairs turned on a lathe to imitate bamboo were particularly popular. The incised rings on the early nineteenth-century side chair, figure 425, are "picked" out in a second color to accent the foreign nature of the piece. Furniture of this nature contrasts sharply with the very elegant, sophisticated New York Sheraton settee, figure 427. On this three-chair-back seating piece, roses and other floral details in natural colors are applied to a black ground.

425. Above: Sheraton side chair. New England. Early nineteenth century. Maple and ash, painted. H. 35″, W. 18½″, D. 15½″. This simple bamboo-turned side chair with cane seat is painted a pale yellow and gilded. (The Metropolitan Museum of Art)

426. Above: Nathan Hawley and his family. Painted by William Wilkie. Albany, New York. 1801. Watercolor on paper. H. 16″, L. 20″. Hawley and his wife sit in turned "fancy" Sheraton chairs. (Albany Institute of History and Art)

427. Below: Federal settee. New York City. Ca. 1800. Chestnut, painted. H. 35½″, D. 19½″, L. 56″. Although this settee has tapering legs more often associated with the designs of Hepplewhite, it is classified as Sheraton because the three-chair-back shape relates to a design published by that master. (The Metropolitan Museum of Art)

428. Below: Fancy Sheraton side chair. New England. Ca. 1830. Maple, hickory, and ash, painted. H. 31⅞", W. 18¼", D. 16½". This chair, one of a set of four, is painted yellow and decorated with brown-and-green freehand painting. (Henry Ford Museum)

429. Above: Fancy Sheraton settee and chair. An illustration from an advertisement by Thomas Ash in David Longworth's *City Directory*. New York City. 1815. (Widener Library)

430. Near right; 431. Far right; 431a. Left: Fancy Sheraton side chairs. New England. 1815–1830. Maple, hickory, and ash, painted. H. 33¼", W. 18", D. 16". These "fancy" chairs are painted with landscape scenes, and the front legs are further embellished with stenciled leaf decoration. (The Peabody Museum of Salem)

Thomas Ash's 1815 advertisement in David Longworth's *City Directory* illustrated a settee and armchair, figure 429, from his "Fancy and Windsor Chair Factory" at 33 John Street, New York City. As this advertisement would indicate, during the years immediately following 1800, "fancy" chairmaking developed into a specialized craft. The New England artist, Samuel Bartoll (ca. 1765–1835), has been tentatively credited with the painted landscape panels and decoration on the pair of fancy chairs, figures 430, 431, and 431a. These distinctive chairs are from a set of six once owned by George Crowninshield of Salem and were used on his impressive yacht, *Cleopatra's Barge*.

277

432. Above: Portrait of Thomas Ash. Painted by John Wesley Jarvis (1780–1840). American. 1816. Oil on canvas. Dimensions unavailable. Thomas Ash was the son of William Ash, a Federal-style chair manufacturer, and a grandson of the more famous Gilbert Ash, the Chippendale furniture-maker of New York. (Parke–Bernet Galleries)

433. Left: Fancy Sheraton armchair. Possibly made by Thomas Ash. New York City. Ca. 1820. Maple and beech, painted. H. 33½″, W. 20¾″, D. 16¾″. The use of applied-metal mounts and the construction of the scrolled arms is unusual on "fancy" chairs. This chair originally belonged to a set of nine pieces, composed of six side chairs, two armchairs, and a settee. Ash either did not mark his work or his labels have not survived. He advertised extensively in contemporary newspapers, and the Museum of the City of New York has one of his trade cards. (The Metropolitan Museum of Art)

434. Top, right: Fancy Sheraton armchair. New York. 1820. Maple and ash, painted. H. 35″, W. 15¾″, D. 15¼″. Although the painted splats in this chair resemble icicles, they were, within the period, referred to as "urn" splats. When found on later country chairs, they are called arrows; hence the term "arrow-back" is used for simple chairs with plank seats. (Henry Ford Museum)

435. Left: Fancy Sheraton armchair. New York or New Jersey. 1825–1850. Maple, birch, and ash, painted. H. 33¼″, W. 20″, D. 16″. Silver, bronze, and gold stenciling is applied over a rosewood-grained finish on this diminutive chair. (The Newark Museum)

436. Above: Fancy Sheraton armchair. Southern New England or New York. 1810–1820. Maple, painted. H. 34¼″, W. 18¾″, D. 15½″. The seat frames of rush-bottomed chairs were finished by the addition of an applied piece of wood once the rushing had been completed. (Winterthur Museum)

437. Above: Fancy Sheraton side chair. Cabinetwork attributed to Thomas Renshaw, decoration attributed to John Barnhart. Baltimore. Ca. 1815. Maple, hickory, and walnut, painted. H. 32½″, W. 18¾″, D. 21″. (Henry Ford Museum)

438. Below: Fancy Sheraton window seat. Baltimore. 1800–1810. Maple and tulipwood, painted. H. 31½″, D. 14″, L. 49″. (Winterthur Museum)

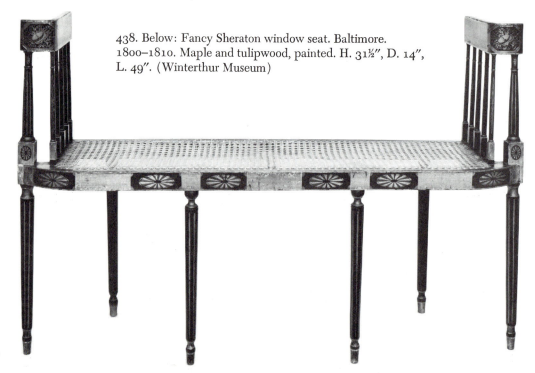

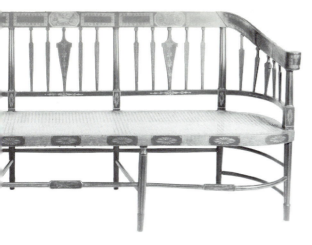

"Elegant fancy furniture . . . painted and gilt in the most fanciful manner" was more popular in Baltimore than perhaps any other area. Thomas Renshaw, John Barnhart, and John and Hugh Finlay were among the numerous makers and painters of "fancy" chairs. Their work is represented in American museums by furniture frequently documented by family association or by their stamped and branded marks or paper labels.

439. Above: Fancy Sheraton settee. Maryland. 1800–1810. Maple and tulipwood, painted. H. 32¾", D. 19", L. 80". (Winterthur Museum)

440. Below: Museum installation. The Imlay Room was named after John Imlay who purchased the wallpaper in 1794 from William Poyntell of Philadelphia. (Winterthur Museum)

CHAPTER 8

THE EMPIRE STYLE 1800-1840

Furniture constructed in the Sheraton and Hepplewhite styles expressed the first phase of the Classical movement in America. The inspiration for the designs were English adaptations of Italian Renaissance examples and forms from the ancient world. The second phase of the American Classical movement was also motivated by foreign fashions. Elegant furniture discovered during French excavations in the ancient world generated an interest in the antique. Egyptian, Greek, and Roman decorative motifs, as well as furniture forms, were freely copied in Paris by *ébénistes*. These same design concepts were popularized in America by immigrant French cabinetmakers who created stylish furniture for wealthy patrons.

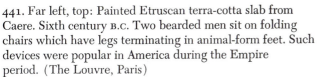

441. Far left, top: Painted Etruscan terra-cotta slab from
Caere. Sixth century B.C. Two bearded men sit on folding
chairs which have legs terminating in animal-form feet. Such
devices were popular in America during the Empire
period. (The Louvre, Paris)

442. Left, bottom: Greek vase. Painting of Achilles resting
upon a couch similar in form to that which the French
painter, Jacques Louis David, made famous in his portrait of
Mme. Juliette Récamier. The form was popular in
France and England as well as America during the
early nineteenth century. (Kunsthistorisches Museum, Vienna)

443. Above: Painting from a Greek vase showing a soldier's
wife seated on a klismos-form chair. Both in Philadelphia
and in New York, such chairs were especially popular during
the late eighteenth and early nineteenth centuries.
(National Museum, Athens)

444. Top, right: Cinerary urn. Fifth century B.C. The figure
of a woman holding a child is seated in a chair with caryatid
armrests and animal-paw feet. (Museo Archeologico, Florence)

445. Right: Statue of General George Washington. By
Horatio Greenough. American. Marble. H. 136″, W. 82½″,
D. 102″. The American sculptor, Horatio Greenough
(1805–1852), chose to portray the toga-clad national hero,
George Washington, in a pose similar to that of the Olympian
god, Zeus. (National Collection of Fine Arts,
Smithsonian Institution)

447. Below: Empire side chair. Probably Philadelphia. Ca. 1820. Poplar, pine, ash. H. 35″, W. 19″. This chair, one of a pair, is painted and decorated with designs and motifs associated with the ancient world. The cane seat is fitted with a tasseled cushion. (Philadelphia Museum of Art)

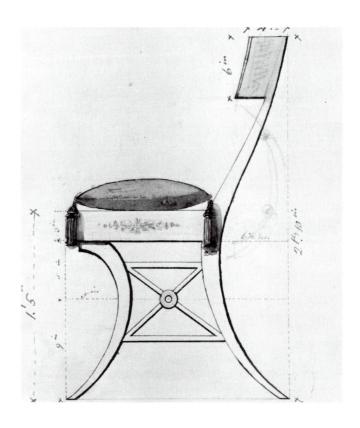

448. Above: Design for a chair. By Benjamin H. Latrobe. American. 1809. Thomas Jefferson, third President of the United States, finding the White House "big enough for two emperors, one Pope, and the grand lama" solicited the aid of Benjamin Henry Latrobe to complete its construction and to furnish it. Latrobe, a favorite at the "Republican Court," outlived the Jefferson era. He designed this chair and other furniture in the Greek manner for "Queen Dolley" (Madison) and assisted in her attempt to make the residence "Habitable but there is not a single apartment finished . . ." Speaking of the great East Room, she said, "I made a drying-room of, [it] to hang up the clothes in." (Papers of B. H. Latrobe, Maryland Historical Society)

Classic Styles

446. Left: Illustration from the book *Designs of Modern Costume. The Card Party* drawn by H. Moses. Published by Henry Setchel and Sons. N.d. London, England. Ca. 1815. This drawing illustrates the great popularity of "antique-style furniture" during the first quarter of the nineteenth century. (The Metropolitan Museum of Art)

449. Right: Empire side chair. Baltimore. 1820. Maple. H. 34¼", W. 17¾", D. 23". The painted and gilded decoration on this Grecian chair is laid over a basic tawny yellow. It is essentially a mixture of the Greek anthemion (honeysuckle), the bellflower, and the Roman fasces motifs. This chair, possibly by the Finlays, is one of a set of twelve. (The Metropolitan Museum of Art)

450. Below: Interior by A. J. Davis. New York City. 1845–1846. Watercolor on paper. H. 13¼", W. 18⅛". This interior is the double parlor of the John C. Stevens residence, College Place and Murray Street, New York City. The Ionic-columned rooms are furnished with Greek Revival furniture. (The New-York Historical Society)

451. Above: Empire couch. New York? 1815–1840. Pine, chestnut. H. 33⅛", L. 78". Many classical motifs, which were popular during the first quarter of the nineteenth century, are incorporated in the decoration on this painted Empire sofa. The abundantly filled gilt cornucopia design on the "hammer end" is repeated on the oblong blocks above the legs of this distinctive piece. (Yale University Art Gallery, The Mabel Brady Garvan Collection)

453. Above: Portrait of Mme. Juliette Récamier. Painted by Jacques Louis David. France. 1800. Oil on canvas. H. 59″, W. 94½″. The French painter, Jacques Louis David, painted the famed beauty, Mme. Récamier, reclining on a Grecian couch. The form is generally known in America today as "Récamier." (The Louvre, Paris)

452. Below: Empire couch. Salem. 1805–1815. Mahogany. H. 38¼″, D. 27⅛″, L. 91½″. Raised carving, which includes a cornucopia and a variety of leafage forms, decorates the surface of this Récamier couch. (Winterthur Museum)

454. Left; 454a. Above: Empire side chair. Possibly by Duncan Phyfe. New York City. 1815–1820. Mahogany. H. 32½". This chair is branded on the inside edge of the front seat rail "P. Gansevoort," for Peter Gansevoort (1788–1876), son of General Peter Gansevoort, Jr., who presented George Washington with a folding bed which Washington used during the American struggle for independence. The splat of this klismos-type chair is sensitively carved with stylized "ancient" motifs. (Albany Institute of History and Art)

455. Left: Empire side chair. Attributed to Duncan Phyfe. New York City. 1810–1815. Mahogany. H. 30¼", W. 18¼", D. 16¼". This chair belonged to the New York City Mayor, DeWitt Clinton, who later became Governor of the state. (Museum of the City of New York)

456. Near left: Empire side chair. New York City. Ca. 1815. Cherry, painted and gilded. H. 32¾″, W. 17″, D. 15″. Gilt decoration is substituted for elaborate carving on this chair. Carved hairy-paw dog feet provide terminals for the front legs. (The Metropolitan Museum of Art)

457. Right: Empire side chair. New York City. 1815–1825. Soft maple and gilt. H. 32″, W. 18¼″, D. 21½″. The carved paw feet and gilt decoration on this scroll-back klismos-type side chair are superior to most. In New York talented furniture decorators used gilt as a substitute for the more costly fire gilt preferred by European craftsmen. (Winterthur Museum)

458. Below: Museum installation. The Empire style was not confined to the products of the cabinetmakers' shops. All the decorative arts of the early nineteenth century were altered in their design by the new vogue. This dining room from the Owens–Thomas house at Savannah, Georgia, is furnished with a banquet table attributed to Henry Connelly. The side chairs are also of Philadelphia origin. The ormolu chandelier is French Empire. (Owens–Thomas House)

459. *The Tea Party*. Painted by Henry Sargent. American. 1821–1824. Oil on canvas. H. 64¼″, W. 52¼″. This expensively carpeted and appointed interior is furnished with Empire armchairs which have carved animal-form supports. Of interest is the window seat being used in a windowless room where chairs are lined up against the wall. The fringed stool is a form that does not seem to have survived. Sargent's nineteenth-century paintings of Boston's upper class are splendid social documents of the era. (Museum of Fine Arts, Boston)

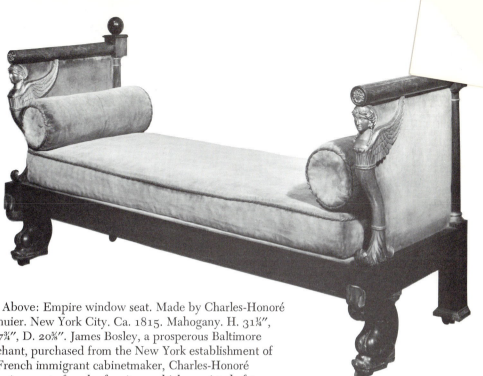

460. Above: Empire window seat. Made by Charles-Honoré Lannuier. New York City. Ca. 1815. Mahogany. H. 31¼", L. 57¾", D. 20⅝". James Bosley, a prosperous Baltimore merchant, purchased from the New York establishment of the French immigrant cabinetmaker, Charles-Honoré Lannuier, a set of parlor furniture which consisted of two armchairs, several side chairs, a pair of card tables, and a pair of settees. The two settees, or window benches, are constructed of mahogany and embellished with black paint and gilt decoration. Lannuier was a Parisian-trained master, and his American work reflects his early Continental background. (Maryland Historical Society)

461. Above: Paper label of Charles-Honoré Lannuier from a rosewood console table. American. Nineteenth century. (The Metropolitan Museum of Art)

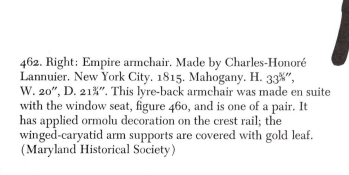

462. Right: Empire armchair. Made by Charles-Honoré Lannuier. New York City. 1815. Mahogany. H. 33⅜", W. 20", D. 21¼". This lyre-back armchair was made en suite with the window seat, figure 460, and is one of a pair. It has applied ormolu decoration on the crest rail; the winged-caryatid arm supports are covered with gold leaf. (Maryland Historical Society)

463. Left, top: Late Sheraton side chair. New York City. Early nineteenth century. Ash, beech, tulipwood. H. 35″, W. 18¼″, D. 16½″. In an illustrated newspaper advertisement of 1815, William Buttre of Albany, New York, offered "Eagle Fancy Chair"[s] not unlike this example. The carved, painted, and gilded decoration on this piece matches that on a related chair in the Winterthur collection. (The Metropolitan Museum of Art)

464. Left, bottom: Late Sheraton side chair. Baltimore. Ca. 1830. Pine and maple, painted and stenciled. H. 31¼″, W. 18¼″, D. 21¾″. This form of elaborately turned and ornately painted side chair is almost always attributed to the chairmaking shops of Baltimore. (Henry Ford Museum)

465. Above: Late Sheraton side chair. New Jersey or Philadelphia. 1815–1825. Maple. H. 32¾″, W. 17¾″, D. 19½″. The bold red-and-black graining on this Grecian-style chair is an attempt to imitate rosewood. (Winterthur Museum)

GEO. H. MUNDAY.
CARVER AND GILDER.

...ove: Trade card of George H. Munday.
...phia. Ca. 1825. On his trade card, Munday
...the attention of the Public to his WARE
...3 Doors Below Library Street, No. 64 Sth
...Craftsmen like Munday not only provided
...or pictures and mirrors, but did
...for chair manufacturers. (The New-York
...al Society)

467. Left: Late Sheraton side chair. Hudson River
Valley, New York. 1825–1850. Pine, maple, hickory.
H. 33¾″, W. 18″, D. 18″. Painted and decorated
Hudson River Valley chairs many times are difficult
to distinguish from the South Jersey types.
(Fenimore House, New York State Historical
Association)

468. Right: Empire altar chair. Designed by
Maximilian Godefroy (working 1806–1824). Made
by William Camp. Baltimore. Ca. 1816.
Bird's-eye maple. H. 32½″, W. 25″, D. 18½″. This
unusual chair was designed en suite with the
lectern, and, since its manufacture, has remained in
use at the First Unitarian Church of Baltimore.
(First Unitarian Church, Baltimore, Maryland)

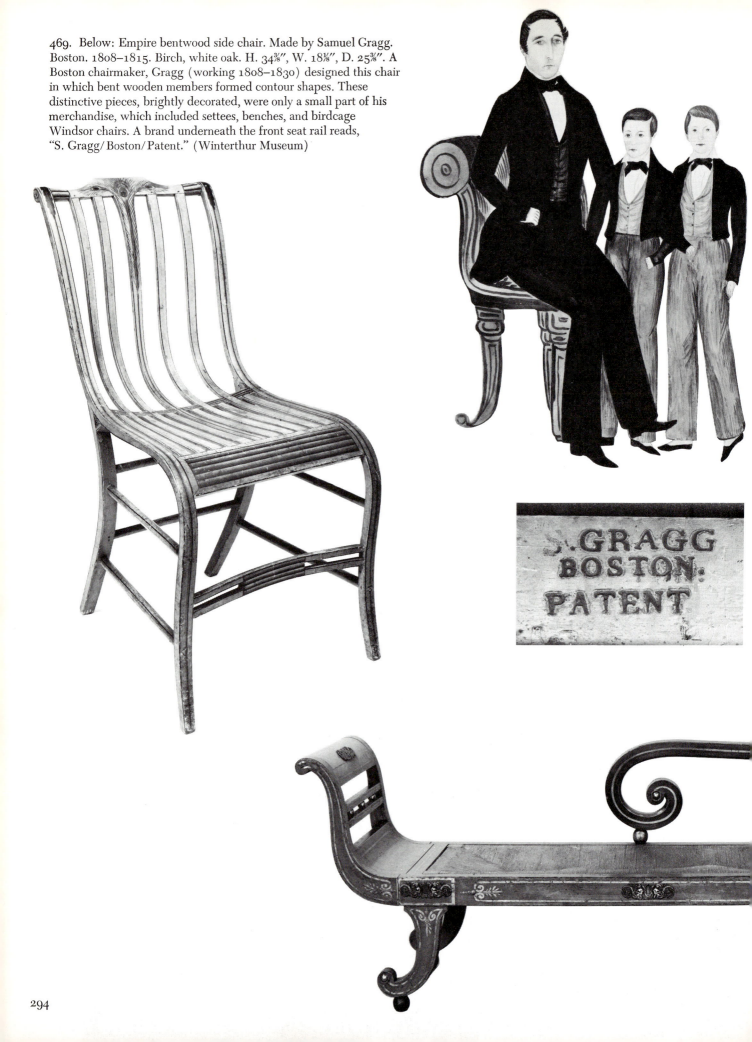

469. Below: Empire bentwood side chair. Made by Samuel Gragg. Boston. 1808–1815. Birch, white oak. H. 34⅜″, W. 18⅛″, D. 25⅜″. A Boston chairmaker, Gragg (working 1808–1830) designed this chair in which bent wooden members formed contour shapes. These distinctive pieces, brightly decorated, were only a small part of his merchandise, which included settees, benches, and birdcage Windsor chairs. A brand underneath the front seat rail reads, "S. Gragg/Boston/Patent." (Winterthur Museum)

S. GRAGG BOSTON. PATENT

470. Left, top: Detail from a family portrait. American. 1840. Watercolor. H. 10⁹⁄₁₆″, W. 17″. It is impossible to know if chairs following this general design were ever actually made; however, since primitive folk artists generally were factual in their representations, it seems quite possible that such a chair did exist. (Museum of Fine Arts, Boston)

471. Center, left: Stamped label from the bottom of a side chair made by Samuel Gragg. Boston. 1815–1820. (Winterthur Museum)

472. Left, bottom: Empire couch. Attributed to P. and B. R. Thomas or to Asher and John Cowperthwaite. New York City. 1815–1820. Maple and oak, painted red. H. 33″, D. 21¼″, L. 77″. The stenciled gilt decoration on this rush-seated Grecian couch is augmented by ormolu mounts. It was made en suite with eight chairs and was used in the music room of a Hudson River home. (The Brooklyn Museum)

473. Near left: Empire side chair. New York City. 1815–1825. Tiger-stripe maple. H. 32″, W. 18½″, D. 19½″. The back rail of this chair, one of a set of four, is painted with a romantic scene in natural colors. Two stylized lyres form the back splats. (The Bayou Bend Collection, The Museum of Fine Arts, Houston)

474. Below: Detail of a portrait of an unidentified gentleman. Painted by Erastus Salisbury Field. American. Ca. 1835. Oil on canvas. H. 32″, W. 28″. The gentleman sits in a "bended chair." (Village Green Antiques)

295

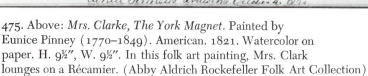

475. Above: *Mrs. Clarke, The York Magnet.* Painted by
Eunice Pinney (1770–1849). American. 1821. Watercolor on
paper. H. 9½″, W. 9½″. In this folk art painting, Mrs. Clark
lounges on a Récamier. (Abby Aldrich Rockefeller Folk Art Collection)

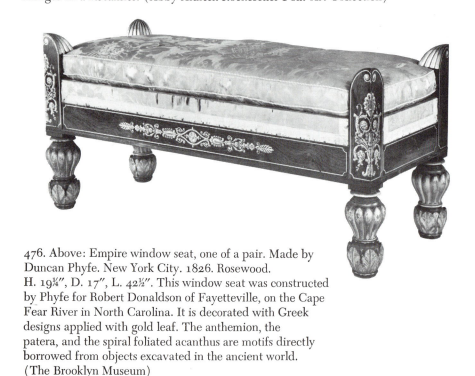

476. Above: Empire window seat, one of a pair. Made by
Duncan Phyfe. New York City. 1826. Rosewood.
H. 19¼″, D. 17″, L. 42½″. This window seat was constructed
by Phyfe for Robert Donaldson of Fayetteville, on the Cape
Fear River in North Carolina. It is decorated with Greek
designs applied with gold leaf. The anthemion, the
patera, and the spiral foliated acanthus are motifs directly
borrowed from objects excavated in the ancient world.
(The Brooklyn Museum)

477. Left: Empire settee. New York City or
Philadelphia. Ca. 1830. Rosewood, maple, poplar, oak.
H. 19½″, D. 19½″, L. 62½″. The beaded banding which
outlines the upper frame of this settee is unusual on such an
early piece. (Museum of Fine Arts, Boston)

478. Above: Empire window stool or bench, one of a pair.
New York City, or Philadelphia, or Baltimore. 1810–1825.
Tulipwood. H. 16⅝″, D. 14″, L. 45″. The antefixes at the
corners of this tulipwood window bench hold the cushion in
place. (Winterthur Museum)

479. Above: Empire window seat. New York City, or Philadelphia,
or Baltimore. 1810–1825. Tulipwood, maple, magnolia. H. 24½″,
D. 22⅜″, L. 61⅛″. This stool, or couch, "with bolster scrolls at each
end" is painted to simulate rosewood. (Winterthur Museum)

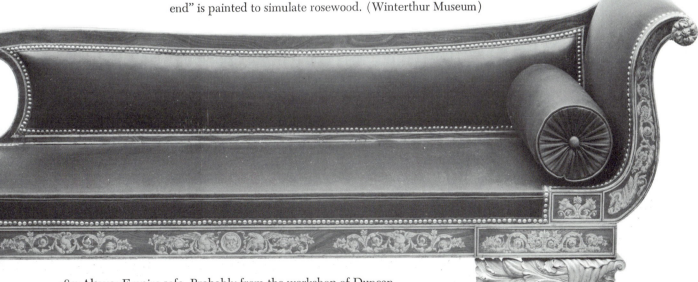

480. Above: Empire sofa. Probably from the workshop of Duncan
Phyfe. New York City. Ca. 1815. Maple. H. 30″, D. 24½″, L. 82½″.
The carved lion's-paw feet and the cornucopia spewing forth leaves,
fruits, and nuts are Empire motifs frequently encountered.
This sleek beauty originally belonged to the Verplanck family of New
York. (The Metropolitan Museum of Art)

481. Below, left: Empire music stool. New York. 1810–1830. Mahogany. H. 33¼″, W. 13¼″, D. 15″. The use of special-purpose chairs, such as music stools and window benches, became popular during the first quarter of the nineteenth century. The earliest examples have reeded legs which relate them to the Sheraton style. (Mrs. Carlos Hepp; photograph courtesy Ginsburg & Levy, Inc.)

482. Right: Empire window bench. New York. Ca. 1815. Mahogany, with brass and ivory inlay. H. 32⅜″, D. 15¼″, L. 45¼″. The brass inlay on this window bench is augmented by a stenciled gilt design on the skirt. (Henry Ford Museum)

483. Below, right: Empire music stool. New York. 1830. Mahogany. H. 30¼″, W. 15″, D. 15½″. Cornucopias, like those carved on the back splat of this stool, were often used as decorative motifs during the 1830's. (Henry Ford Museum)

484. Right: Empire music stool. New York. 1820. Mahogany.
H. 19″, Diameter 13″. Boldly carved leafage decorates the
legs of this adjustable music stool which is one of the finest
examples of this form known. (Henry Ford Museum)

485. Right: Empire window seat with matching
footstool. Attributed to Duncan Phyfe. New York
City. 1810–1820. Native hardwood, grained
rosewood, gilt stenciling. Window seat height 30″,
L. 41½″. Footstool dimensions unavailable. Gilt paint
is used as a substitute for carving on the legs of
these pieces. They are from a set of four, consisting
of twin window seats and footstools. (Photograph
courtesy Ginsburg & Levy, Inc.)

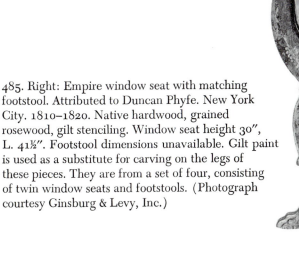

486. Above; 486a. Top, left; 486b. Below: Empire sofa. New
England. 1820–1830. Mahogany, pine. H. 34½″, D. 20¼″,
L. 99″. During the late 1820's and early 1830's, craftsmen,
working in the Empire style, produced ornate, exuberantly
carved chairs and sofas. As always, those working in or
close to urban centers were responsible for the more
sophisticated examples. Only a master craftsman could have
created this eagle-and-cornucopia-back piece. (Henry
Ford Museum)

487. Above; 487a. Right: Empire sofa. New York? 1835–1840. Mahogany, pine. H. 35″, D. 23″, L. 78¾″. The combination of the flat veneered planes, the carved Greek motifs, and the ornate carved feet indicate that this Late Classical piece is transitional in nature. The inclusion of the S-scrolled bracket next to the leg anticipates the style of Late Classical furniture popular during the 1840's. (Henry Ford Museum)

488. Left; 489. Left, center; 490. Left, bottom: Views of furniture-making establishments. China. 1813. Watercolors. H. 11¾", W. 15". These three Chinese paintings, from a set of four, depict Oriental craftsmen making furniture in the hongs for European merchants. The top painting illustrates the various forms of bamboo furniture that might be traded with Yankee sea captains. The second painting shows a furniture-maker planing a piece of wood. A saw rests on the floor beside him. Furniture popular during the nineteenth century is shown in the bottom painting. A craftsman is caning the daybed in the center of the picture. (Ginsburg & Levy, Inc.)

491. Above: Armchair. China. 1790–1850. Bamboo. H. 40⁹⁄₁₆", W. 20⅞", D. 21⅛". This Chinese bamboo armchair has a cane seat. (Winterthur Museum)

492. Left: *Sailors' Tavern*. American or English. Late eighteenth century. Watercolor drawing. H. 12″, W. 6″. This charming view and the accompanying verse are taken from a navigation exercise book. (The Peabody Museum of Salem)

493. Below: Captain's bed. Probably Rhode Island. Ca. 1798. Mahogany. H. 26⅝″, D. 32″, L. 84½″. This type of bed often was used on board ship. (Winterthur Museum)

494. Below: A detail of *The Launching of the Ship Fame*. Painted by George Ropes (1788–1819). American. Ca. 1802. Oil on canvas. H. 33½″, W. 44″. This early nineteenth-century painting shows the 1802 launching at the Crowninshield Wharf of the ship *Fame* built in the nearby shipyard of Retire Becket in Salem, Massachusetts. Ships such as this carried on a brisk trade with the Orient during the 1800's. (Essex Institute)

495. **Above:** Museum installation. The original furnishings of George Crowninshield's bedroom on his famous yacht *Cleopatra's Barge* included this bed, desk, and Windsor chair. A cane which belonged to the Salem, Massachusetts, dandy leans against the Windsor chair. (The Peabody Museum of Salem)

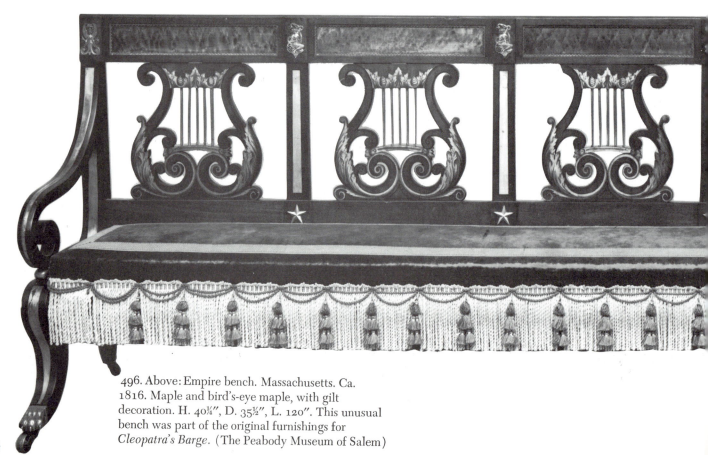

496. Above: Empire bench. Massachusetts. Ca. 1816. Maple and bird's-eye maple, with gilt decoration. H. 40¼", D. 35½", L. 120". This unusual bench was part of the original furnishings for *Cleopatra's Barge.* (The Peabody Museum of Salem)

497. Above: Museum installation. The dining room of
Crowninshield's yacht is now part of the collections at the
Peabody Museum. The Empire lyre-back bench is decorated
with gilt and has a tassel and fringe skirt. (The Peabody
Museum of Salem)

498. *Cleopatra's Barge.* Painted by George
Ropes. American. 1818. Gouache. H. 17½",
W. 22¼". Ropes specialized in marine
painting at Salem, Massachusetts, during
the early nineteenth century. This detail
shows the Crowninshield yacht which was
built at Salem in 1816. (The Peabody
Museum of Salem)

499. Left: Empire armchair. Made by Henry Connelly. Philadelphia. Ca. 1818. Mahogany. H. 33⅛", W. 22", D. 22". The carved dolphins and other devices on this Classical Revival chair, one of a pair made for Stephen Girard, are substitutes for the metal ornaments one would expect to find on French and English furniture of the same period. (Charles H. and Mary Grace Carpenter; photograph courtesy Ginsburg & Levy, Inc.)

500. Below: Empire side chair. Attributed to Anthony Quervelle. Philadelphia. 1840. Mahogany. H. 35", W. 20", D. 18". Dolphins and other nautical motifs decorate this unique chair. (Joseph T. Butler)

501. Below: Empire sofa. Probably New York. 1820–1840. Mahogany. H. 34", D. 27", L. 85". The carved dolphins which form the legs and arms on this sofa are decorated with gilt. (The White House)

502. Right: Portrait of Miss Gilmore. Painted by Erastus Salisbury Field. American. 1835–1845. Oil on canvas. H. 54", W. 34". Miss Gilmore sits in a scale-carved Empire chair. (Museum of Fine Arts, Boston)

503. Left: Classical armchair. Made by William King. Georgetown, Washington, D.C. 1817. Mahogany. Dimensions unavailable. President James Monroe ordered this and twenty-three matching armchairs and two settees for the White House. They are constructed in the Late Sheraton style. (The White House)

504. Above: Zanzibar armchair. Boston or Salem. 1830. Ebonized mahogany. H. 33½″, W. 18″, D. 18½″. Zanzibar chairs were popular in New England seaport towns during the first and second quarters of the nineteenth century. (James Gwynn)

505. Right: Classical armchair. Made by William Hancock. Boston. 1829–1831. Mahogany. H. 41½″, W. 24″, D. 28½″. Constructed in the Late Regency style, this library chair was labeled by the Boston cabinetmaker, William Hancock. It was constructed with brass ratchets that permit the back to recline. The front rail pulls out to form a footrest. The design is an early forerunner of the leather or vinyl lounge chairs made during the 1950's. (Dr. and Mrs. Roger Gerry)

506. Late Classical armchair. Baltimore. 1830–1840. "Whitewood." H. 34½″, W. 20½″, D. 20½″. The flat shape of the arms and legs of this Southern chair anticipates the "scroll style" of the 1840's. Gilt stencil decoration of acanthus and anthemion motifs enriches much of the surface. (The Baltimore Museum of Art)

Carvers & Turners

Duncan Phyfe, while selecting designs for his furniture, is reputed to have pointed to the ceiling, from which hung paper patterns that he had drawn, and instructed his workman to "Use a combination of this and this and that." The tool chest, figure 508, completely fitted with the finest tools of the time, belonged to this distinguished New York cabinetmaker. The bow and tenon saws, spokeshaves, and marking gauge clearly visible in the illustration would have been most useful in the production of chairs. Phyfe, "strict in his habits," enjoyed financial success. His house, directly across the street from the workshop, warehouse, and salesroom, was "most elegant."

507. Left: *The Cabinetmaker*. An illustration from *The Book of Trades or Library of Useful Arts*. Published in Philadelphia by Jacob Johnson. 1807. Patterns for chair-backs hang on the wall behind the craftsman. (The New York Public Library)

508. Above: Tool chest that belonged to Duncan Phyfe. New York. Nineteenth century. Phyfe is known to have used this chest in 1829. (The New-York Historical Society)

509. Below: Self-portrait sketch by Lewis Miller (1796–1882). York, Pennsylvania. Miller shows himself working with a plane on a tool bench. The original inscription which accompanied this drawing states, "Lewis Miller Carpenter, Working . . . At the Trade for Thirty years, In South Duke Street, York, p.a. done Work for the Citizens, and County Commissioners . . ." (The Historical Society of York County)

510. Far right: *The Turner*. An illustration from *The Book of Trades or Library of Useful Arts*. 1807. In this illustration the turner works at a treadle lathe which is powered by a pumping foot motion. The speed could be adjusted by moving the drive belt to different settings on the spindle pulley. (Library of Congress)

511. Far left: Museum installation. Empire parlor from an Albany, New York, house dating about 1830. High ceilings, long windows, and a marble mantel flanked with carved caryatids provide an appropriate background for the Late Classical furniture. (Winterthur Museum)

512. Left: Advertisement from the firm of Joseph Meeks & Sons. Lithograph by Endicott & Swett. New York City. 1833. (The Metropolitan Museum of Art)

513. Below, left: Late Empire side chair. American. 1820–1830. Mahogany. H. 33¾″, W. 18″, D. 18″. This chair is part of a set made en suite with a sofa. (The Metropolitan Museum of Art)

Late Classical or "Pillar and Scroll" furniture was most often constructed of pine or other inexpensive woods and veneered with rich, matched-grain mahogany. This style, popular during the 1830's and early 1840's, was one of the first to be manufactured by machine. Mass production of furniture was made possible by the technological advancements of the machine age. During the first years of this phenomenon, the small cabinetmaking shops which had created handcrafted furniture were totally phased out since they could not compete with the machine's gigantic productivity.

Late Classical

514. Above: Late Empire side chair. Probably New York. 1825–1840. Mahogany, ash, cherry. H. 34″, W. 17¾″, D. 18″. Shown in the interior, figure 511, this side chair is one of a pair. (Winterthur Museum)

313

515. Top: Late Classical window seat, one of a pair. H. 16¼″, L. 44¾″. 516. Above: Late Classical footstool. H. 15¼″, W. 30¾″, D. 15¼″. 517. Right, bottom: Late Classical méridienne. H. 38½″, D. 24½″, L. 74″. 518. Right, top: Late Classical "Gondola" chair, one of a set of four. H. 30¼″, D. 16½″. All of this mahogany furniture is from a suite of fourteen pieces manufactured in the workshop of Duncan Phyfe, New York City, in 1837. According to family tradition, Samuel A. Foot, a New York lawyer, purchased the furniture for use in the parlor of his new home at 678 Broadway, New York City. (The Metropolitan Museum of Art)

Duncan Phyfe, like his competitors Joseph and Edward Meeks (later Joseph Meeks & Sons) of New York, and John Needles of Baltimore, had to adapt his production to incorporate the manufacturing procedures of the time. The architect, John Hall, published his *The Cabinet-Maker's Assistant* in 1840. In this manual, which was intended as a guide for furniture-makers, he illustrated numerous examples which could be crafted in the "Pillar and Scroll" style. That same year the steam-driven band saw, with the capability of cutting intricate curves for almost any thickness of wood, came into common use. The scrolled style continued to be popular, and in 1850, A. J. Downing wrote in his *The Architecture of Country Houses* that "the furniture most generally used in private houses is some modification of the classical style." It had "the merit of being simple, easily made and very moderate in cost."

519. Above: Late Classical sofa. New York. 1825–1830. Mahogany, mahogany veneer. H. 34″, D. 26″, L. 80″. The carved feet on this sofa illustrate the influence of the French Restoration style. The pillared front posts are fitted with ormolu capitals and bases. (James Ricau)

520. Below: Late Classical music stool. New York. 1830–1850. Mahogany veneer on pine. H. 29¼″, W. 15⁵⁄₁₆″, D. 14½″. True Pillar and Scroll construction was used when this music stool was made. (Henry Ford Museum)

521. Above: Late Classical side chair. Possibly by Joseph Meeks. New York City. 1835–1840. Mahogany and mahogany veneer. H. 33″, W. 19½″, D. 16½″. A prototype for the curvaceous, continuous-stile-and-rail construction of this lyre-splat side chair was published by George Smith in his *Household Furniture* in London, 1826. (Edgar de N. Mayhew; photograph, The Newark Museum)

522. Right: Museum installation. The Late Classical side chair in this interior is almost identical to those illustrated in Joseph Meeks's 1833 advertisement lithographed by Endicott & Swett, in which he offers "Cabinet and Upholstery Articles." (The International Garden Club, Bartow Mansion, Pelham Bay, New York)

523. Victorian rocking chair. American. Mid-nineteenth century. Black walnut. H. 42½″, W. 23″, D. 39″. This flat-cut, scrolled armchair is the one in which Lincoln was sitting when he was assassinated. It is upholstered in the original red damask, and its design incorporates elements of both the Scrolled and Rococo Revival styles. (Henry Ford Museum)

524. Above: Early photograph of the interior of Ford's Theatre, Washington, D.C., where Abraham Lincoln was assassinated while attending a performance of *Our American Cousin* on April 14, 1865. (Henry Ford Museum)

525. Right: Museum interior of Logan County Courthouse where young Abraham Lincoln practiced law while serving as a "rider" on the Illinois "mud circuit." The Logan County Courthouse was built in Pottsville, Illinois, in 1840. Several of the Late Classical chairs which were used in its restoration are part of the original furnishings. The armchair before the desk is attributed to Abraham Bouvier of Philadelphia. (Henry Ford Museum)

CHAPTER 9

THE VICTORIAN STYLES 1820-1900

529. Above: Museum installation. The dining room of Lyndhurst is Gothic both in its architectural concept and its furnishings. The addition of this room in 1864–1865 was supervised by Alexander Jackson Davis, the designer of the original house. (Lyndhurst, National Trust for Historic Preservation; photograph courtesy Louis Reens)

526. Far left: Drawing of the hundred-foot Gothic Revival tower, a later addition to the Hudson River mansion, Lyndhurst. By Alexander Jackson Davis. New York. (Avery Library, Columbia University)

527. Near left (opposite page): Photograph of St. Luke's Church, built in Isle of Wight County, Virginia. 1632. This church is one of America's oldest examples of Gothic architecture. (Library of Congress)

528. Bottom, left (opposite page): Museum installation. The eighteenth-century English interior is furnished with chairs constructed in Chippendale's Gothic taste. (Victoria and Albert Museum)

530. Below: View of Lyndhurst. American. Wood engraving from a Davis drawing titled *A View of Paulding Manor from the Southeast*. The facade of Lyndhurst as shown in this print was greatly altered when Davis redesigned the "Country Mansion" for George Merritt in 1864. (Lyndhurst, National Trust for Historic Preservation)

When Alexander Jackson Davis (1803–1892) built the country house Lyndhurst in 1838–1841 for William Paulding, Mayor of New York, and his son Philip R. Paulding, his use of the Gothic style was not without precedent. "Pointed" architecture first developed as a cohesive style in the early part of the twelfth century in France. In that country it was used extensively in the construction of cathedrals adorned with elaborate stained-glass windows. During the latter half of the twelfth century, English church builders incorporated Gothic designs into their buildings. The use of Gothic motifs on furniture was emphasized in Thomas Chippendale's mid-eighteenth-century *Director*. In America, the early nineteenth-century Gothic movement was essentially an architectural one. A. J. Downing, author of the 1842 edition of *Cottage Residences or a Series of Designs for Rural Cottages and Cottage-Villas and Their Gardens and Grounds Adapted to North America*, stated that the Gothic style was reserved for a man "with strong aspirations after something higher than social pleasures."

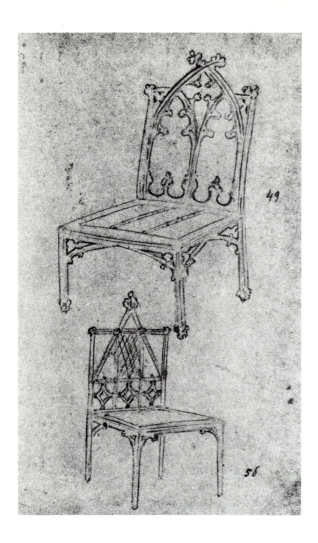

531. Left: Drawing of Victorian side chairs in the Gothic style. By Alexander Jackson Davis. New York. Philip Hone, when visiting the still unfinished Lyndhurst in 1841, predicted that the "Gothic monastery will one of these days be designated as 'Paulding's Folly.'" These designs are for chairs intended to be used in the Paulding residence. Burns and Trainque of New York City are known to have made some of the furniture for Lyndhurst. A. J. Downing, a competitor of Davis, described their pieces as "the most correct Gothic furniture . . . executed in this country." (Lyndhurst, National Trust for Historic Preservation)

Gothic Revival

532. Right: Victorian side chair in the Gothic style. American. 1847. Walnut. H. 57", W. 27", D. 25". This and matching chairs were designed by James Renwick, Jr., for use in the Smithsonian Institution Building, Washington, D.C. (Smithsonian Institution)

534. Right: Victorian armchair in the Gothic style, one of twelve. Probably New York. 1864–1866. Oak. H. 45½″, W. 20″, D. 21″. This chair appears to have been designed for George Merritt by Davis when he completed the additions at Lyndhurst. It has remained in the house since the 1860's. (Lyndhurst, National Trust for Historic Preservation)

533. Left: Victorian wheel-back side chair in the Gothic style. New York. 1838–1841. Oak. H. 37″, W. 18¼″, D. 17½″. This chair, one of a pair, was designed for Paulding by Davis for use at Lyndhust in the "Saloon." The four-lobed designs in the back of this chair are known as quatrefoils. The lobes that surround the wheel-back are called crockets. (Lyndhurst, National Trust for Historic Preservation)

535. Above: Room interior. The front parlor of the carpenter Gothic home, Roseland, built for Henry Chandler Bowen (1813–1896) by the architect Joseph C. Wells at Woodstock, Connecticut. The furnishings include Gothic tall-back chairs. (Roseland)

536. Left; 536a. Far right: Victorian side chair in the Gothic style. Designed by Alexander Jackson Davis. New York. 1840. Oak. H. 39¼″, W. 18½″, D. 15¼″. The flattened cabriole leg and cloven foot accent the Neo-Gothic design of the back of this chair. (Museum of the City of New York)

537. Near right: Victorian side chair in the Gothic style, one of a pair. Designed by Alexander Jackson Davis. New York. 1840. Oak. H. 45″, W. 18¾″, D. 18″. Oak was preferred for the best Gothic Revival chairs since its strength was thought to be superior to mahogany and rosewood. (Lyndhurst, National Trust for Historic Preservation)

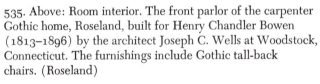

538. Right: Advertisement of Gardiner's Ware Rooms.
Published in *Rode's New York City Directory*. 1853–1854.
During the Victorian era, numerous furniture styles, mostly
revivalistic in nature, coexisted. In this advertisement,
furniture with both Gothic and Rococo design elements is
immediately identifiable. (The New-York Historical Society)

539. Above: Victorian side chair and table, in the Gothic
style. New York. 1855. Rosewood. Chair Height 34″,
W. 16½″, D. 16½″. Gothic leaf carvings and other motifs are
freely used as decorative elements on this essentially Rococo
New York chair. It retains the original red-and-buff
needlepoint covering in a modified fleur-de-lis pattern.
(The Metropolitan Museum of Art)

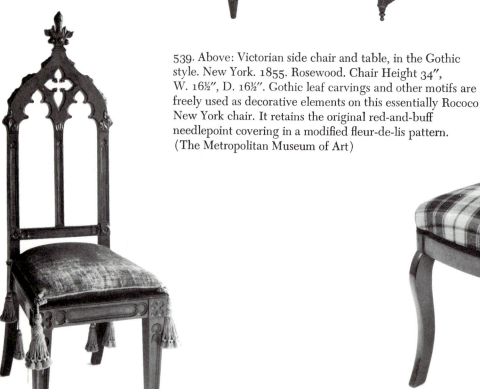

540. Far left: Victorian side chair in the Gothic style. Made by Daniel & Hitchins. Troy, New York. 1856. Mahogany. H. 55¼″, W. 20¼″, D. 19″. This hall chair was originally purchased from the 199 River Street shop of Daniel & Hitchins by Mr. R. J. Milligan of Saratoga Springs, New York. (The Brooklyn Museum)

541. Near left: Victorian side chair in the Gothic style. New York. 1850. Mahogany. H. 33¾″, W. 18″, D. 17¾″. Chairs almost identical to this example were made by Alexander and Frederick Roux of New York City. Joseph Meeks & Sons supplied a dozen of these chairs to the White House in

1846–1847. They were later used by Abraham Lincoln in his Cabinet Room. (The Brooklyn Museum)

542. Above: Portrait of Mr. and Mrs. Charles Henry Augustus Carter. New York City. 1848. Probably painted by Nicholas Biddle Kittell. Oil on canvas. H. 21½″, W. 23½″. Mr. and Mrs. Carter are sitting in the drawing room of their home on Bleecker Street in New York City's Greenwich Village. A sofa, armchair, and window bench, upholstered in a vibrant blue fabric, indicate this young couple's awareness of the fashionable Gothic style. (Museum of the City of New York)

327

Rococo Revival

During the early 1840's Late Classical designs were gradually phased out by the insistent use of the "modern" or Rococo styles. Professor Benjamin Silliman, Jr., in his review of New York's 1853 Crystal Palace Exhibition, wrote scathingly about "the ponderous and frigid monstrosities" of the Classical period. The name most frequently associated with the American Rococo Revival Movement is John Henry Belter (1804–1863), a German immigrant who came to America as a fully-trained cabinetmaker. He worked at several different New York City locations before 1858 when he opened his J. H. Belter and Company Cabinet Factory on Third Avenue. In 1856 Belter patented a laminating process which involved gluing thin layers of rosewood together at right angles, so that the grain of each layer was alternating. Once pressed and shaped by steaming in a special matrix, the veneer layers, sometimes as few as three but oftentimes as many as sixteen, were ready for carving. Belter's process was not totally original, for the Egyptians had used laminated wood panels in the construction of their sarcophagi. It was, however, soon imitated by other furniture manufacturers who, like the patentee himself, worked predominantly in the Rococo Revival style. Charles A. Baudouine, active in New York from 1845 through 1900, manufactured chairs in his huge furniture factory. Though identical in style to Belter's, they were distinguished by a seam running down the back—a method of construction he devised to circumvent Belter's patent.

543. Left: Room interior. The parlor of Melrose, the Natchez, Mississippi, Greek Revival home built in 1845 by Judge Edward Turner for his daughter, is furnished with Rococo Revival furniture, including a "courting set"— a double-chair love seat, which enabled the chaperone to sit between the young woman and her gentleman caller. (Mrs. George Malin Davis Kelly)

544. Right: Detail of a slipper chair. Attributed to John Henry Belter. New York City. Mid-nineteenth century. Rosewood. H. 43⅛", W. 18½", D. 18". (The Metropolitan Museum of Art)

FACTORY 76 ST. ON 3ᴿᵈ AVENUE.

545. Above: Detail of a Victorian sofa in the Rococo style. Probably made by John Henry Belter. New York City. 1855–1860. Rosewood. H. 47¼″, D. 27¼″, L. 56½″. (Museum of the City of New York)

546. Above and below: Details from a billhead of John Henry Belter. New York City. Dated May 20, 1864. This bill was rendered to Mrs. Elliott at 27 West 33rd Street and included "3 small Blkw Chairs" for $17.00 each. The purchase price of $51.00 would today represent approximately $510.00. Belter's Third Avenue and 76th Street, New York City, factory opened in 1858. (Museum of the City of New York)

MANUFACTURERS OF
ALL KINDS OF Cabinet Furniture.
Warehouse 722 Broadway

547. Left; 547a. Above: Victorian armchair in the Rococo style. Made by John Henry Belter. New York City. 1850. Rosewood. H. 48½″, W. 25¾″, D. 24½″. This chair was owned by Abraham Lincoln. Like all of Belter's chairs, the back is not divided by a seam. (Henry Ford Museum)

548. Right: Patent model made by John Henry Belter. New York City. 1858. Mahogany. This tiny model accompanied Belter's application for a patent on his laminating process. It was assigned Patent No. 19405. Once, in a fury over an infringement upon this patent, Belter entered his shop and smashed the molds from which his chairs were being constructed. (Smithsonian Institution)

549. Above; 550. Below; 551. Near right; 552. Far right, top:
Pencil sketches of chair designs. Drawn by John Jelliff
(1813–1893). Newark, New Jersey. Ca. 1850. Jelliff, a
talented cabinetmaker, followed the eighteenth-century
tradition of handcrafting furniture. Using primarily rosewood
and walnut, he constructed his pieces in both the Rococo
and Gothic styles. These original pencil sketches are an
indication of the facile talent which this man possessed.
(The Newark Museum)

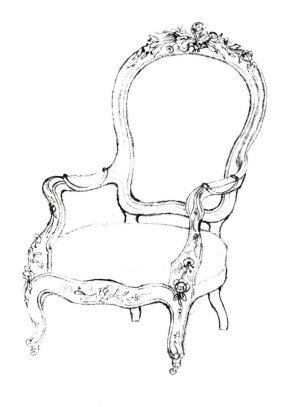

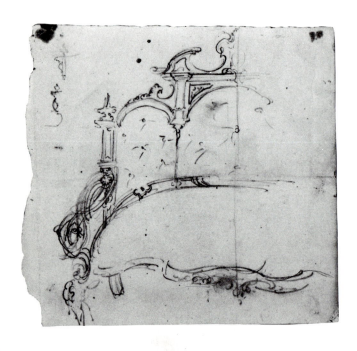

553. Below: Silhouette of the John Jelliff family. Newark, New Jersey. Ca. 1844. H. 20⅛", W. 23½". The Jelliff family included his mother, Mrs. Nancy Jelliff, standing next to the Gothic-inspired fireplace mantel; his wife, holding their baby, Carrie, and sitting in a Late Classical chair; and his daughters, Elizabeth Mary, born in 1841, holding a basket, and Harriette, standing before her father. The framed picture on the wall is a view of Mount Vernon and Washington's Tomb and possibly is a print by Currier and Ives. (The Newark Museum)

554. Above: Portrait of Joseph Meeks. American. Ca. 1800. Pastel. H. 24¾″, W. 19¾″. Meeks, founder of the New York Meeks furniture firm, would have been twenty-nine years old in 1800. Most of the furniture associated with him is in the Late Classical style as shown in his advertisement of 1833 on page 313. (Mr. and Mrs. Bradford A. Warner)

555. Above: Trade card published by John Meeks. New York City. Ca. 1860. This card lists Meeks's address as 333 and 335 Fourth Street. His furniture manufactory was located there from 1860 through 1864. (The New-York Historical Society)

556. Above: Victorian armchair in the Rococo style. Attributed to Joseph Meeks. New York City. Mid-nineteenth century. Rosewood. H. 43½″, W. 27″, D. 24″. In his plant, Meeks, like his contemporaries Belter, Baudouine, and Jelliff, manufactured furniture in numerous styles. His 1833 lithograph, printed by Endicott & Swett, illustrated over forty pieces which were constructed for the most part in the scrolled, Late Classical style. Labeled pieces in the Elizabethan style are known. This Rococo armchair is similar to those in a suite that was a gift from the firm to Joseph W. Meeks's daughter, Sophia Teresa, when she married Dexter A. Hawkins in 1859. (The Metropolitan Museum of Art)

557. Detail from a broadside. Published by Endicott &
Swett, New York City. 1833. This building housed the
Meeks & Sons Manufactory of Cabinet Furniture in 1833.
(The Metropolitan Museum of Art)

558. Above: *Entertaining in the Parlor*. By A. J. Volck. American. 1861–1865. Pencil drawing. H. 8$\frac{5}{16}$″, W. 11$\frac{2}{16}$″. Volck was a dentist by profession, and a resident of Baltimore. Politically his sympathies were with the South and he drew many caustic cartoons lampooning President Lincoln. A large part of the population of Baltimore was pro-Southern; this drawing illustrates a group of ladies engaged in mending and knitting in behalf of Southern servicemen. A military jacket lies on the floor beside the chair of one young woman; another is reading *The Maryland News*. In the foreground is a low circular table with a bust of the President of the Confederate States, Jefferson Davis, prominently displayed on it. (Maryland Historical Society)

559. Above, left: Victorian armchair in the Rococo style. American. Mid-nineteenth century. Rosewood. H. 45″, W. 27$\frac{1}{4}$″, D. 35″. During the 1850's, American craftsmen, working in the "modern" style, preferred to minimize framework in favor of colorful upholstery. (T. B. Buckles, Jr.)

560. Left, bottom: Victorian armchair in the Rococo style. American. 1847–1850. Mahogany. H. 37″, W. 32″, D. 28″. The continuous-arm

construction of this upholstered chair is not common. (Sunnyside,
Sleepy Hollow Restorations)

561. Right, top: Victorian armchair in the Rococo style. Possibly by
Leon Marcotte. New York. Ca. 1860. Pearwood. H. 37¾″, W. 22″,
D. 21¾″. John Taylor Johnston and Frances Colles were married
in 1850, and in 1855 began building their home on Fifth Avenue at
8th Street, New York City. It is thought that the Johnstons
bought a suite of furniture, including this chair, for their newly
completed home from the French émigré cabinetmaker, Leon
Marcotte. The application of metal decorations in the Rococo period is
rare. (The Metropolitan Museum of Art)

562. Right, bottom: Victorian armchair in the Rococo style. American.
Mid-nineteenth century. Mahogany, painted white and gold.
H. 42½″, W. 25½″, D. 26″. This armchair is part of a set from the
New York home of Robert Kelly. Other forms in the suite are a
piano, center table, additional armchairs, side chairs, and a tête-à-tête
—a sofa with chair-back ends and a low center. Richard Upjohn,
the distinguished nineteenth-century architect, assisted Mr. Kelly with
the selection of his furniture. (Munson–Williams–Proctor Institute)

563. Above, left: Victorian tête-à-tête in the Rococo style. Attributed to John Henry Belter. New York City. Mid-nineteenth century. Rosewood. H. 44½″, D. 43″, L. 52″. Romantic mid-Victorians relished the opportunity of spending an evening on the "conversational." (The Metropolitan Museum of Art)

564. Below: Victorian parlor furniture in the Rococo style. Made by G. Vollmer. Philadelphia. 1859. Gilt, wood unknown. Settee: H. 48″, D. 24″, L. 88″. Chair: H. 45¼″, W. 27″, D. 24″. President James Buchanan purchased this parlor suite and installed it in the White House where it remained until 1937. (Smithsonian Institution)

565. Above, right: Victorian sofa in the Rococo style. Attributed to John Henry Belter. New York City. Mid-nineteenth century. Rosewood. H. 48½″, D. 29½″, L. 89¾″. In 1854 Professor Benjamin Silliman, Jr., of Yale observed, "We are no longer contented with the plainness that was once satisfactory." Perhaps he was speaking of furniture such as this sofa which once had been gilded. (The Metropolitan Museum of Art)

566. Right: *In the Parlor*. Painted by Charles S. Connor (1857–1905). American. 1885. Oil on canvas. H. 23″, W. 18″. Connor included a Late Rococo sofa in this interior of his betrothed wife's home at Fountain City, Indiana. Though cluttered by today's taste, the room is rather austere when compared to typical Victorian interiors. (Indianapolis Museum of Art)

567. Below: Victorian méridienne in the Rococo style. Made by John Henry Belter. New York City. Ca. 1850. Rosewood. H. 44½″, D. 32″, L. 52″. This piece was used by Abraham Lincoln in his Springfield, Illinois, home. It was sold at auction by his widow, Mary Todd Lincoln. (Henry Ford Museum)

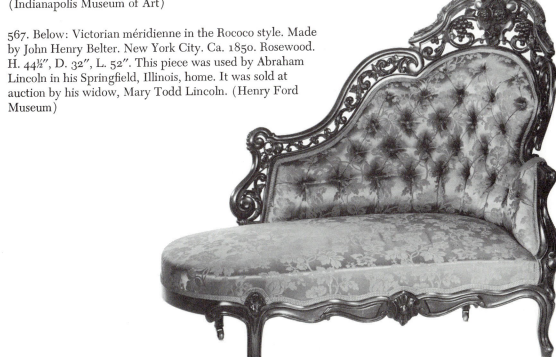

568. Left: Victorian side chair in the Rococo style. American. Ca. 1850. Rosewood. H. 38″, W. 16½″, D. 21″. The flat carving on the back of this chair indicates that it is somewhat later in date than the more exuberant, deeply carved examples previously shown. (Henry Ford Museum)

569. Above: Pencil drawing by John Jelliff. Newark, New Jersey. Ca. 1850. Jelliff consistently refused to machine-make furniture. The pierced splat on the chair in this sketch is similar in design to figure 568. (The Newark Museum)

570. Left: Victorian side chair in the Rococo style. New York. 1850. Walnut. H. 41½", W. 18¾", D. 18½". Gothic designs are cut into the back of this chair. (Henry Ford Museum)

571. Right: Victorian armchair in the Rococo style. Attributed to Moore and Campion. Philadelphia. Ca. 1860. Walnut. H. 64", W. 28", D. 21". Though the front legs of this piece are cabriole, the back is centered with a shield like device associated with the somewhat later Renaissance Revival style. (Smithsonian Institution)

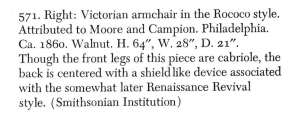

572. Left: Victorian side chair in the Rococo style. Possibly made by Leon Marcotte. New York. Ca. 1850. Walnut. H. 43½", W. 20", D. 23". The essence of Rococo carving and design is asymmetry. This chair is an example of Baroque or Mannerist-Revival design in that the carving is balanced and regular. The tapestry upholstery is original. (Lockwood–Mathews Mansion)

573. Below: Portrait of Lucinda Warren Goddard (1811–1895). Painted by J. T. Evans (1802–1874). American. 1833. Watercolor on board. H. 12½″, W. 9″. Miss Goddard married Mr. Sullivan Lucion Carpenter and they lived at 47 Monroe, Roxbury, Massachusetts. She stands beside a piano bench with cabriole legs. (Museum of Fine Arts, Boston)

574. Right: Victorian side chair in the Rococo style. American. 1850–1870. Mahogany. H. 32½″, W. 18½″, D. 22¼″. Balloon-backs, constructed of solid and not laminated wood, were the most popular chairs of the mid-nineteenth century. (Sunnyside, Sleepy Hollow Restorations)

576. Left: Victorian side chair in the Rococo style. American. Ca. 1850. Rosewood. H. 38″, W. 19″, D. 22″. Very few Rococo chairs were constructed with cane seats and backs. (Smithsonian Institution)

577. Below: Victorian side chair in the Rococo style. American. 1860–1870. Walnut. H. 34½″, W. 20″, D. 23½″. The short arms on this chair, one of a set of six, give added strength. (Henry Ford Museum)

575. Above: Victorian sofa in the Rococo style. New England. 1859. Rosewood. Dimensions unavailable. This and nine other red plush sofas were purchased for $35.00 each for use in the Hall of Representatives and Senate Chamber in the Vermont State House at Montpelier. (Vermont State House)

578. Below: Photograph of the Cheap Furniture Store located at 905 State Street, Chicago, Illinois. This early photograph, taken in 1868 or 1869, shows balloon-back side chairs, an armchair, and a sofa from the 1850's as part of the store's secondhand merchandise. (Chicago Historical Society)

579. Right, top: Victorian sofa in the Rococo style. American. 1860–1870. Mahogany. H. 37⅛″, D. 22¼″, L. 62″. This sofa is upholstered in black horsehair and is typical of furniture used in "Queen Anne" Revival-style houses built during the second half of the nineteenth century. (Henry Ford Museum)

580. Right, bottom: Victorian lady's rocker in the Rococo style. American. 1860–1870. Walnut. H. 32½″, W. 22¼″, D. 34¾″. Ladies' rockers were diminutive in size. (Henry Ford Museum)

581. Right, top: Advertisement of Gould & Co., "Furniture Manufacturers and Dealers." Published in 1876. Philadelphia. Visitors to the Philadelphia Centennial were offered a seven-piece Rococo Revival suite, including a sofa, a gentleman's chair, a lady's chair, and four balloon-back side chairs, at a cost of $65.00 upholstered in haircloth or any color wool terry, or $125.00 in plush or silk. (The New York Public Library)

582. Right, bottom: Victorian side chair in the Rococo style. American. 1860–1870. Mahogany. H. 37½", W. 20", D. 23". Simplified Rococo Revival chairs were sold at the annual furniture marts in Grand Rapids, Michigan, as late as the middle 1880's. This example is one of the most sophisticated of its type. (Henry Ford Museum)

583. Below: Photograph of the cabinetmaking shop of Henry W. Jenkins & Son. Taken in 1864. Craftsmen and more noble gentlemen peer from the windows of the Baltimore establishment. (Jenkins Collection)

584. Near right: Design for an Elizabethan chair made of "Old Church Wood" submitted by Henry W. Jenkins & Son, Funeral Directors and Cabinetmakers, in 1861, to the Presbyterian minister, Dr. Backus. H. 9⅛", W. 12½". The Jenkins firm also specialized in interior decoration and a large number of their drawings for suggested room settings exist. (Jenkins Collection; photograph courtesy Winterthur Museum)

The "Elizabethan" revival is elusive. During the 1840's and 1850's "Elizabethan" furniture was advertised, but actually, the manufacturers had no coherent understanding of how authentic furniture dating from Elizabeth's reign, 1558–1603, looked. Victorian chairs which have spiral or ball turnings are loosely classified as Elizabethan. These turnings are actually anachronistic and were not part of the decoration of Elizabethan period pieces.

Elizabethan Revival

585. Above: Victorian side chair in the Elizabethan style. American. Ca. 1850. Rosewood, mahogany. H. 42½″, W. 18¼″, D. 17¼″. This chair has spiral-turned front legs and stiles. The needlework seat was worked by Mrs. Richard Van Wick (née Catherine Bergen Johnson, married in 1851). (Museum of the City of New York)

586. Right: Victorian armchair in the Elizabethan style. American. Ca. 1900. Mahogany. H. 39⅜″, W. 24″, D. 18½″. The Baroque spiral-twist turnings relate this armchair to one illustrated in Downing's *Country Houses.* (The Brooklyn Museum)

587. Below: Victorian armchair in the Elizabethan style. New York. 1840–1850. Ebonized wood. H. 48″, W. 24″, D. 24″. Bobbin- or ball-turned members were used in the construction of this chair. (Miss Frances K. Talbot)

588. Left: Victorian davenport-bed in the Elizabethan style. Made by Kindel Bed Company. Grand Rapids, Michigan. Ca. 1913. Oak. H. 33″, D. 36″, L. 61½″. The Elizabethan style continued to be popular during the early years of the twentieth century. This patented bed was created by Charles J. Kindel, founder of the firm. In 1915 the Kroehler Manufacturing Company, in order to obtain the patent, bought the company at a price that allowed Kindel to retire. Later Kroehler sold the plant to outside interests. In 1924 Kindel decided to go back into business; he repurchased the plant and started manufacturing "Colonial" bedroom furniture. (Grand Rapids Public Museum)

589. Left: Victorian "spool" armchair in the Elizabethan style. American. 1865–1885. Walnut. H. 38″, W. 23″, D. 25″. The flattened-ball turnings on this armchair are called spool turnings. Because a bed with similar turnings was used by "The Swedish Nightingale," Jenny Lind, all spool furniture became known as "Jenny Lind style" pieces. (Mrs. J. Balfour Miller)

590. Right: Victorian slipper chair, in the Elizabethan style. American. 1840–1860. Walnut. H. 41¾″, W. 17½″, D. 19″. The upholstery on this Baroque spiral-twist or corkscrew-turned chair is velvet and tapestry. In 1878 Harriet Prescott Spofford, author of *Art Decoration Applied to Furniture*, mentioned Elizabethan chairs, indicating that they were still much in favor. (Henry Ford Museum)

592. Right: Victorian side chair in the Cottage style. American. 1860–1875. Maple. H. 28⅝″, W. 15¼″, D. 13⅞″. Bobbin-turned and spool chairs were inexpensive substitutes for more formal seating pieces. (Henry Ford Museum)

591. Left: Victorian side chair in the "Cottage" style, one of a set of four. American. Ca. 1860. Pine. H. 34″, W. 17½″, D. 17½″. This green-and-gilt-decorated chair is from a bedroom suite. The use of a cane back on a Cottage chair is unusual. (Smithsonian Institution)

Sarah & Eliza Russell's room at Mrs Smith's N E Broad & Spruce Philad' 1854

593. Above: Interior view of Sarah and Eliza Russell's room at Mrs. Smith's located on Northeast Broad and Spruce Streets, Philadelphia. 1854. Watercolor on paper. H. 7″, W. 9″. The room is furnished with spindle-turned Cottage side chairs in front of the windows, a lady's rocker flanking the fireplace, a piano, and a tripod-base piano stool. (Nina Fletcher Little)

594. Below: Advertisement of Merriam & Parsons. Published in *Business Encyclopedia and Commercial Directory*. Alvord & Co. New York. 185? This firm, which manufactured and dealt in "Cottage Chamber Furniture," also offered an endless variety of bureaus, wardrobes, sinks, tables, wash-stands and toilets, and cane and wood seat chairs. Chairs were also available in packages and cases for shipping. (The New-York Historical Society)

MERRIAM & PARSONS,
Manufacturers and Dealers in Cottage Chamber Furniture,
ALSO, EVERY VARIETY OF

Bureaus, Wardrobes, Sinks, Tables, Wash Stands & Toilets, Cane & Wood Seat Chairs.

Chairs in packages and cases for shipping.

Nos. from 121 to 137 FULTON STREET, Boston.

O. W. Merriam.   W. A. Parsons.

595. Above: Victorian armchair in the Renaissance style. Made by
Thomas Brooks & Co. Brooklyn, New York. 1872. Walnut. H. 38¼″,
W. 32½″, D. 31″. The ornately carved roundel and escutcheon on the
top rail of this "puffed" armchair are flanked by dolphins. This piece
was originally purchased by Mr. N. H. Clement at the Upholstery
Warehouse, Nos. 127 and 129 Fulton Street, maintained by the Brooks
firm. Curtains, mattresses, and "Spring Pilliasses, Feathers, &c"
were also available. (The Brooklyn Museum)

596. Above: Victorian armchair and two "demi-arm" chairs in the Renaissance style. New York? Ca. 1860. Walnut and burl. Armchair: H. 44¾", W. 25", D. 24½". Mammoth suites of Renaissance furniture often contained chairs of many different sizes. (Henry Ford Museum)

Charles Wyllys Elliott, writing on household art in the mid-1870's, spoke of Renaissance Revival furniture in this way: "The most miserable wretch could not lie on it, and no man would try to sit on it if the earth were near." Then going on to speak of sofas, "Do people wish to look at them? Do they please the eye? But they buy them!" And buy them they did. The Renaissance style was an immensely popular one. Furniture constructed with elegantly turned trumpet legs, massively carved roundels, and paneled medallions set off by the use of fine contrasting inlay and gilded incised lines appealed to the rising middle class seeking a visual way to demonstrate its newly gained affluence. Vibrant upholstery fabrics were frequently used. Mr. Elliott noted that "'The beautiful' and 'good taste' are words, and do not and cannot be made to convey the same sense to widely-differing minds. . . . What we want, or need, is the application of 'good sense' and 'good taste' to the art of living."

597. Right: Victorian armchair in the Renaissance style. American. 1870–1880. Walnut. H. 37¼", W. 20⅛", D. 19¼". An almost identical chair is illustrated in an 1875 issue of *The Art Journal*. (Henry Ford Museum)

353

599. Below: Victorian side chair in the Renaissance style. Made by Leon Marcotte. New York City. Ca. 1865. Satinwood, rosewood. H. 39″, W. 17½″, D. 17½″. Tradition maintains that Theodore Roosevelt's parents, Theodore and Martha, ordered from Leon Marcotte a suite of bedroom furniture for their East 20th Street home in New York. It consisted of a bed, a dresser, a wardrobe, this chair, and matching tiebacks for the curtains. (Theodore Roosevelt Birthplace)

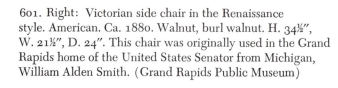

598. Above: Detail of a portrait of Martha J. Lamb. Painted by Cornelia A. Fassette (1831–1898). American. 1878. Oil on canvas. H. 15″, W. 24″. Like so many Victorian matrons, Mrs. Charles A. Lamb (1829–1893) chose Renaissance furniture and deliberately created an organized clutter, a furnishing idea cherished by women of the day. (The New-York Historical Society)

601. Right: Victorian side chair in the Renaissance style. American. Ca. 1880. Walnut, burl walnut. H. 34½″, W. 21½″, D. 24″. This chair was originally used in the Grand Rapids home of the United States Senator from Michigan, William Alden Smith. (Grand Rapids Public Museum)

602. Far right: Victorian footstool in the "Style Antique." Made by Alexander Roux. New York City. 1865. Polychromed wood. H. 23¾″. The Victorian predilection for eclecticism did not escape furniture-makers. "Greek," "Roman," "Turkish," "Elizabethan," are all terms that were indiscriminately applied to numerous styles of furniture in an effort to make them more salable to a romantically inclined public. (The Metropolitan Museum of Art)

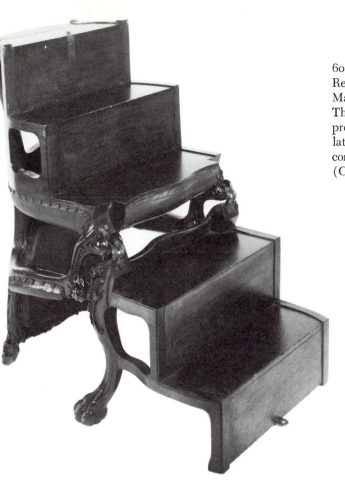

600. Below; 600a. Left: Victorian library step-chair in the Renaissance style. Made by Auguste Eliaers. Boston, Massachusetts. 1853. Mahogany. H. 37″, W. 24″, D. 27″. The ornate carving and massive proportions of this piece predate by some forty years the golden oak movement of the late nineteenth century. The design is an interesting combination of the Rococo and Renaissance Revival. (Chicago Historical Society)

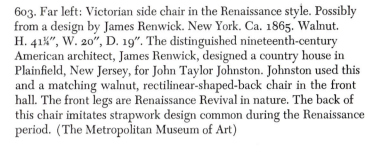

603. Far left: Victorian side chair in the Renaissance style. Possibly from a design by James Renwick. New York. Ca. 1865. Walnut. H. 41¼", W. 20", D. 19". The distinguished nineteenth-century American architect, James Renwick, designed a country house in Plainfield, New Jersey, for John Taylor Johnston. Johnston used this and a matching walnut, rectilinear-shaped-back chair in the front hall. The front legs are Renaissance Revival in nature. The back of this chair imitates strapwork design common during the Renaissance period. (The Metropolitan Museum of Art)

604. Near left: Victorian daybed in the Renaissance style. American. 1875–1900. Mahogany veneer. H. 38½", D. 22", L. 72". The turned urn support on the back of this sofa or daybed is a motif that was frequently used on Late Renaissance furniture. (Grand Rapids Public Museum)

605. Below: Victorian sofa in the Renaissance style. Made by Mitchell, Vance & Co. New York City. 1868–1870. Rosewood, mother-of-pearl. H. 45⅞", D. 31", L. 76¾". Incised lines, picked out with gilt, and a mother-of-pearl center medallion add elegance to this sofa. It is from a large suite of "Marie Antoinette" sitting room furniture used in the Jedediah Wilcox house, Meriden, Connecticut. (The Metropolitan Museum of Art)

606. Left, top: Victorian side chair in the Renaissance style. H. 38¼″, W. 19½″, D. 21½″. 607. Left, bottom: Victorian armchair in the Renaissance style. H. 40½″, W. 28¾″, D. 26″. 608. Center: Victorian sofa in the Renaissance style. H. 42″, D. 26½″, L. 63″. These walnut pieces are from a large suite of furniture probably made in Grand Rapids, Michigan, between 1850 and 1870. The arms are carved in the form of swans' heads. High-style Renaissance furniture was first manufactured in the Eastern cities. With few exceptions, Midwestern examples, like these, are less pretentious in design. (Henry Ford Museum)

609. Above: *Chess Players.* Painted by Thomas Eakins. American. 1876. Oil on wood. H. 11¾″, W. 16¾″. The opponents in Eakins painting have drawn Renaissance chairs to their game table. (The Metropolitan Museum of Art)

At the beginning of the nineteenth century, Paris replaced London as the center of cultural inspiration for Americans. Immigrant French craftsmen introduced in the Eastern cities furniture made in the latest, most up-to-date style. The Rococo Revival, during the late 1840's and 1850's, was based on the eighteenth-century Louis XV furniture. By mid-century, French craftsmen dominated New York's furniture industry. Baudouine, Roux, Marcotte, Dessoir, and Ringuet Le Prince were offering to the affluent elegant furniture that, in design, mirrored the latest fashions of Paris.

610. Left: Victorian side chair in the Louis XVI style. Made by Leon Marcotte. New York City. Ca. 1860. Ebonized maple and fruitwood, gilt and bronze. H. 37¾", W. 17½", D. 20¾". (The Metropolitan Museum of Art)

611. Below: Victorian sofa in the Louis XVI style. Made by Leon Marcotte. New York City. Ca. 1860. Ebonized maple and fruitwood, gilt and bronze. H. 42½", D. 34½", L. 73". This sofa and figure 610 are from a suite that included two sofas, a pair of small cabinets, a large cabinet, six side chairs, two lyre-back chairs, two armchairs, and a firescreen. Ernest Hagen, a late nineteenth-century cabinet-maker, recognized Marcotte's great skill in creating fine furniture—"This style is really the best of all and will never go out of fashion, and, if not overdone . . . is simply great." (The Metropolitan Museum of Art)

612. Left: Victorian side chair in the Louis XVI style. Perhaps by Leon Marcotte. New York City. 1860–1865. Maple, brass, mother-of-pearl. H. 35¾″, W. 17½″, D. 21″. Engraved inlaid brass and mother-of-pearl marquetry decorate the back, seat rail, and legs of this "French" chair. (The Metropolitan Museum of Art)

613. Below: Victorian slipper chair in the French Second Empire style. Possibly made by Herter Brothers. New York City. Ca. 1865. Maple. H. 30¼″. This chair is ebonized and inlaid with rosewood bead moldings on the rails. (The Metropolitan Museum of Art)

French
Revivals

614. Right: Victorian sofa in the Louis XVI style. New York or possibly English. 1876. Ebonized mahogany with bands of bird's-eye maple inlaid with mother-of-pearl. H. 48¼", D. 26¼", L. 76". This sofa is from a large suite that is said to have been awarded First Prize at the Philadelphia Centennial in 1876. (Museum of the City of New York)

615. Left: Victorian armchair in the Louis XVI style. New York or possibly English. 1876. Ebonized mahogany with bands of bird's-eye maple inlaid with mother-of-pearl. H. 43", W. 20½", D. 23¼". This chair and the accompanying sofa, figure 614, belonged to Mr. and Mrs. James Lancaster Morgan, 7 Pierrepont Street, Brooklyn, New York. (Museum of the City of New York)

616. Right: Photograph of the front parlor in the residence of Mr. and Mrs. James Lancaster Morgan. This view was taken about 1885 after Mr. James L. Morgan, Jr., and his wife went to live there. The room contains many articles brought by them from their former home at 39 Pierrepont Street, Brooklyn. The armchair, figure 615, is at the right of the fireplace. A table, another chair, and a matching side chair are scattered throughout the cluttered Victorian room. (Museum of the City of New York)

617. Right: Lucy Hooper in her Paris apartment. Painted by Edward Lamson Henry (1841–1919). American. 1876. Oil on canvas. H. 12″, W. 15″. Americans frequently traveled to France and, succumbing to the charms of Paris, they stayed. (The Newark Museum)

618. Below: Victorian side chair in the Louis XV style. American. Nineteenth century. Oak. H. 39½″, W. 20″, D. 18″. Nineteenth-century "French" furniture was often gilded. This example, left natural, is upholstered with tapestry. (The Newark Museum)

619. Below: Photograph of a Victorian sofa in the French style. Sold by The Brooks Household Art Company of Ohio. Ca. 1885. Undoubtedly such an ostentatious piece was destined to be used in a "Marie Antoinette" room of the late nineteenth century. (The Metropolitan Museum of Art)

620. Right: Photograph of a bedroom suite in the Waldorf-Astoria Hotel, Fifth Avenue and 34th Street, New York City. This photograph, taken ca. 1900, illustrates the epitome of high style and luxury. An amusing note is that the pillows which have been tied in a bolster are adorned by a large ribbon and bow. The room is furnished with Victorian furniture in the Louis XV and Louis XVI styles. Inlay, painting, and marquetry decorate these metal-mounted pieces. (Museum of the City of New York)

621. Right: Victorian side chair in the Louis XV style. American. 1890–1900. Maple and oak. H. 32¾", W. 17", D. 16". At the close of the nineteenth century, many of America's wealthiest families, oftentimes nouveau riche, thought French-inspired furniture the finest. Not only authentic reproductions, figure 619, but also vague approximations flooded the market. This gilded side chair is such an approximation and originally belonged to Mr. and Mrs. Andrew Carnegie. (Museum of the City of New York)

Greek and Egyptian motifs occur on American furniture throughout the nineteenth century. Sparked first perhaps by Thomas Hope's 1807 publication, *Household Furniture and Interior Decoration,* this movement, though never a popular one, was persistent. Even in Hope's day, his design concepts were not unchallenged. The July edition of *The Edinburgh Review* spoke of Hope's work in this way: "Many of the objects, being exactly copied from the fine remains of ancient art, are unquestionably beautiful in themselves . . . but quite unsuitable for articles of household furniture.

622. Above: Victorian footstool in the Egyptian style. American. 1875–1900. Oak and hickory. H. 15″. Ancient tomb paintings were the inspiration for the designs of much Egyptian Revival furniture. (The Newark Museum)

Egyptian Revival

623. Left: Illustration from *Household Furniture and Interior Decoration.* Written by Thomas Hope. Published in London, England. May, 1807. Plate 8 from Hope's book illustrates many of his ideas for adapting ancient motifs to modern furniture forms. (Museum of the City of New York)

625. Below: Victorian footstool in the Egyptian style. New York. Ca. 1880. Maple, painted. H. 12″, W. 15½″, D. 12″. Egyptian designs, such as the clustered columns with a lotus capital on the legs, are much in evidence on this small painted-and-polychromed footstool. (The Metropolitan Museum of Art)

626. Left; 626a. Far left, top: Victorian settee in the Egyptian style. American. 1875–1885. Rosewood with ebonized wood and inlay. H. 42½″, D. 25″, L. 48″. The notorious financier, Jay Gould, purchased this Neo-Egyptian settee and matching chairs for use in the Davis-designed Gothic manor, Lyndhurst, during the 1880's. Painted medallion inserts center the top rail. (Lyndhurst, National Trust for Historic Preservation)

624. Left: Victorian side chair in the Egyptian style. Probably New York City. 1850–1875. Rosewood, with burl maple borders. H. 28½″, W. 25″, D. 21¾″. The Egyptian Revival movement received fresh impetus in America when *Cleopatra's Needle*, a sculpted obelisk, was installed in New York's Central Park in 1881. Egyptian ornamentation, when applied to the decoration of furniture, was seldom architecturally correct. The motifs on this chair only approximate those popular in the ancient world. The cabinetmaker, Ernest Hagen, had very definite opinions about the Egyptian Revival style. Writing of his competitors, Pottier & Stymus, he said, ". . . their work was nearly all done in the 'Neo Grec' most awfull gaudy style with brass gilt Spinx head on the sofas and arm chairs, gilt engraved lines all over with porcailaine painted medalions on the backs, and brass gilt bead moldings nailed on. Other wise, their work was good; but the style horrible." (The Metropolitan Museum of Art)

Invention and Utility

627. Left: Victorian spring chair. American. 1860–1870. Iron and wood. H. 40¾″, W. 18″. A metal spring chair was patented in 1849 by Thomas B. Warren and made by the American Chair Company of Troy, New York, manufacturer of reclining seats for railroad cars. A similar chair was exhibited at the Crystal Palace at London, England, in 1851 where these "novelties which ever increase the luxury and convenience of this necessary article of furniture" received much attention. (Privately owned)

During the late 1830's and early 1840's chair manufacturers developed new designs which took advantage of machine manufacturing techniques, and they incorporated structural members made of iron and other metals into the construction of their products. The United States Patent Office was flooded with requests for exclusive rights to manufacture such innovative furniture. Describing the seemingly never-ending parade of styles, Washington Irving, the popular American author, felt that ". . . style has ruined the peace and harmony of many a worthy household; for no sooner do they set up for style, but instantly all the honest old comfortable, sans cérémonie furniture is discarded."

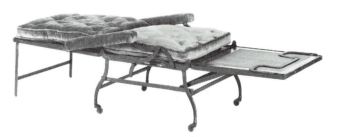

629. Left; 629a. Above: Victorian invalid chair. Manufactured by the Marks A.F. Chair Company. New York. 1876. Iron, walnut. H. 46″, W. 29⅞″, D. 25½″. This reclining invalid's chair was designed by C. B. Sheldon and patented on February 1, 1876. (Henry Ford Museum)

630. Below, right: Victorian metal rocking chair. American. 1850–1860. Iron. H. 39½″. For several years, this chair was thought to be the personal property of Peter Cooper (1791–1883), the great American philanthropist who was also an innovator in the use of structural ironwork in the building industry. Recent studies indicate that this might be incorrect. (Cooper–Hewitt Museum of Design, Smithsonian Institution)

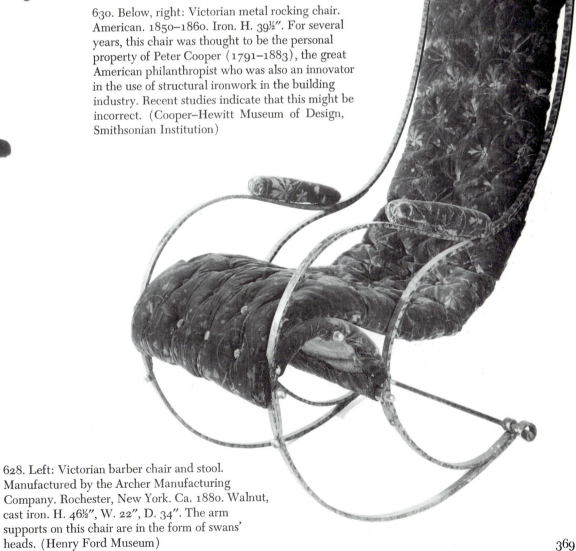

628. Left: Victorian barber chair and stool. Manufactured by the Archer Manufacturing Company. Rochester, New York. Ca. 1880. Walnut, cast iron. H. 46½″, W. 22″, D. 34″. The arm supports on this chair are in the form of swans' heads. (Henry Ford Museum)

631. Left: Photograph of Miss Lula Hassal. Taken by Altenburg, Genesee and Elliott Streets, Buffalo, New York. 1885–1895. Little Lula sits on a twisted metal frame chair and rests her bejeweled shoe on a matching metal footstool. (Privately owned)

632. Above: Victorian metal bathtub. American. Ca. 1900. Tin, iron. H. 39″, W. 24″, D. 25″. Countless teakettles and buckets of hot water were required to fill such an elementary bathing facility. (Henry Ford Museum)

633. Right: Illustration of an adjustable reclining and reading chair. Manufactured by the Sargent Manufacturing Company. New York City. 1885. From the fashionable American magazine, *Decorator and Furnisher*, July, 1886. (Privately owned)

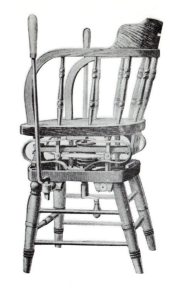

634. Right: Advertisement for a Health Jolting Chair. Manufactured by the Sargent Manufacturing Company, 814–816 Broadway, New York City. From a company sales catalogue issued in 1888. Victorian Americans were fascinated with magical health cures, potions, and "beneficial devices." "The Health Jolting Chair," offered for $25.00, "strengthens the arms, expands the chest, develops the lungs, and . . . exercises all the important internal organs." (Privately owned)

635. Below: Patent drawing for an invalid's exercising chair. Patent No. 775. Issued June 12, 1838. This chair is a very early example of metal-and-wood patent furniture. The apparatus was intended to be used in a stationary position or it could be swung on suspended rods from the ceiling. (United States Patent Office)

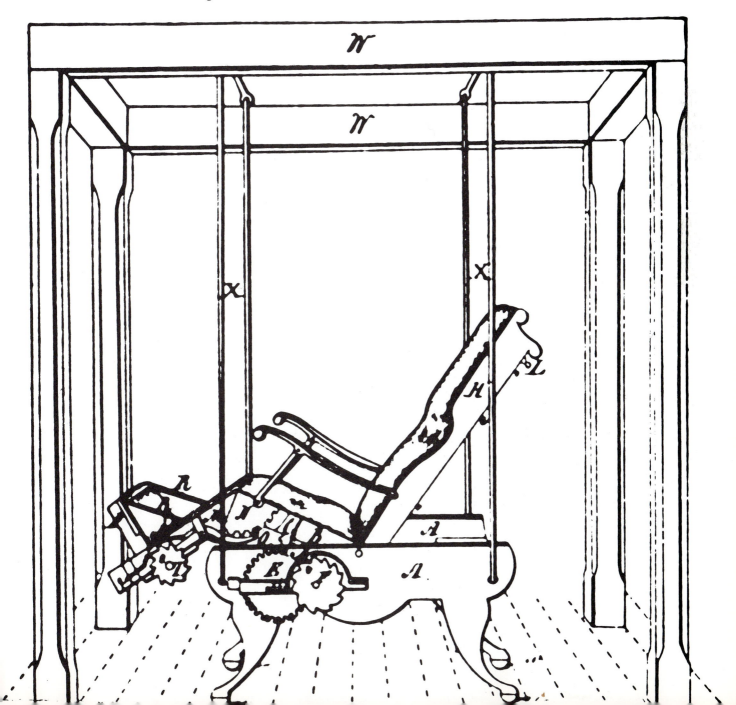

636. Below: Victorian swivel armchair. American. Ca. 1900. Oak. H. 43″, W. 22″, D. 23″. This desk chair was constructed with a device that allowed it to tilt backward. Arrow-back spindles frequently appear on golden oak pieces. (Henry Ford Museum)

637. Right: Photograph of the Tennessee State Library. 1910. The room was furnished with several patented chairs constructed from wood and metal. Tilting chairs, like the one at the desk in the foreground, were manufactured during the 1870's and 1880's. A cast-iron spiral staircase and radiator cover attest to the increasing use of metal as an acceptable ingredient for interior decoration. (Tennessee State Library and Archives)

638. Left: Victorian schoolroom desks. Manufactured by the American S.F. Company. Buffalo, New York. Ca. 1900. Maple, birch, iron. H. 30½″, W. 24¼″, D. 27½″. This firm manufactured desks and shipped them to schools throughout the country. (Henry Ford Museum)

639. Right, top: Victorian swivel side chair. American. 1900. Oak, iron. H. 37″, W. 17½″, D. 17″. This desk chair has a shaped seat and square spindles in the back. The height could be adjusted and the chair was fitted with casters for easy movement. (Henry Ford Museum)

640. Right, bottom: Victorian swivel armchair. American. 1870–1890. Oak, cast iron. H. 42½″, W. 25½″, D. 23¾″. A cane seat and back provided comfort for the sitter in this desk chair. Incised reeding and circle motifs, popular on oak furniture during the 1870's, are evident on the base. (Henry Ford Museum)

The Morris Style

The English designer William Morris, dissatisfied with contemporary furniture design, in 1861 founded a firm through which he hoped to offer to the public examples of good taste. Associating himself with some of the Pre-Raphaelite artists, he attempted to create by hand furniture similar in style to that found in thirteenth-century England. American chairmakers seized on the idea and adapted the general form, manufacturing endless variations at numerous price levels.

641. Above: Victorian Morris chair. Manufactured by Morris & Company. English. 1866 or after. Ebonized oak, iron. Upholstered, with embossed Utrecht velvet. H. 38½″, W. 28″, D. 36″. The bobbin- and spool-turned arm supports and stretchers on this English Morris chair are typical of the Elizabethan Revival style popular during the 1860's. Morris, a large man, found the ornate chairs of his Victorian age uncomfortable. He was one of the first to attempt to build adjustable comfort into a chair. A metal rod rests on a projecting rack at the rear of this chair; it can be moved to raise or lower the hinged back. (Victoria and Albert Museum)

642. Left: Victorian Morris chair. American. 1885–1895. Mahogany, iron. H. 44½″, W. 26¾″, D. 30″. The carved panel with leafage and floral motifs on this armchair is Art Nouveau in inspiration. (The Newark Museum)

643. Above: Victorian Morris chair. American. 1880's. Golden oak, iron. H. 40½″, W. 31″, D. 39″. This adjustable-back piece was constructed in a simplified version of the Egyptian style. (Grand Rapids Public Museum)

644. Below, left: Victorian lady's Morris chair. American. Late nineteenth century. Mahogany. H. 29¼″, W. 25¾″, D. 37½″. Carved animal masks form the handrests on this diminutive lady's chair. (Grand Rapids Public Museum)

645. Below, right: Victorian Morris chair. American. 1900–1910. Golden oak, iron. H. 38″, W. 27″, D. 28″. Chairs constructed of flat, sawed boards, as in this example, would originally have been inexpensive to purchase. (The Brooklyn Museum)

Following the teachings of the English art critic and author John Ruskin, designer William Morris and artist Burne-Jones jointly created "artistic furniture" which served as the prototype for much of the American furniture made during the 1870's and 1880's. Elegant inlaid and painted pieces, designed and crafted by decorating and furnishing firms, were available to members of America's wealthiest class. Harriet Prescott Spofford in her 1878 New York publication, *Art Decoration Applied to Furniture*, illustrated furniture in the Gothic, the Renaissance, the Elizabethan, the Jacobean, the Louis Seize, the Pompeian, the Moorish, the Eastlake, the Queen Anne, the Oriental, and the "modern" styles. Inlay was seldom used in the medley which she so highly recommended, even though it "has become a matter of universal pride."

646. Left: Detail of back of Victorian armchair. American. 1875. Ebonized rosewood veneer with inlay of lighter woods and mother-of-pearl. H. 38⅝″, W. 26⅛″, D. 26½″. This chair was made for James Lenox (1800–1880) who resided at 53 Fifth Avenue, New York City. The back of the chair is inlaid with the Lenox coat of arms and crest. (Museum of the City of New York)

647. Below: Photograph of the library of the David Sproat Kennedy house. 41 Fifth Avenue, New York City. 1887. Taken by John Wallace Gillies. Chairs similar to the Lenox chair were used in this home. (Museum of the City of New York)

The Artistic Chair

648. Left: Victorian inlaid side chair. Made by Pottier and Stymus Manufacturing Company. New York City. Ca. 1880. Mahogany with inlay. H. 34″, W. 19¼″, D. 17½″. Delicately inlaid leaves and flowers form the decoration on this chair. (Museum of the City of New York)

649. Right: Victorian inlaid armchair. Made by Pottier and Stymus Manufacturing Company. New York City. Ca. 1880. Mahogany with inlay. H. 35¼″, W. 22″, D. 19⅜″. This chair and figure 648 were made for the home of Mr. Auguste Pottier, president of the furniture firm, and were part of a set of dining room chairs. (Museum of the City of New York)

650. Left, top: Victorian inlaid side chair. New York. 1885–1890. Mahogany. H. 34¼", W. 15", D. 16¼". Finely inlaid panels accentuate the eclectic nature of the design of this chair. (Museum of the City of New York)

651. Left: Victorian inlaid side chair. Made by Herter Brothers. New York City. Ca. 1876. Ebonized maple, inlaid. H. 37½", W. 17¼", D. 18". This side chair was made for the Philadelphian, William T. Carter. It is part of a large suite which includes a bed, dresser, table, and mirror. (Philadelphia Museum of Art)

652. Above: Museum installation. Dressing room in the home of John D. Rockefeller, Sr., at 4 West 54th Street, New York City, built ca. 1880. Inlaid designs on the doors and other woodwork echo the inlaid decoration on the furnishings. (Museum of the City of New York)

653. Right: Victorian side chair. American. 1900–1910. Cherry. H. 36¾", W. 19", D. 20". The carving on the back of this chair is a three-dimensional version of popular inlaid motifs. The decorative designs relate to the Art Nouveau movement. (Henry Ford Museum)

654. Below: Victorian inlaid side chair. New York. Ca. 1880. Maple, with mahogany inlay. H. 37″, W. 18⅜″, D. 17¾″. The tufted seat and back add elegance to this side chair, originally part of a suite used by Mrs. Collis P. Huntington in the New York town house she sold to John D. Rockefeller, Sr. (Museum of the City of New York)

379

The Eastlake Style

The Eastlake style derives its name from the similarity between American furniture manufactured during the 1870's and 1880's and illustrations included in the English book, *Hints on Household Taste in Furniture, Upholstery and Other Details*, by Charles Locke Eastlake, an architect, artist, and author. This book, published in 1868, a recasting of earlier articles for the periodical, *The Queen*, was intended "to suggest some fixed principles of taste for the popular guidance of those who are not accustomed to hear such principles defined." Eastlake's book was immensely popular with the American Victorian public which was keenly interested in self-improvement. The American application of Eastlake's name to the diverse products distressed Mr. Eastlake. "I find American tradesmen continually advertising what they are pleased to call 'Eastlake' furniture, with the production of which I have had nothing to do, and for the taste of which I should be very sorry to be considered responsible." American furniture constructed in the Eastlake style is generally rectilinear in form, often constructed from contrasting woods, and, many times, ebonized. Panels of inlay and shallow-carved incised lines are the principal forms of decoration. Often a multitude of turned spindles are an integral part of the design of these massive, but simple, pieces.

655. Above; 656. Below: Illustrations from *Hints on Household Taste in Furniture, Upholstery and Other Details* by Charles Locke Eastlake. England. 1868. (Privately owned)

No. 168.   No. 164.

No. 166.   No. 124.

657. Above: Advertisement of Gardner and Company. *The Asher and Adams Commercial Atlas.* New York City. 1870–?. The Gardner and Company display at the 1876 Philadelphia Centennial included "Eastlake" chairs with perforated seats. (The New-York Historical Society)

658. Right: Victorian platform rocker in the Eastlake style. American. Ca. 1875. Ebonized wood. Dimensions unavailable. This chair is from a suite of bedroom furniture which includes a bed with porcelain-tile panels set into the headboard. (Smithsonian Institution)

659. Below: Early photograph of a Victorian tête-à-tête in the Eastlake style made by Kimbel & Cabus. New York. 1865–1895. This unusual piece was constructed with decorated panels and embellished with incised decoration picked out in gilt. (Cooper–Hewitt Museum of Design, Smithsonian Institution)

660. Left: Detail of an advertisement by George Hunzinger. Published in *The Asher and Adams Commercial Atlas*. New York. 1871. This illustration shows George Hunzinger's firm at 323–327 West 16th Street, New York City. The sign indicates that at this time he was involved in the manufacture of furniture other than chairs since it reads "Fancy Chairs and Ornamental Furniture." (The New-York Historical Society)

661. Right: Victorian side chair. Manufactured by George Hunzinger. New York City. 1869. Walnut. H. 32½", W. 19¾", D. 20". (The Metropolitan Museum of Art)

662. Below: Price list of George Hunzinger. Published in *The Asher and Adams Commercial Atlas*. New York. 187?. Folding and reclining chairs are specifically mentioned on this list. (The New-York Historical Society)

GEORGE HUNZINGER,
MANUFACTURER OF
Fancy Chairs, Folding and Reclining Chairs, and Ornamental Furniture,
141 and 143 SEVENTH AVE., NEW YORK.

PLATE No 2.—Universal Chair Walnut Frame, finished, price, 89.33; in muslin, 812.00; in plain Terry, 816.00; in Terry with nice Tapestry style, 818.67; in figured Tapestry, $20.00.

PLATE No. 2.—Large Rocker, No. 2, Frame in Walnut, 813.33; in Muslin, 824.00; in Terry, with nice bordering, $33.33.

PLATE No. 4.—Chair No. 4, Frame in Walnut, 818.67; upholstered in different colored Satin, with Star, $40.00.

PLATE No. 6.—Rocker No. 32, in Maple or Walnut, with any color, braided wire seat and back, 88.00.

PLATE No. 7.—All Gilt Chair Frame, No. 5, price, 825.33.

PLATE No. 7.— "   "   "   " 6, " 25.33.

PLATE No. 17.—Manhattan Chair, in any colored Terry, with Tapestry stripe, price, 89.33.

PLATE No. 17.—Carved Reclining Chair, frame Walnut and Gilt, 834.66; Tufted in Muslin, 844.00; Tufted in Terry with Marquette or fine Tapestry stripe, 853.33; in Satin, with Satin Stripe, Silk Fringe in front, 872.00.

PLATE No. 23.—Dining or Library Chair, No. 43, in Walnut with any color, braided Wire Seat and Back, 810.67.

PLATE No. 23.— "   "   "   " 44, "   "   "   "   "   "   " 10.67.

The Reclining Chairs are made in turned frames in different sizes and shapes, ready Upholstered from 820.00 upward. These are only a few selected specimens of my work. For full Catalogue and Price List please apply to GEO. HUNZINGER, 141 and 143 7th Ave., N. Y.

663. Top: Victorian side chair. Manufactured by George Hunzinger. New York City. 1869. Walnut. H. 34″, W. 19″, D. 17½″. (Lyndhurst, National Trust for Historic Preservation)

664. Right: Victorian side chair. Manufactured by George Hunzinger. New York City. 1869. Walnut. H. 33″, W. 16½″, D. 14″. Both this chair and figure 663 retain their original upholstery. (Lyndhurst, National Trust for Historic Preservation)

665. Below: Illustration of a chair by George Hunzinger from *The Asher and Adams Commercial Atlas*. New York City. 187?. A folding and reclining chair was offered in walnut and gilt for $34.66. It was also available upholstered in satin with satin stripe, silk fringe in front, for $72.00. (The New-York Historical Society)

Spindles, pistons and knobs, ship's wheels, club feet and cogs—all are structural parts of the now famous eclectic chairs made by George Hunzinger, a German immigrant. Defying specific classification (some feel they are Renaissance Revival; others, Eastlake), these extraordinary examples of chairmaking are much sought after both by museums and private collectors. Often these pieces, though stationary, give the general appearance of having folding capabilities. The chairs which Hunzinger patented in 1861 and 1866 were so popular that for years he was content to manufacture only chairs. Hunzinger's pieces were praised in *The Asher and Adams Commercial Atlas* published during the 1870's where it was said that his chairs were "as strong as they are beautiful and as comfortable to sit in as they are graceful in appearance. . . . In this establishment the useful and ornamental are so thoroughly combined as to draw acknowledgement from all who examine them."

666. Left: *Portrait of a Young Woman.* Painted by Winslow Homer. American. 1872. Oil on mahogany board. H. 6″, W. 8¼″. This beautiful young woman in Homer's painting sits in a folding chair much like the one illustrated in Gervase Wheeler's New York publication, *Rural Homes*, 1852. (Current whereabouts unknown)

667. Above: Victorian folding rocking chair. Made by E. W. Vaill. Worcester, Massachusetts. 1876. Walnut. H. 32″, W. 18″, D. 25″. Brass caps top the back posts and finish the side rails on this chair. (Smithsonian Institution)

668. Left: Victorian folding rocker. American. 1880–1890. Maple, painted black. H. 39¾″, W. 19¼″, D. 29¾″. The turnings on this rocker are similar to those on "East Lake" rocking chairs manufactured by Alfred E. Stacey. (Henry Ford Museum)

670. Right: Trade card of Alfred E. Stacey. Elbridge, Onondaga County, New York. 1875–1895. (The New-York Historical Society)

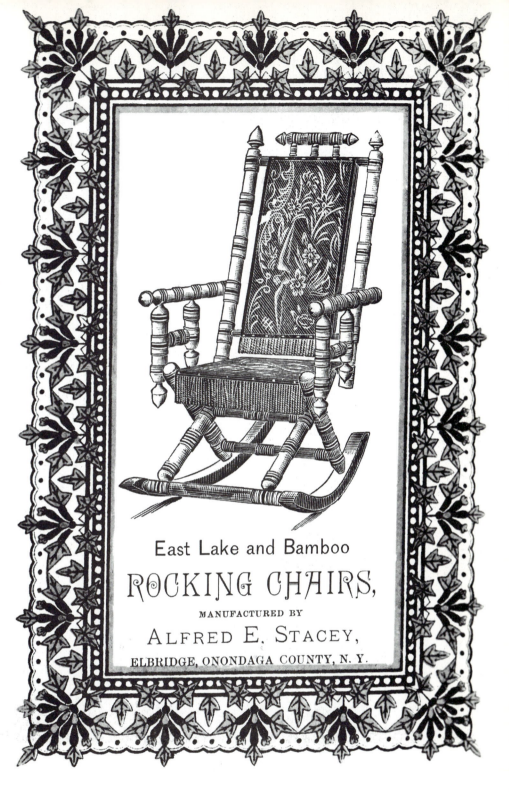

East Lake and Bamboo
ROCKING CHAIRS,
MANUFACTURED BY
ALFRED E. STACEY,
ELBRIDGE, ONONDAGA COUNTY, N. Y.

669. Below: Folding chairs. American. Early twentieth century. Maple. H. 31½″, W. 16″, D. 16″. These chairs were used on the S.S. *Ticonderoga*, a side-wheel steamer built in 1906. It plied Lake Champlain and Lake George until 1953. (Shelburne Museum, Inc.)

Writing in his 1878 "Essays on Beds and Tables, Stools and Candlesticks," published in *The House Beautiful,* New York art critic Clarence Cook said, "Whenever the designs obey the law of the material employed, and do not try to twist or bend it out of its own natural and handsome curves, they are sure to be pleasing to look at and serviceable to use." He also mentioned bamboo furniture and the then raging Eastlake style. Almost as if on cue, the firm of Alfred E. Stacey from Elbridge, New York, advertised "East Lake" and bamboo chairs. Since neither really related to Eastlake's theories as expressed in his *Hints on Household Taste,* it seems that Mr. Stacey capitalized on a good thing.

671. Above: Early photograph of the picture gallery at the Malden Public Library. Designed by H. H. Richardson. Woburn, Massachusetts. 1878. The gallery is furnished with a turned-spindle bench much like those shown in Eastlake's *Hints*. (Museum of Fine Arts, Boston)

672. Left: Victorian armchair. Designed by H. H. Richardson for the Crane Memorial Library. Quincy, Massachusetts. 1880. Oak. H. 42″, W. 14¾″, D. 19½″. This chair was originally upholstered with leather. Its design is essentially "modern." (Museum of Fine Arts, Boston)

673. Right: Photograph of the interior of the Burlington, Vermont, library. Designed by H. H. Richardson. Built in 1888. The huge center table is surrounded by Richardson adaptations of the seemingly ageless Windsor chair. (Museum of Fine Arts, Boston)

During the 1880's, the American architect and furniture designer, Henry Hobson Richardson (1836–1886), designed numerous public buildings in the Boston area. The ideas for the furnishing of these buildings were also from this highly creative man's drawing board. Chairs with turned spindles and bobbins, which relate them to the Eastlake illustrations in *Hints*, were often used to contrast with striking architectural effects. Later building commissions in the Albany, New York, area include the State Capitol in 1881. Even though the Senate Chamber in that building is Romanesque in nature, typical Richardson Eastlake-like chairs and tables were used to furnish it.

674. Above: Victorian armchair. Probably New York City. 1880's. Oak. H. 36″, W. 24″, D. 24″. This Eastlake-style armchair appears in an 1880's photograph of the dining room of Jay Gould's magnificent Hudson River yacht, *Atalanta*. It also is pictured in 1904–1910 photographs of Helen Gould's art gallery at Lyndhurst. (Lyndhurst, National Trust for Historic Preservation)

675. Right: Photograph of Charles and Anna Dole. Taken by the Buffalo Photo. Co. Buffalo, New York. Late nineteenth century. Casting aside Victorian etiquette, Charles Dole sits (in an Eastlake chair) while his wife, Anna, stands. (Cornercopia)

676. Below, left: Early photograph of furniture offered for sale by the Kimbel & Cabus Company. New York City. 1880's. Their chairs were considered to be the best examples of the American Eastlake style. (Cooper–Hewitt Museum of Design, Smithsonian Institution)

677. Below, right: Victorian armchair. Massachusetts. 1879. Chestnut. H. 47″, W. 27″. The children of Cambridge, Massachusetts, presented this ebonized armchair to Henry Wadsworth Longfellow on his seventy-second birthday. It was constructed of wood taken from "the spreading chestnut tree" immortalized in his famous poem, "The Village Blacksmith." (Longfellow House)

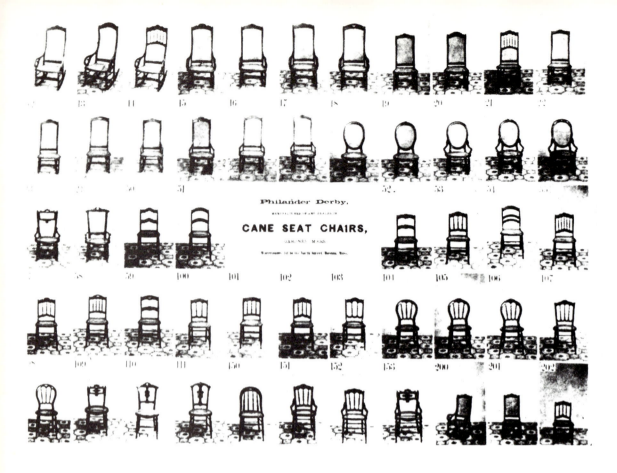

Easily manufactured components were designed for speedy assembly by chairmakers all across the country during the 1870's and 1880's. Oftentimes factories such as Philander Derby's, operating in Gardner, Massachusetts, from 1868 until after 1878, specialized in the production of "cane seat chairs." Unless pieces are marked or labeled, it is impossible to assign their origin to a specific factory or region. They were constructed of local woods and offered for sale in almost every small city in America.

678. Top: Early advertisement of the Philander Derby firm. Gardner, Massachusetts. 1875. Philander Derby, who manufactured and dealt in cane seat chairs, maintained warehouses on North Street in Boston. (Privately owned)

679. Left: Victorian armchair in the Renaissance style. American. 1860–1880. Walnut. H. 39½″, W. 21″, D. 22″. This armchair is now part of the furnishings of Sarah Jordan's boarding house, the first home in the world to be lighted by Thomas Alva Edison's incandescent light. (Greenfield Village and Henry Ford Museum)

Factory Chairs

680. Above, center; 680a. Above, right: Victorian side chair. Made by the Detroit Chair Factory. Detroit, Michigan. Ca. 1875. Maple, painted black. H. 32¼″, W. 17¼″, D. 17″. The Detroit Chair Factory was in operation from 1865 through 1878 and produced an array of chairs quite similar to those shown in the Philander Derby advertisement, figure 678. (Henry Ford Museum)

681. Above, left: Victorian child's chair. Made by the Detroit Chair Factory. Detroit. Ca. 1870. Pine, maple. H. 26″, W. 14¼″, D. 13½″. The Detroit Chair Factory specialized in the production of inexpensive seating pieces. Its variety of styles offered Michigan residents the opportunity of selecting one that most pleased their personal taste. This diminutive piece is painted and grained. (Privately owned)

682. Right: Victorian balloon-back side chair. Made by the Detroit Chair Factory. Detroit. Ca. 1870. Walnut. H. 34″, W. 17¼″, D. 21″. This chair is one of a pair. (Privately owned)

683. Left: Victorian armchair in the Renaissance style. American. 1860–1880. Walnut and oak with maple panels. H. 35″, W. 20″, D. 22″. Numerous mid-Victorian chairs were constructed with "demi" arms which not only provided strength but were thought to be decorative as well. Two thin slices of bird's-eye maple veneer were applied to the top rail of this chair. Incised lines surround the veneer, creating an illusion of greater depth. (Henry Ford Museum)

684. Top: Victorian "fancy" side chair. American. 1860–1880. Maple, beech. H. 33½″, W. 16″, D. 15¾″. (Henry Ford Museum)

685. Above, right: Victorian rocking chair. Made by H. D. Hankerson. Massachusetts. 1850–1875. Maple. H. 35¾″, W. 19½″, D. 28½″. The manufacturer selected a grained finish for this rocking chair. Working near Waltham, Massachusetts, Hankerson made products that were "inexpensive and sturdy." (Henry Ford Museum)

686. Right: Victorian armchair. American. Ca. 1865. Curly maple. H. 45½″, W. 18½″, D. 20″. General Robert E. Lee sat in this armchair when he surrendered his army at the Appomattox Court House on April 9, 1865. (Smithsonian Institution)

687. Left: Photograph of Abraham Lincoln. Taken by Matthew B. Brady. Washington, D.C. Ca. 1860. This early photograph of Lincoln shows him sitting in an oak chair originally made en suite with desks. They were designed in 1857 by Quartermaster-General Montgomery C. Meigs for use in the United States House of Representatives. The firm of Bembe & Kimmel in New York City manufactured the furniture. The pieces were too heavy and were sold at auction in 1859. Popular Washington photographers Matthew B. Brady and Alexander Gardner purchased some of the furniture and it frequently appears in their photographs of the period. (Henry Ford Museum)

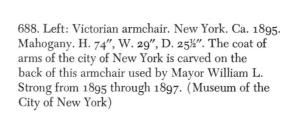

688. Left: Victorian armchair. New York. Ca. 1895. Mahogany. H. 74″, W. 29″, D. 25½″. The coat of arms of the city of New York is carved on the back of this armchair used by Mayor William L. Strong from 1895 through 1897. (Museum of the City of New York)

689. Right: Victorian armchair. New York. 1899–1900. Oak. H. 53″, W. 34″, D. 25″. Original furnishings of Theodore Roosevelt's Oyster Bay, Long Island, home, Sagamore Hill, include this ornately carved armchair. It was made by the prisoners at Sing Sing State Prison for T.R. while he was Governor. (Sagamore Hill)

690. Right: Victorian armchair. Made by Bembe &
Kimmel. New York City. 1857. Oak, oak veneer.
H. 40½″, W. 26″, D. 23½″. For the history of this
chair, see figure 687. (Henry Ford Museum)

Special Orders

Special-order furniture, incorporating the symbols
chosen to represent America, was always popular with
political leaders. Abraham Lincoln used a Renaissance
Revival secretary-desk and matching armchair with a
shield and star carved into the elaborate cornice. It remained in use in the Cabinet Room at the White House
through the Theodore Roosevelt Administration. Special-
order furniture, however, was not exclusively the pre-
rogative of Presidents. Fraternities, and even hotels, commissioned furniture that would be uniquely theirs.

691. Left; 691a. Above: Victorian armchair. New York. Ca. 1885. Oak, walnut. H. 46¼″, W. 26″, D. 23¼″. The original furnishings of the lobby of New York's famed Chelsea Hotel on West 23rd Street included this ornately carved Romanesque armchair. Since these photographs were taken, the pieces have been refurbished—painted with white enamel and upholstered in shining red plastic, a monument to modern taste. The dining room of Henry Villard's fabulous Fifth Avenue mansion, designed by McKim, Mead and White, also contained in 1885 furniture similar in design to this extraordinary piece. (Chelsea Hotel)

692. Right: Victorian hall chair. American. 1870–1890. Walnut. H. 48″, W. 21″, D. 18½″. The seat of this chair lifts up, revealing a place to store books or papers. (Henry Ford Museum)

HAVERHILL MASONIC CHAIRS.
Master's Chair, 6 ft. 9 in. ; Warden's Chairs, 6 ft. 3 in.   The most elaborate Chairs made in the country.

693. Top: Illustration from a trade catalogue. Published by Shaw, Applin & Co., 27 Sudbury Street, Boston, Massachusetts. 1880. This company offered "Lodge" and "Masonic" chairs, claiming them to be "the most elaborate chairs made in the country." (The Metropolitan Museum of Art)

694. Above: Early advertisement. Stickley & Simonds Co. Syracuse, New York. 1895. This firm advertised that it could provide "Parlor Suites and Occasional Pieces in Marqueterie, etc., etc., in the Most Artistic Styles." This chair obviously was one of the "artistic" pieces. (Privately owned)

695. Below: Early advertisement. M. Walker & Sons. Philadelphia, Pennsylvania. 1870–1880. A twisted-metal chair was offered in their general line of garden furniture. (Smithsonian Institution)

696. Right: Illustration of the Iron Warehouse of John B. Wickersham at 312 Broadway, New York City. 1854. This establishment featured cast- and wrought-iron furniture intended for both outdoor and indoor use. (Library of Congress)

697. Near right, bottom: Victorian garden seat. American. 1880. Cast iron and wire. H. 38½", W. 36½", D. 22½". Woven-wire-and-metal furniture was preferred for gardens because it could endure adverse climatic conditions and was cool on hot summer days. (Henry Ford Museum)

698. Far right, bottom: Victorian garden chair. American. 1875–1880. Iron and wire. H. 38", W. 16", D. 14¾". Such pieces were usually fitted with cushions for comfort. (Henry Ford Museum)

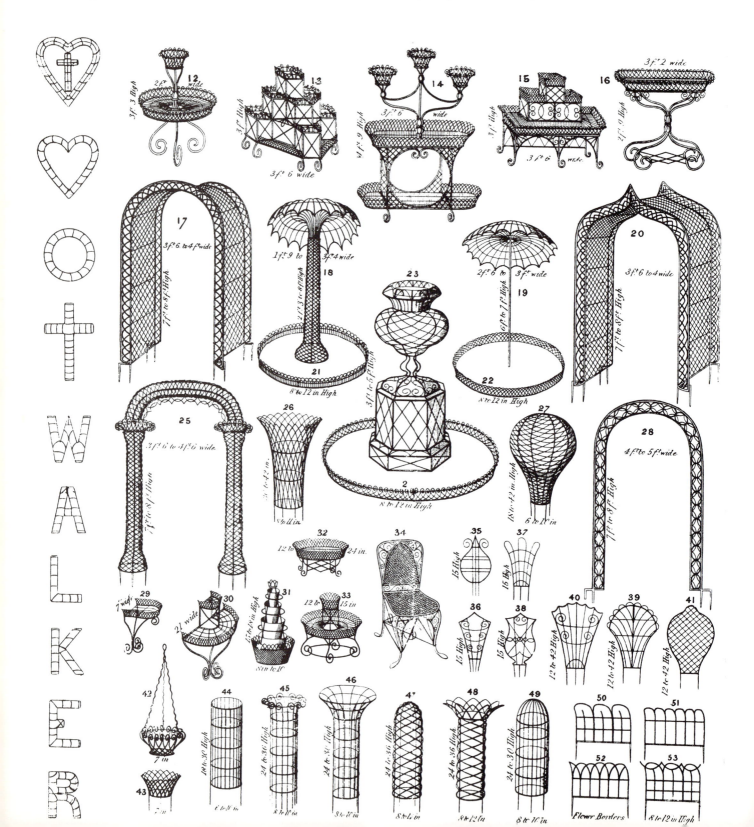

Garden Seats

During the nineteenth century, revolutionary milling and iron-founding techniques in the production of metals enabled furniture manufacturers to adapt this malleable substance for their own purposes. Mass-produced cast-iron and reinforced-steel-wire chairs and benches provided seating furniture for gracious verdant gardens.

699. Above: Victorian tête-à-tête. New York. Late
nineteenth century. Driftwood or tree stumps. H. 31½″,
D. 22½″, L. 66″. Handcrafted "organic furniture" contrasted
sharply with products of the machine age. Reflecting
Victorian taste, this tête-à-tête was constructed from tree
branches and roots and used at Lyndhurst. A popular
magazine during the 1850's, *The Horticulturist,* in 1852
featured two articles on this type of construction for outdoor
seating pieces. (Lyndhurst, National Trust for Historic
Preservation)

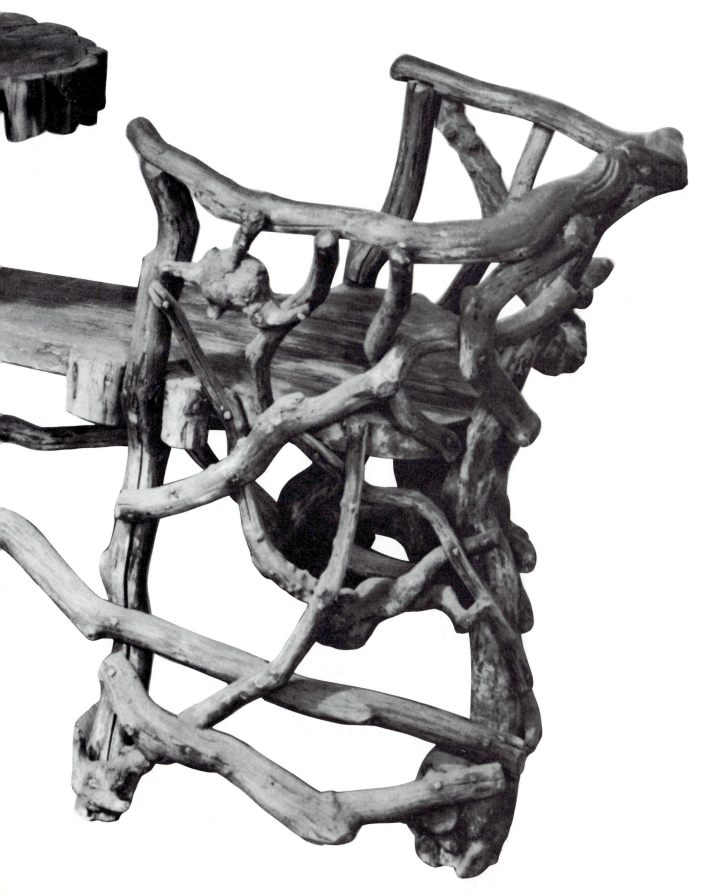

700. Left: Victorian rocking chair. American. Late nineteenth century. Wicker with maple and hickory. H. 38½″, W. 25⅛″, D. 33¼″. The Mentzer Read Company of Grand Rapids, Michigan, and Hong Kong, sold imported "sea grass" furniture in direct competition with the "Willow and Rattan Furniture" offered by Jones Smith of New York. This example relates closely to a chair shown by Smith in an 1882 advertisement which also offered "Tables, Settees, Etc." (Henry Ford Museum)

701. Below, left: Photograph of Little Lulu Byard. American. Ca. 1900. Wicker furniture intended for indoor use was generally very elaborate. It was a favorite prop for early photographers specializing in portraiture. The child has placed her toy horse on the end of a wicker chaise. (New York State Historical Association)

702. Above: Photograph of child sitting on a wicker bench. American. Ca. 1890. This bench was used as a studio prop by the Cooperstown, New York, photographer, Arthur "Putt" Telfer. (New York State Historical Association)

The raw materials used in the construction of organic furniture were not exclusively of American origin. Cane, imported during the late seventeenth century, was used for the seats and backs of Flemish-style chairs. During the eighteenth century, wicker and rattan chairs are known to have been exported from the Orient to American ports. Ships sailing from Germany and Holland in the mid-nineteenth century brought to New York bamboo and cane pieces which competed with the furniture woven from indigenous materials by "unfortunate orphans."

703. Above: Early photograph of Louis Comfort Tiffany. The famed creator of Favrile glass and countless leaded-glass lampshades and windows sits in a wicker chair. (Lillian Nassau Ltd.)

704. Below: Advertisement of Bloomingdale Brothers. Published in *Decorator and Furnisher*. March, 1896. Bloomingdale's, located at Third Avenue and 59th Street, in New York City, sold reed rockers, "very comfortable, nothing better made," for $4.96. (Privately owned)

705. Right: Victorian platform rocker. American. Late nineteenth century. Cane, maple, and pine, with metal springs. H. 40¾", W. 20¾", D. 18½". Platform rockers were much in style during the late 1800's. This example is rare, since they were usually constructed of wood and comfortably upholstered. Large springs mounted under the rocker and on top of the platform base prevented the sitter from tipping too far forward or backward. (Shelburne Museum, Inc.)

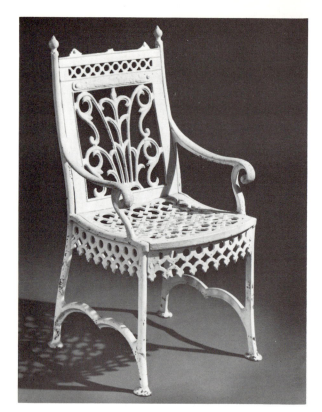

706. Above: Victorian armchair. Made by B. Chambers. American. Ca. 1870. Cast iron. H. 34⅜", W. 19½", D. 18". Gothic motifs decorate the skirt of this cast-iron chair which was used at Longwood Gardens in Kennett Square, Pennsylvania. (Henry Ford Museum)

707. Below: Victorian side chair. Made by Robert Wood & Co. Philadelphia. Ca. 1850. Cast iron. H. 33", W. 17", D. 20½". One of a set of six, this cast-iron garden chair relates to the popular Rococo Revival. (Henry Ford Museum)

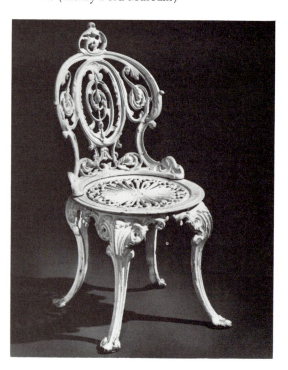

708. Below, left: Victorian settee. Designed by Washington Irving. American. 1836. Cast iron. H. 31", D. 18", L. 47½". Gothic design permeates this garden piece which was used at Sunnyside, Washington Irving's home on the Hudson. (Sunnyside, Sleepy Hollow Restorations)

709. Right: Detail of the painting *View From Hyde Park on the Hudson River, New York*. Attributed to Victor DeGrailly. American. Oil on canvas. Ca. 1840. H. 21¼", W. 28¾". Certainly the grandeur of the Hudson was the subject of conversation between the young lady with the parasol and her beau while they sat on the cast-iron bench. (The New-York Historical Society)

Bentwood chairs were first manufactured in the Viennese plant of Michael Thonet during the 1840's. The parts were shipped throughout the world and, once they had reached their destination, assembled with screws. During the years immediately following London's Crystal Palace Exhibition in 1851, American manufacturers mass-produced the original Thonet forms. The Sheboygan Chair Company of Sheboygan, Wisconsin, sold rockers in "Mahogany, Walnut, Ebony or Antique Elm. Polished." These domestic pieces competed directly with original Thonet furniture sold in New York at 808 Broadway and in Chicago at the Palmer House in "Depot[s] for the United States of America."

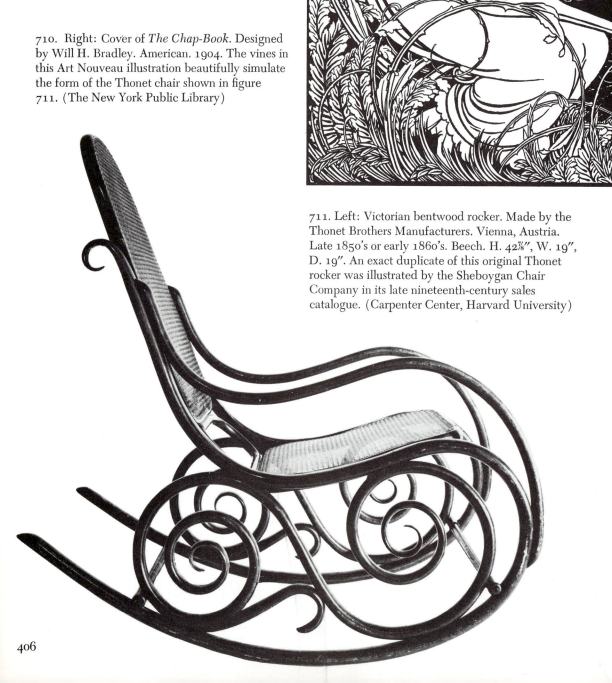

710. Right: Cover of *The Chap-Book*. Designed by Will H. Bradley. American. 1904. The vines in this Art Nouveau illustration beautifully simulate the form of the Thonet chair shown in figure 711. (The New York Public Library)

711. Left: Victorian bentwood rocker. Made by the Thonet Brothers Manufacturers. Vienna, Austria. Late 1850's or early 1860's. Beech. H. 42⅞", W. 19", D. 19". An exact duplicate of this original Thonet rocker was illustrated by the Sheboygan Chair Company in its late nineteenth-century sales catalogue. (Carpenter Center, Harvard University)

Bentwood Forms

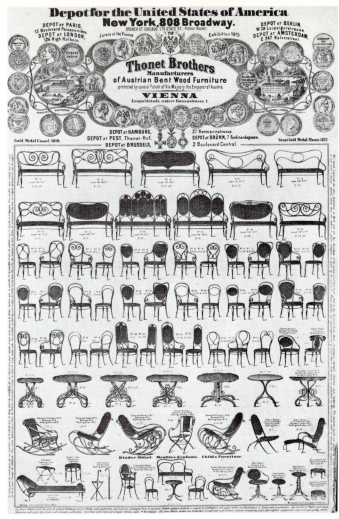

712. Above, left: Bentwood side chair. Czechoslovakia. 1915. Hickory, willow, ash. H. 34½″, W. 14″, D. 18″. American bentwood furniture is identical in form to European imports and, unless labeled, is impossible to distinguish from the European examples. Cane-back chairs were used to furnish the House of Delegates in the Maryland State House in 1880. President Herbert Hoover, Thomas Edison, and numerous other world dignitaries sat on these bentwood chairs when Henry Ford opened his Museum and Greenfield Village on October 21, 1929, in Dearborn, Michigan. Manufacturers still produce these simple forms, copying exactly the early designs of the European firm. (Henry Ford Museum)

713. Above, right: Advertisement of the Thonet Brothers. New York. Ca. 1874. This advertisement indicates that Thonet furniture had won prizes in international expositions the world over, and at home in Vienna enjoyed the royal patronage of the Emperor of Austria. Thonet pieces were made of beech and might be obtained either "polished in their natural color or stained like rosewood, walnut or mahogany." (The New-York Historical Society)

714. Left: Bentwood side chair. American. Ca. 1915. Hickory, ash, willow. H. 37″, W. 16″, D. 18″. The front legs of this chair are shaped and carved. (Henry Ford Museum)

715. Left: Illustration of a settee from a trade catalogue published by the Charles P. Limbert Company of Grand Rapids and Holland, Michigan, in 1907. Much Oriental- or Japanese-inspired furniture was actually made in the United States. (The Metropolitan Museum of Art)

716. Below: Design for a bamboo chair illustrated by Kilian Brothers. New York. 1876. These chairs could be purchased for $8.67. (The Metropolitan Museum of Art)

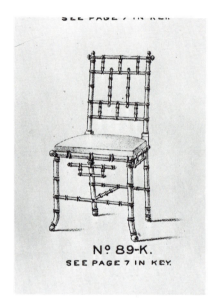

717. Below: Early photograph of a Japanese-style settee manufactured and sold by Kimbel & Cabus. New York City. Ca. 1880. (Cooper–Hewitt Museum of Design, Smithsonian Institution)

The Japanese Craze

In the Japanese exhibit at the Philadelphia Centennial of 1876, ancient as well as modern objects were shown. Americans found the exotic nature of these "curios" fascinating. The Japanese bazaar and teahouse, attended by natives in kimonos, was much heralded by the national press, and the Japanese craze that followed permeated every form of the decorative arts. Homemakers with an artistic bent were guided by such publications as *Decorator and Furnisher* in the creation of wall hangings consisting of Japanese fans bound together with woven strips of bamboo. Bamboo furniture, the editors noted in 1886, was popular "among people of artistic taste." William H. Vanderbilt included in his block-long house on New York's Fifth Avenue a fantastic Japanese room, which he filled with a clutter of things Oriental.

718. Above, right: Child's rocking chair. American. Ca. 1900. Cane, maple. H. 22¾", W. 17½", D. 19⅜". A Japanese fan design is worked into the back of this woven rocker. (Henry Ford Museum)

719. Below, left: Paper label of Nimura & Sato Co., from a chest of drawers. Brooklyn, New York. Ca. 1915. This company constructed furniture in America from imported bamboo. (The Brooklyn Museum)

720. Below, right: Japanese-style side chair. American. Ca. 1900. Maple. H. 33¾", W. 17¼", D. 15½". This chair is from a bedroom suite consisting of a bed, a table, two side chairs, a chest of drawers, and a mirror. The wood has been turned to resemble bamboo, and the rings have been stained to achieve a realistic effect. (Cary F. Baker, Jr.)

721. Left, top; 722. Left, bottom: Japanese-inspired side chairs. Made by George W. Maher (1864–1926). Chicago, Illinois. 1897. Mahogany. H. 43½″, W. 23″, D. 20⅞″. Part of a set of sixteen dining-room chairs, these were made for the home of John Farson, Oak Park, Illinois. (Park District of Oak Park, Illinois)

723. Above: Museum installation. Peter Hall, working from drawings created by the California architects, Charles and Henry Greene, crafted Oriental-inspired pieces intended for use in the interior of homes which the brothers were designing. The furniture in this interior was made for use in a house commissioned by David Gamble in 1907 and built in 1908. (Photograph courtesy The Metropolitan Museum of Art)

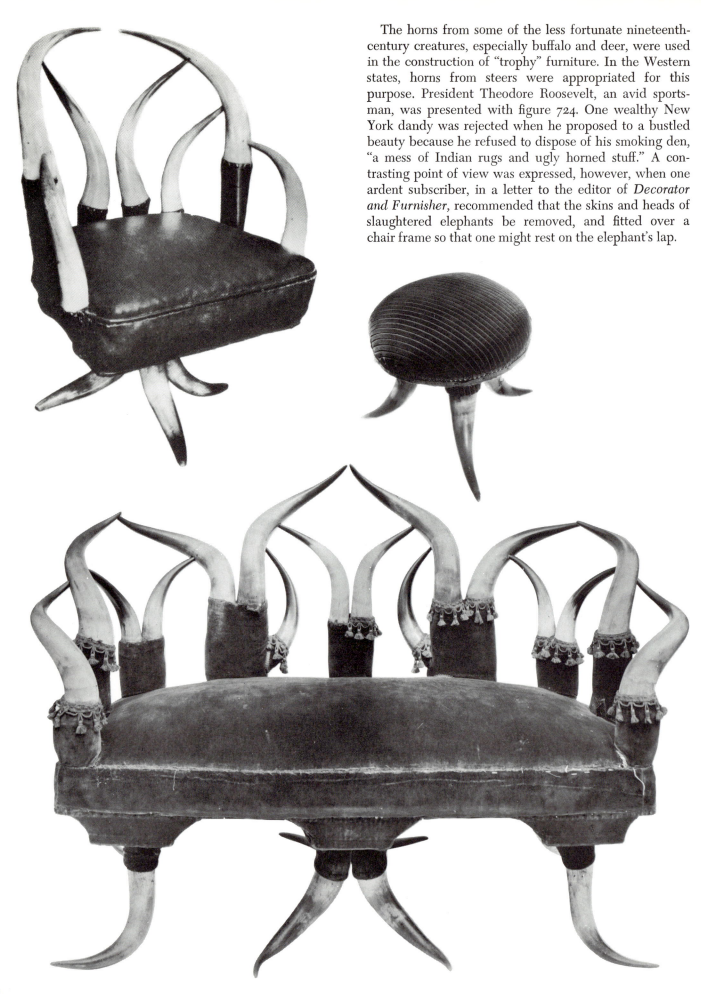

The horns from some of the less fortunate nineteenth-century creatures, especially buffalo and deer, were used in the construction of "trophy" furniture. In the Western states, horns from steers were appropriated for this purpose. President Theodore Roosevelt, an avid sportsman, was presented with figure 724. One wealthy New York dandy was rejected when he proposed to a bustled beauty because he refused to dispose of his smoking den, "a mess of Indian rugs and ugly horned stuff." A contrasting point of view was expressed, however, when one ardent subscriber, in a letter to the editor of *Decorator and Furnisher,* recommended that the skins and heads of slaughtered elephants be removed, and fitted over a chair frame so that one might rest on the elephant's lap.

Chairs of Horn

724. Far left, top: Victorian armchair. American. Ca. 1885. Steer horns and leather. H. 34½″, W. 26½″, D. 22½″. This desk chair was presented to President Theodore Roosevelt by a Western admirer. (Sagamore Hill)

725. Near left, top: Victorian footstool. American. Ca. 1900. Steer horns. H. 9″, Diameter 10½″. (Henry Ford Museum)

726. Left, bottom: Victorian settee. American. Late nineteenth century. Steer horns and velvet. H. 42″, L. 64″. This three-chair-back settee is appropriately upholstered with green velvet and trimmed with fringe. (Decorative Accents, New York City)

727. Above: Victorian armchair. American. Ca. 1900. Steer horns. H. 37⅛″, W. 30½″, D. 26⅛″. The feet, in the form of four-pronged brass claws enclosing glass ball casters, are similar to those used on pieces created by the firm of Louis C. Tiffany and Associated Artists. This decorating adventure was founded in 1879 by the painters Samuel Coleman and Lockwood deForest; the textile designer, Candice Wheeler; and Louis Comfort Tiffany, scion of the well-known jewelry and silver firm in New York City. (Henry Ford Museum)

728. Left: Advertisement of Carrington, DeZouche & Co. Philadelphia. 1876. For those attending the Centennial, a "Turkish Room" upholstered in a gaily printed floral fabric trimmed with a red binding and accented by red-and-black fringe and tassels was a real showstopper. (The Metropolitan Museum of Art)

729. Right: Drawing of a tufted-seat hall glass. Executed by the decorating firm of Henry W. Jenkins & Son. Baltimore. Late 1870's. Ink and wash. H. 13⅜", W. 9⅜". Much nineteenth-century furniture is classified as Turkish when it is upholstered and tufted even though the forms have no known Eastern prototypes. Widespread acceptance of the Turkish style by the American public was encouraged by furniture manufacturers. (Jenkins Collection; photograph courtesy Winterthur Museum)

Turkish Trifles and Treasures

730. Right: Advertisement from the Sears, Roebuck & Company catalogue. American. 1897. This firm offered to their customers an "elegant Turkish parlor suit . . . by mail," consisting of "one tête-à-tête, one rocker, one gents' easy chair, one parlor or reception chair, all guaranteed to be one of the best parlor suits ever put on the market." (Henry Ford Museum)

$23.00 BUYS A

OUR SPECIAL OFFER: SEND US $5.00 as a guarantee can examine it at your freight depot
Three per cent. discount allowed if cash in full accompanies you

No. 9503 This elegant Turkish parlor suit consists of 1 Tetê 1 Rocker, 1 Gents' Easy Chair, 1 Parlor or Reception Chair. pieces are made in extra large size, high backs and large comforta and are very latest design. The upholstering or cover of this suit latest design and pattern of imported goods; each piece is co a different color. We will be pleased to mail you samples of six colors to select from, or if left to us to make selection in colors o sterer will in all cases give you colors on this suit that will plea every respect. The suit is finely upholstered, with plush band on top and sides of back and trimmed with a heavy worsted frin

731. Below: Victorian love seat in the Turkish style. American. Nineteenth century. H. 33″, D. 20″, L. 45″. Draped tassels, fringe, and gimp conceal the legs of this heavily padded and tufted, oval-back, silk-upholstered love seat. (Grand Rapids Public Museum)

732. Above: Victorian armchair. American. Ca. 1880. H. 30⅛″, W. 30¾″, D. 24½″. Turkish rugs were especially popular with American homemakers. This adjustable armchair is covered with a fabric woven in imitation of such a rug. Cords and tassels probably were draped from the top corners of the back to the top rear corners of the arms. (Smithsonian Institution)

5.00 PARLOR SUIT

...nd we will send you the suit by freight. C. O. D., subject to examination; you ... perfectly satisfactory pay the freight agent the balance, $18.00 and freight. ... $22.31 pays for the suit.

suit is made with good steel spring seats and spring edges and every piece is made with spring backs. This is without a doubt one of **the best parlor suits ever put on the market** at the price we ask for it and will be an ornament in any home. We can furnish this same parlor suit upholstered in good grade of crushed plush, assorted colors, and other styles of covering.

4 piece Parlor Suit, price in cotton tapestry	$23.00
4 piece Parlor Suit, price in crushed plush	25.50
4 piece Parlor Suit, price in silk brocatelle	29.50
4 piece Parlor Suit, price in silk damask	34.00

During the last third of the nineteenth century, Turkish-style furniture was constructed by manufacturers with the belief that upholstery was more important than the structural frame. Metal coil springs enclosed within a hidden frame, once properly upholstered, created a kind of sitting comfort previously unknown. This exotic style, probably first sparked by Eastern displays at the Philadelphia Centennial, extended beyond furniture design. "Smoking dens" and "Turkish corners" were built into private homes and public buildings. Even Eastern dress was occasionally affected.

733. Above, right: 734. Right: Early photographs of Victorian armchairs in the Turkish style displayed at the World's Columbian Exposition. Chicago, Illinois. 1893. Numerous exhibitions of the "wonderous" electricity competed with displays of historic furniture. Featured was a William and Mary high chest which once belonged to George Washington's mother, Mary Ball Washington, and which is now at the Henry Ford Museum. These Turkish chairs were exhibited by an unidentified American manufacturer. (Library of Congress)

735. Above: Early photograph of Victorian couch in the Turkish style displayed at the World's Columbian Exposition. Chicago, Illinois. 1893. The overstuffed elegance of such extraordinary pieces was accentuated by the selection of lavish upholstery materials, such as silk, imported satin, and leather. (Library of Congress)

736. Below, right: Victorian armchair in the Turkish style. American. Ca. 1880. H. 35″, W. 31″, D. 37″. This chair retains its original upholstery showing a pastoral scene on the seat and back. Elaborately twisted rope and fringe provide definition of form. (Smithsonian Institution)

737. Below, left: Victorian armchair in the Turkish style. American. 1880's. Walnut. H. 38½″, W. 31″, D. 26″. The shield-shaped back and exposed casters on the legs of this Oriental-inspired chair are unusual details. (Henry Ford Museum)

Advertising in the October, 1884, issue of *Decorator and Furnisher,* the G. E. Sparmann Company of 58–64 Clinton Street, New York City, offered "Fine Furniture Frames [Turkish]." Available with either "iron backs" or "ash backs," the armchairs illustrated in the advertisement have massive carved claw feet.

Combined Sofa and Bath Tub.

THE COMMON SENSE INVENTION OF THE AGE.

Is Practical, Convenient, Economical, Comfortable, Portable, Complete and Cheap.

In presenting this valuable combination to the public we are supplying a long-felt want, and placing a household necessity within the reach of all. It is not only a handsome and desirable piece of household furniture, but combines with it the best of bathing facilities. A full-sized Bath Tub, with water tank of 18 gallons capacity, the most improved Heating Device and complete Waste Water Attachments.

There is also provided a large rubber apron, that buttons on to the inside of outer edge of Bath Tub. folding over the front and covering the carpet one yard, thereby forming a perfect protection to the upholstery and carpet.

The combination can be upholstered appropriately for any room, and the bath used as satisfactorily as if taken in the most modern of bath-rooms.

For full particulars, as to styles of Upholstering, Prices, etc., address,

BRUSCHKE & RICKE,

Sole Manufacturers,

257 Division Street, Chicago, Ill.

738. Above: Photograph of an interior in the home of David Belasco. New York City. 1904. Belasco, a famous American dramatist and producer, lived at 247 West 70th Street where he maintained a "Turkish corner" in the very latest style. (Museum of the City of New York)

739. Left: Advertisement of Bruschke & Ricke, 257 Division Street, Chicago, Illinois. Published in *Decorator and Furnisher*. December, 1883. These Midwestern manufacturers created ingenius devices like pianos and chests of drawers that converted into beds, and a bathtub-sofa, the "common sense invention of the age." (Privately owned)

419

740. Above; 742. Right: Museum installation. The Moorish smoking room (ca. 1880) of the John D. Rockefeller, Sr., home at 4 West 54th Street, New York City, was one of the most sophisticated American interiors inspired by the Orient. Rich inlay and painted and gilded decoration accent the splendid ebonized furniture. An Indian-type garniture, consisting of a dragon-mounted clock and two urn-shaped, multiple-armed candelabra, attests to Mr. Rockefeller's awareness of the latest fashions. (The Brooklyn Museum)

741. Left: Victorian daybed in the Turkish style. American. Ca. 1880. H. 28", D. 32", L. 75". The Rockefeller home was redecorated around 1880 and part of the new furnishings included this sumptuous tasseled lounge. (Museum of the City of New York)

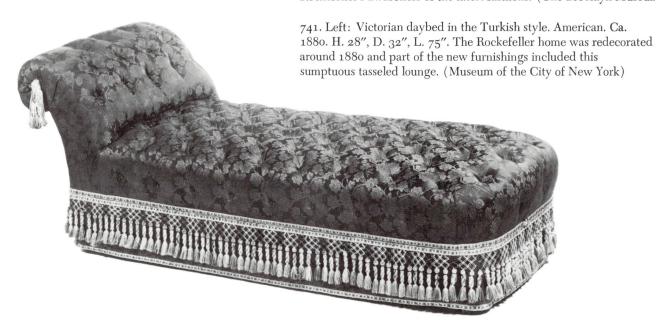

CHAPTER 10
THE COUNTRY STYLE
1800-1900

Shaker Classics

743. Museum installation. The Shakers, a celibate, religious, communal society founded by the English millworker, Ann Lee, established some thirty colonies across America by 1840. Talented craftsmen, who thought of work as a form of prayer, created some of America's simplest, yet most beautiful, furniture. The room interior shows slat-back chairs hanging from pegboards, a Shaker practice that created more interior living space. (Milwaukee Art Center)

744. Below, left: Shaker rocking chair. Made at the Mount Lebanon, New York, community. Ca. 1875. Maple. H. 42″, W. 22½″, D. 18½″. The Shakers produced furniture for sale to the "world's people" as a means of financial support. The woven red-and-black tape seat indicates that this rocking chair was intended for use outside of the Shaker community. (Colin Hall)

745. Below, right: Shaker foot bench. Made at the Mount Lebanon, New York, community. Ca. 1875. Maple, pine. H. 6¾″, W. 11¼″, D. 11½″. This piece retains the original stain-and-varnish finish. (Henry Ford Museum)

747. Above: Illustration from *The Shaker Almanac*. American. 1886. Shaker sisters sit in ladderback chairs while they label and wrap bottles of Seigel's Syrup, a product offered to "the outside world" by the industrious sect. (The New York Public Library)

746. Above: Shaker settee. American. Mid-nineteenth century. Maple. Dimensions not available. The pegs were strung with rope, and a fitted cushion served as the seat on this rare Shaker piece. (Current whereabouts unknown)

748. Above, left: Shaker dining chair. Probably Hancock, Massachusetts. Ca. 1830. Maple. H. 26″, W. 18″, D. 14½″. (Henry Ford Museum)

749. Above, right: Shaker bench. Canterbury, New Hampshire. 1855–1865. Maple, pine. L. 56″. (Henry Ford Museum)

750. Below, left: Shaker rocking chair. Mount Lebanon, New York. 1840–1860. Maple. H. 41″, W. 25⅛″, D. 31″. The flat arm capped with a round, mushroom-like finial is found on many Shaker chairs. (Henry Ford Museum)

751. Near right: Shaker rocking chair. Mount Lebanon, New York. Ca. 1850. Maple, with ash rockers. H. 43″, W. 25″, D. 26″. This chair was constructed with a turned top rail. The gold-and-olive-green-striped plush cushion is original. (Henry Ford Museum)

752. Right, center: Shaker high chair. American. 1840–1860. Maple, pine, hickory, ash. H. 29″, W. 16″, D. 14″. This child's chair has a threaded metal device that enables the seat to be raised or lowered. (Henry Ford Museum)

753. Left: Shaker side chair. Canterbury, New Hampshire. 1830–1870. Curly maple. H. 40¾″, W. 19½″, D. 13½″. The back legs of this chair are fitted with rounded bottoms secured in a socket so that the sitter can tilt backward; hence, the name "tilting chair." (Philadelphia Museum of Art)

754. Top: Sketch of a Shaker cobbler. Probably Sabbathday Lake, Maine. Nineteenth century. Pencil. H. 5½″, W. 7″. A four-legged stool, pegboards on the wall, and a Shaker stove are included in this drawing of a Shaker bootmaker's shop. (Privately owned)

755. Above: Shaker cobbler's bench. Mount Lebanon, New York. Walnut. H. 30″, W. 24″, D. 18″. This bench was made and owned by the North Family of Shakers at Mount Lebanon. The bulbous-turned legs are typical of Shaker craftsmanship. (Mr. and Mrs. James A. Keillor)

Zoar and Others

Religious communal societies were founded and prospered in numerous areas in America during the nineteenth century. The most successful, of course, were the Shakers who, in scattered communities from Maine to Ohio, created severe, beautifully proportioned furniture. The German Separatist leader, Joseph Baumler, with a band of some three hundred followers, in 1817 established a village at Zoar, Ohio. By 1835 self-sustaining farms and small, diverse craft shops provided a source of revenue for community members. Followers of the Rappite Society of New Harmony, Indiana, and the Swedish Jansonites who settled at Bishop Hill, Illinois, also made furniture. Craftsmen at Bishop Hill, clinging tenaciously to the handcraft traditions they brought with them, created chairs with a distinct European flavor. Not always, however, were the furniture-makers in these isolated communities unaware of the successive stylistic changes being dictated by current vogues in Eastern urban areas. The klismos form of figure 756 relates directly to the Empire style.

BISHOP HILL in 1855.

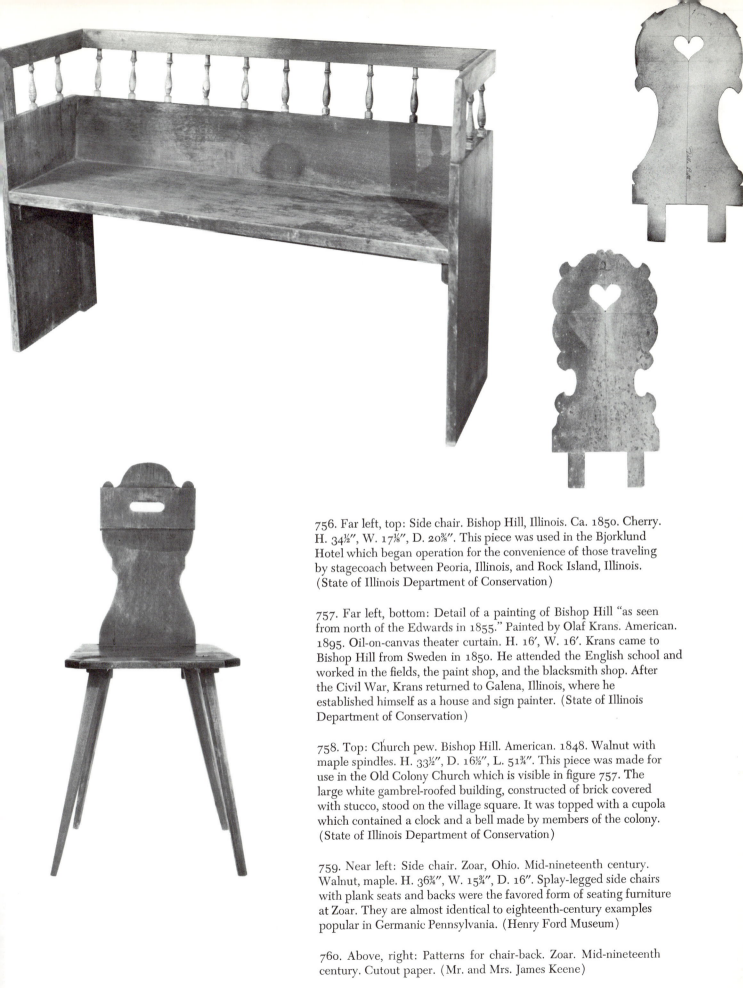

756. Far left, top: Side chair. Bishop Hill, Illinois. Ca. 1850. Cherry. H. 34½″, W. 17⅛″, D. 20⅜″. This piece was used in the Bjorklund Hotel which began operation for the convenience of those traveling by stagecoach between Peoria, Illinois, and Rock Island, Illinois. (State of Illinois Department of Conservation)

757. Far left, bottom: Detail of a painting of Bishop Hill "as seen from north of the Edwards in 1855." Painted by Olaf Krans. American. 1895. Oil-on-canvas theater curtain. H. 16′, W. 16′. Krans came to Bishop Hill from Sweden in 1850. He attended the English school and worked in the fields, the paint shop, and the blacksmith shop. After the Civil War, Krans returned to Galena, Illinois, where he established himself as a house and sign painter. (State of Illinois Department of Conservation)

758. Top: Church pew. Bishop Hill. American. 1848. Walnut with maple spindles. H. 33½″, D. 16½″, L. 51¾″. This piece was made for use in the Old Colony Church which is visible in figure 757. The large white gambrel-roofed building, constructed of brick covered with stucco, stood on the village square. It was topped with a cupola which contained a clock and a bell made by members of the colony. (State of Illinois Department of Conservation)

759. Near left: Side chair. Zoar, Ohio. Mid-nineteenth century. Walnut, maple. H. 36¾″, W. 15¾″, D. 16″. Splay-legged side chairs with plank seats and backs were the favored form of seating furniture at Zoar. They are almost identical to eighteenth-century examples popular in Germanic Pennsylvania. (Henry Ford Museum)

760. Above, right: Patterns for chair-back. Zoar. Mid-nineteenth century. Cutout paper. (Mr. and Mrs. James Keene)

761. Left: Plank side chair. Zoar. 1850–1875. Pine, oak. H. 38″, W. 18″, D. 19½″. The legs which extend through the seat are split and wedged much like Windsors of a century earlier. (Henry Ford Museum)

762. Right: Plank side chair. Zoar. 1850–1875. Pine, oak. H. 38½″, W. 18″, D. 18″. Handholds are cut into the backs of most Zoar plank chairs. Oftentimes they are in fanciful designs. (Henry Ford Museum)

763. Right; 763a. Above: Carved side chair. Zoar.
Ca. 1850. Walnut. H. 34¼", W. 16⅞", D. 16½".
Numerous punched designs, including a basket
containing a large tulip and buds, decorate the back,
the rails, and the seat of this unique piece.
(Henry Ford Museum)

764. Left: Portrait of Charles Mortimer French. Painted by Asahel Powers. American. Ca. 1820. Oil on panel. H. 35¾″, W. 22¼″. Master French sits in a step-down Windsor which, like most nineteenth-century country chairs, was painted and decorated. The Windsor-type footstool appears to be painted and grained. (New York State Historical Association)

765. Above: Portrait of an unidentified Vermont woman. Painted by Asahel Powers. American. Ca. 1825. Oil on panel. H. 35″, W. 26⅛″. The painted and decorated armchair was probably a rocker. (New York State Historical Association)

Windsor chairs, probably the type most frequently made in the eighteenth century, continued to be very popular in the nineteenth century. Once acceptable in the most elegant interiors, their general use during the 1800's was confined to the homes of the less affluent urban dwellers and, of course, the dwellings of the country people. The structural use of various kinds of wood, each best serving its purpose, necessitated the painting of these forms. Messrs. H. H. Morgan and R. Charles, advertising in *The Indiana Farmer* in November of 1825, advised the subscribers that they "have established a Paint Shop in Salem, where they intend carrying on the Painting Business in its different branches, as follows: — Sign, House and Ornamental Painting, — Glazing, Mahoganising doors and Marbling Stair cases. — Windsor chair painting and ornamenting. Canvass painting. — Constant supply of putty on hand. Furniture cleansed and Varnished." Furniture cleaning is seldom mentioned in early newspaper advertisements; however, it is noted in woodworkers' account books and it usually refers to the refinishing of oil or shellac surfaces. New Windsor forms appeared during the nineteenth century. As before, Windsor chairmakers specialized in the production of these inexpensive seating forms.

Nineteenth-century Windsors

766. Above, left: Detail from *The Sportsman's Last Visit*. Painted by William S. Mount. American. Ca. 1835. Oil on canvas. H. 21½″, W. 17½″. The young woman's suitor sits in an arrow-back Windsor side chair. (Suffolk Museum and Carriage House, Stony Brook, New York)

767. Above, right: Sketch of mother and child. By the Baroness Hyde de Newville. New York. 1808. Detail of a watercolor. H. 7¼″, W. 13⅜″. This stylish matron from Amsterdam, New York, sits in a bamboo-turned Windsor side chair, while her child stands on a Windsor "cricket." (The New-York Historical Society)

768. Below, right: *Good Company*. Painted by J. Wells Champney. American. 1879. Oil on canvas. H. 18″, W. 26″. The Philadelphia Centennial of 1876 kindled an interest in things early American. Up-to-date painters were quick to romanticize the picturesque life-style of the past. The man in this painting sits in an eighteenth-century-type Windsor armchair; the woman, in a mid-nineteenth-century example. (Paul Nelson; photograph courtesy Vose Galleries)

769. Far left: Windsor high chair. New England. 1820–1840. Pine, maple, hickory, poplar. H. 33⅞", W. 15⅛", D. 15⅜". Because the top terminals of the back posts on this chair resemble "rabbit ears," this form is often referred to by that term. (Henry Ford Museum)

770. Near left: Windsor side chair. New England. Ca. 1800. Hickory, oak, pine. H. 37⅞", W. 23¾", D. 16¾". The X-shaped stretchers on this bow-back Windsor are an unusual device that appeared late in the eighteenth century. (Henry Ford Museum)

771. Left: Windsor high chair. New England. Ca. 1815. Pine, hickory, maple. H. 34¼", W. 13¼", D. 13¾". Bamboo-turned legs and shaped rod spindles suggest that this chair was made by a rural chairmaker. (Henry Ford Museum)

772. Above: Windsor side chair. Massachusetts. 1795–1815. Ash, oak, white pine, maple. H. 36⅞", W. 19⅜", D. 21¼". The concave front stretcher on this loop-back side chair is joined to the back legs by turned spoke-like stretchers. The design of early nineteenth-century Windsors often relate them to Fancy Sheraton chairs. (Winterthur Museum)

773. Left: Museum installation. The Charles Fowler Barber Shop in the Street of Shops is furnished with a Windsor barber chair. (Henry Ford Museum)

774. Below, left: Windsor barber chair. New England. 1840–1860. Poplar, maple, oak. H. 37½", W. 22⅛", D. 25". Arrow-back Windsors are constructed with spindles that are shaped like those in the back of this chair. (Henry Ford Museum)

775. Below, right: Windsor commode chair. Eastern Massachusetts. Ca. 1810. Pine, maple. H. 38¼", W. 18¾", D. 15½". The deep, shaped skirt on this unusual chair was designed to conceal a chamber pot. (Privately owned)

776. Above, left: Windsor writing-arm chair. New England. 1825. Maple, pine, hickory. H. 35¼″, W. 35¾″, D. 25¼″. The dramatic splay or great outward thrust of the back on this rare form is most desirable. (Henry Ford Museum)

777. Below, right: Salem rocker. Massachusetts. Ca. 1840. Maple, pine. H. 42⅛″, W. 22⅞″, D. 24¾″. The top rail of this Salem rocker is painted and decorated with a charming rural scene. (Henry Ford Museum)

778. Below, left: Boston rocker. New England. Ca. 1832. Maple, pine. H. 45″, W. 26¾″, D. 28″. Boston rockers were universally popular from the 1830's through the 1860's. When found in antique shops today, their heavily scrolled pine seats, which distinguish them from the Salem variants, are often split. This example is painted, grained, and stenciled. The arms were left unpainted. (Henry Ford Museum)

779. Above, right: Windsor side chair. New England. 1830. Pine, maple. H. 33⅜″, W. 16⅞″, D. 17¼″. This rabbit-ear Windsor is painted a bright yellow. (Henry Ford Museum)

780. Right: Double-seated, Hitchcock-type rocker. New England. 1825–1830. Hickory, or ash and pine. H. 30½", L. 34". Country furniture often combines design elements from several different styles. This rocking bench might be classified either as Hitchcock or Windsor. (Old Sturbridge Village)

781. Above: Windsor armchair. Made by Joel Pratt, Jr. Sterling, Massachusetts. 1820–1830. Pine, maple. H. 34", W. 21½", D. 15¼". This painted arrow-back, rabbit-ear armchair bears a paper label which indicates that it was "Warranted . . . Made and Sold" by Mr. Pratt. (Henry Ford Museum)

782. Right: Windsor rocker. New England. 1830–1840. Maple, white pine. H. 45", W. 25", D. 34". Vigorous spindles, arm supports, and splayed legs give strength to this massive rocking chair. The deeply saddled seat attests to a country origin. The legs dowel into the rocker, a method of construction that differs from that used on the Salem and Boston rockers. Chairs of such individuality were never mass-produced. (Privately owned)

783. Above: Windsor side chair. Made by Park & Co. Cleveland, Ohio. 1860–1890. Pine, maple, ash. H. 31½″, W. 17½″, D. 17″. "Kitchen" Windsors were manufactured all across the United States between 1860 and 1915. This example is almost identical to those sold through the mail by the Sears, Roebuck & Company during the early years of the twentieth century. (Henry Ford Museum)

784. Left: Windsor armchair. American. Ca. 1850. Pine and maple, painted. H. 31½″, W. 21½″, D. 17″. "Captain's chairs" or "Firehouse" Windsors are eagerly sought by young collectors today. This example retains traces of the original red paint. (Henry Ford Museum)

785. Above: *The House of the Charles Hawkins Family
Located West of Onsted, Michigan.* American. Ca. 1880.
Oil on canvas. H. 18″, W. 24″. Chairs of the kitchen and
firehouse variants dot the front yard. One can only wonder
what use the stove under the tree might serve. (Mr.
and Mrs. David Claggett)

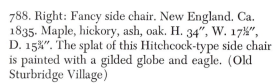
786. Left: Fancy side chair. Attributed to David Alling. New Jersey. 1820–1835. Maple, hickory, ash. H. 34½″, W. 17¾″, D. 15¼″. This is one of a pair of chairs that originally belonged to Alling's first cousin, John Alling III, who lived in Newark, New Jersey. (The Newark Museum)

787. Below, left; 787a. Above: Fancy side chair. Made by L. Hitchcock. Hitchcocksville, Connecticut. Ca. 1830. Maple, hickory, ash. H. 34″, W. 17⅛″, D. 18″. The back rail of this chair is stenciled with the maker's name and address. Like most Hitchcocks, it is painted black and decorated with colored and gilt stenciled paintings. Hitchcock chairs were made in numerous patterns and sometimes shipped great distances to purchasers. (Henry Ford Museum)

788. Right: Fancy side chair. New England. Ca. 1835. Maple, hickory, ash, oak. H. 34″, W. 17½″, D. 15¾″. The splat of this Hitchcock-type side chair is painted with a gilded globe and eagle. (Old Sturbridge Village)

789. Above: Advertisement of the Hitchcock Chair Company. Published in *The Connecticut Courant.* 1831. Hitchcock's views on the use of "ardent spirits" are easily determined in this early advertisement. (Hitchcock Chair Company)

Paint & Stencils

790. Above; 790a. Top: Metal mallet and mark used by Jule Chalk. Ohio. 1850–1870. Wrought iron. L. 12⅞″. (Henry Ford Museum)

791. Right: Side chair. Made by Jule Chalk. Ohio. 1850–1870. Maple, pine. H. 33″, W. 16¼″, D. 18″. This chair, one of four, is painted and stenciled, and is stamped on the bottom "Jule Chalk." (Henry Ford Museum)

792. Left: Painted rocking chair. New England. 1830–1840. Maple, hickory, ash. Dimensions unavailable. Elaborate stenciled designs in the form of baskets of fruit and stylized leafage decorate this tall-back, rush-seat, Hitchcock-type rocking chair. (Index of American Design)

793. Right: Chairmaker's trade sign. New England. Ca. 1835. Maple, pine, oak, ash. H. 64″, W. 28″, D. 26″. This oversized painted-and-decorated chair once sat on the roof of a New England chair manufacturing firm. (Shelburne Museum, Inc.)

794. Left: Convertible armchair. Found in Watertown, New York. 1830–1850. Maple. H. 41″, W. 17″, Depth of seat 17″. During the 1850's, patent furniture was manufactured in most cities. One ingenious inventor sold his device for converting a straight chair to a rocking chair and left the actual construction of the piece to others. (Mr. and Mrs. James A. Keillor)

795. Left: *Baby With Doll.* Attributed to Sturtevant J. Hamblin. Massachusetts. 1840–1850. Oil on board. H. 15½″, W. 12¼″. Dolls of the nineteenth century were always dressed according to the prevailing fashion. In this painting the neckline of the doll's gown matches that on the dress of the child. She sits in a painted-and-decorated country chair similar in form to figure 796. (Abby Aldrich Rockefeller Folk Art Collection)

796. Right: Side chair. New England. Mid-nineteenth century. Pine, maple. H. 34″, W. 16⅝″, D. 15″. Painting and graining were used to decorate this country side chair which has an urn-shaped splat. (Henry J. Prebys)

797. Below: Painted settee. New England. 1830–1850. Maple, pine. H. 34¾″, D. 22⅜″, L. 82¼″. This brightly painted bench was constructed with solid lyre splats. Stenciled designs accent the shape of this piece. Painted shells and cornucopias embellish the crest rail. Stylized flowers and butterflies are used on the edge of the seat which is formed from a single plank of pine. (Henry Ford Museum)

798. Left: Portrait of Levi B. Tasker. Painted by Joseph H. Davis. Stratford Ridge, New Hampshire. March 20, 1836. Pen, ink, and watercolor. H. 11", W. 9⅜". Davis shows Mr. Tasker sitting in a painted-and-grained country chair of the Late Empire style. Notice the gaily figured carpet and painted-and-decorated table. (Old Sturbridge Village)

799. Below: Empire side chair. New England. 1830–1840. Maple, pine, ash. H. 33", W. 17½", D. 19". The boldly grained-and-stenciled decoration on this dramatic country chair is superlative. (Mr. and Mrs. Charles V. Hagler)

800. Right: *Man of Science.* By M. Kranz(?) New York. 1839. Oil on canvas. H. 39", W. 33". This nineteenth-century Isaac Newton sits in a chair with a rush seat. (Edgar William and Bernice Chrysler Garbisch)

802. Right; 802a. Left: Worshipful Master's chair. Made by John Luker. Ohio. Nineteenth century. Pine, maple. H. 72″, W. 29¼″, D. 30″. As the American frontiers expanded westward in the nineteenth century, the Masonic fraternity moved with the people. Every Midwestern community of any size had a Masonic lodge in which secret fraternal meetings were held. This chair is a significant piece of American folk art. Painted on a deep blue ground are various Masonic symbols, as well as the names of the manufacturer, John Luker, and the Worshipful Master, J. H. M. Houston, for whom the piece was made. (Mr. and Mrs. Charles V. Hagler)

801. Below: Modern-day photograph of a nineteenth-century Masonic Temple located at Mount Pleasant, Ohio. (Mr. and Mrs. Charles V. Hagler)

Manuf^d by JOHN LUKER

CHAPTER 11

THE COLONIAL REVIVAL 1876-1970

803. Top: Installation at the Philadelphia Centennial Exposition. Taken from *Frank Leslie's Illustrated Weekly Newspaper.* June 10, 1876. Notice that a bed with a checked coverlet is visible in the second story. (The New York Public Library)

804. Above: Photograph of the New England Kitchen at the Philadelphia Centennial Exposition. 1876. This picture illustrates the truly eclectic point of view held by most Victorians in respect to Colonial furnishings. (The New York Public Library)

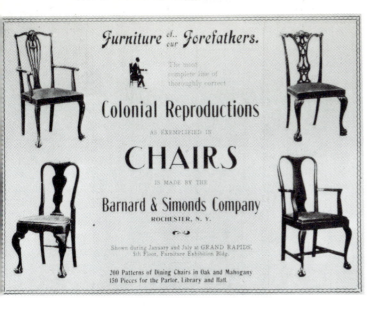

807. Below: Colonial Revival side chair. American. Late nineteenth century. Mahogany with mahogany veneer. H. 34½″, W. 22″, D. 22″. This unusual dining chair was constructed with design elements from the Chippendale, Federal, and Late Emipre styles. (The Newark Museum)

The Colonial Revival movement competed with the numerous other eclectic styles of the late nineteenth century for dominance of the American furniture market. In 1881 Clarence Cook estimated that the movement was some twenty years old, and by 1884 contemporary publications indicate that the manufacturing of antiques had become a modern industry. These "new antiques" were, however, not always faithful reproductions. More often elements of many furniture styles would be combined, sometimes with rather extraordinary results. The popularity of reproduction Colonial furniture has never waned. Even today young newlyweds clamor for these approximations of yesterday's furnishings.

805. Left: Colonial Revival armchair. Made by Hale and Kilburn Manufacturing Company. Philadelphia. 1910. Oak. H. 43″, W. 24¾″, D. 24″. This piece, from a set of four side chairs and two armchairs, was used in the Merion, Pennsylvania, home of Mrs. Laura L. Barnes. (The Brooklyn Museum)

809. Right: Colonial Revival armchair. Made by the Baker Furniture Company. Holland, Michigan. Ca. 1920. Walnut with inlay. H. 40″, W. 28″, D. 22″. The production of William and Mary pieces was the stock-in-trade of the Baker Furniture Company during the 1920's and 1930's. (Grand Rapids Public Museum)

808. Above: Colonial Revival armchair. American. Ca. 1915. Mahogany. H. 53¼″, W. 25½″, D. 20″. This armchair in the William and Mary style was used in the dining room at Fair Lane, the Dearborn, Michigan, home of Henry Ford. (Henry Ford Museum)

810. Below: Advertisement of William B. Savage. Boston. Published in *Decorator and Furnisher*. 1887. Novelties were an important aspect of the Colonial Revival period. The "Old Flax Spinning Wheel Chair" was recommended as a beautiful wedding or birthday present. (Privately owned)

Distinguishing between authentic period furniture and faithfully constructed revival pieces or reproductions can sometimes be most difficult, especially if the reproductions were produced during the late nineteenth century when individual craftsmen of great skill made superb reproductions of Colonial-style chairs. Over a period of approximately seventy-five years, these later pieces have developed wear marks and general coloration similar to original examples. When buying in the marketplace, dealers and auctioneers usually classify a reproduction as "in the style of." The entry "Chippendale Style Armchair" would indicate that the chair had not originated during the middle eighteenth century, but was a later copy.

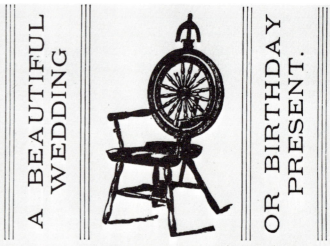

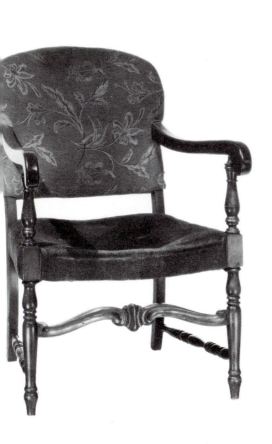

812. Above: Photograph of the library in
Henry Villard's residence. New York City. 1885.
This mansion, designed by McKim, Mead & White,
New York architects, was furnished with Pilgrim and
Chippendale Revival furniture. (The New-York
Historical Society)

811. Above: Colonial Revival armchair. Grand
Rapids, Michigan? 1900–1915. Mahoganized cherry.
H. 33½", W. 23½", D. 31½". This armchair, one
of a pair, was considered to be in the Queen Anne
style. (Henry Ford Museum)

813. Above: Colonial Revival settee. American. Ca. 1900. Mahogany, stained a deep
cherry color. H. 36", D. 23", L. 34½". The ends of this sofa are constructed from wood
that has been laminated and shaped in a steam press. (Henry Ford Museum)

816. Right: "Colonial Parlor Rocker." A detail from a sales catalogue published by the Bishop Furniture Company. Grand Rapids, Michigan. 190?. The firm said of this quartered-oak-and-mahoganized birch piece, "We can safely say that there has never been placed on the market a rocker of similar design and equal quality at so low a price as we ask for this . . . C O D–$7.65, Price Cash with order–$7.27." (The Metropolitan Museum of Art)

815: Below: Colonial Revival Windsor armchair. Made by Wallace Nutting. Framingham, Massachusetts. 1917–1922. Pine, maple, hickory. H. 48″, W. 21″, D. 16½″. Wallace Nutting manufactured faithful reproductions of Pilgrim and eighteenth-century furniture. This marked Windsor chair is one of many used in the library at the Theodore Roosevelt Birthplace, New York City. Nutting pieces are occasionally identified with a printed paper label; more often, however, they are stamped or branded, such as is this example. (Theodore Roosevelt Birthplace)

814. Above: Colonial Revival Windsor rocking chair. American. Ca. 1900. Mahogany, stained. H. 42½″, W. 27½″, D. 33½″. Like so much Colonial Revival furniture, this piece is constructed of mahogany; however, a heavy coat of cherry stain greatly alters the appearance of the wood. The fourth article in *The Ladies' Home Journal* 1897–1898 picture series, "Inside of a Hundred Homes," illustrates the library of an unidentified Philadelphia house. Colonial Revival furniture, including a chair identical to this one, "contrasts admirably with the plain walls of the room." (Sagamore Hill)

817. Right: Colonial Revival rocking chair. American. 1900–1915. Mahogany, stained red. H. 33¼", W. 23½", D. 31½". Chairs of this general nature were frequently offered in mahogany, golden oak, or mahoganized birch. (Henry Ford Museum)

818. Below: *At the Fender*. Published by Wallace Nutting. American. 1904. Print. H. 8", W. 10". Wallace Nutting's activities extended far beyond the manufacturing of reproduction furniture. His finely colored prints of picturesque New England landscapes were the products of his picture-publishing business. A seemingly endless group of "Colonial Interiors" from early houses, furnished with authentic antiques and peopled by ladies in period costumes, were popular decorating additions. (Privately owned)

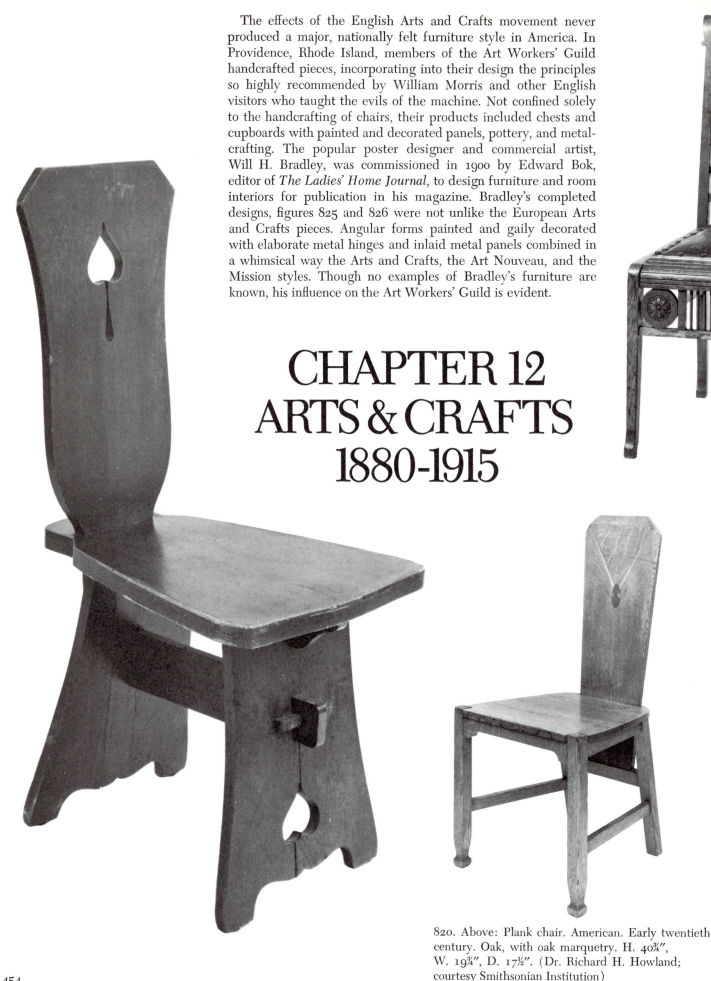

The effects of the English Arts and Crafts movement never produced a major, nationally felt furniture style in America. In Providence, Rhode Island, members of the Art Workers' Guild handcrafted pieces, incorporating into their design the principles so highly recommended by William Morris and other English visitors who taught the evils of the machine. Not confined solely to the handcrafting of chairs, their products included chests and cupboards with painted and decorated panels, pottery, and metalcrafting. The popular poster designer and commercial artist, Will H. Bradley, was commissioned in 1900 by Edward Bok, editor of *The Ladies' Home Journal,* to design furniture and room interiors for publication in his magazine. Bradley's completed designs, figures 825 and 826 were not unlike the European Arts and Crafts pieces. Angular forms painted and gaily decorated with elaborate metal hinges and inlaid metal panels combined in a whimsical way the Arts and Crafts, the Art Nouveau, and the Mission styles. Though no examples of Bradley's furniture are known, his influence on the Art Workers' Guild is evident.

CHAPTER 12
ARTS & CRAFTS
1880-1915

820. Above: Plank chair. American. Early twentieth century. Oak, with oak marquetry. H. 40¾", W. 19¾", D. 17½". (Dr. Richard H. Howland; courtesy Smithsonian Institution)

819. Far left: Plank chair. Made by Charles P. Limbert Company. Grand Rapids and Holland, Michigan. Early twentieth century. Oak. H. 38¼″, W. 18½″, D. 18″. It is interesting that this chair is similar in design to the eighteenth-century pieces crafted by the Pennsylvania-Germans and the mid-nineteenth-century examples created by the German Separatists at Zoar, Ohio. (Providence Art Club)

821. Left: Eastlake side chair. American. Late nineteenth or early twentieth century. Oak. H. 32″, W. 18″, D. 18″. The stylized carved roundels on this chair are similar in design to those on chairs made by Sydney R. Burleigh, a leading spirit in the Art Workers' Guild, Providence, Rhode Island. (The Brooklyn Museum)

822. Left: Eastlake side chair. Made by Sydney R. Burleigh for his compatriot, John G. Aldrich. Providence. 1887. Mahogany. H. 32½″, W. 18½″, D. 19″. John G. Aldrich, an artist and craftsman, and Charles M. Stetson, an industrialist, together with Burleigh, were the prime movers in the Providence Arts and Crafts efforts. (Mr. and Mrs. David Aldrich)

823. Above: Modern photograph of the Providence Art Club. Providence. This building is perhaps unique in America in that it is an architectural expression of the American Arts and Crafts movement. (Providence Art Club)

824. Above: Photograph of the interior of the New York Yacht Club. 1901. The dining room, which was decorated in the manner of a ship's interior, was furnished with "craft" furniture. (Library of Congress)

825. Right: Designs for a table and chair. Drawn by Will H. Bradley. Published in *The Ladies' Home Journal*. 1901 and 1902. Bradley was one of the few American designers who attempted to reconcile the Mission, the Arts and Crafts, and the Art Nouveau styles and at the same time create a definite style of his own. (The New York Public Library)

826. Right: Design for a dining room. Drawn by Will H. Bradley. Published in *The Ladies' Home Journal.* 1901 and 1902. Bradley's design concepts were closely related to those created by the celebrated Scottish designer, Charles Rennie Mackintosh. (The New York Public Library)

827. Below: Modern furniture designed by John E. Brower and made by the Sleigh Furniture Company, Grand Rapids. 1907. Brower's chair, chest of drawers, and dresser anticipate modern furniture forms by almost twenty years. (Grand Rapids Public Museum)

CHAPTER 13
ART NOUVEAU
1895-1915

828. Above: Art Nouveau settee. Attributed to Edward Colonna. French. Late nineteenth century. Walnut. H. 39½", L. 45". Colonna, an American, emigrated to France and became one of the leading designers in the Art Nouveau style. Most of Colonna's work was for the French dealer, Samuel Bing, whose shop, L'Art Nouveau, provided the name for the late nineteenth-century movement. Colonna returned to America in later life and might have influenced young designers. Though little high-style Art Nouveau furniture was crafted in America, it certainly would have been available at shops in New York and other major Eastern cities. (Lillian Nassau Ltd.)

829. Left: Art Nouveau armchair. Attributed to Edward Colonna. French. Late nineteenth century. Walnut. H. 39", W. 24". (Lillian Nassau Ltd.)

830. Right, top: Art Nouveau side chair. Attributed to Edward Colonna. French. Late nineteenth century. Walnut. H. 36", W. 19". The carving on the top rail of this chair matches that on the armchair, figure 829, and the settee, figure 828. (Lillian Nassau Ltd.)

831. Right: Photograph of the French Pavilion at the St. Louis Exposition, St. Louis, Missouri. 1904. Americans were "awed by this orgy of curvilinear woodwork." (Cooper–Hewitt Museum of Design, Smithsonian Institution)

The American Art Nouveau movement was essentially limited to areas other than furniture. Louis Comfort Tiffany's Favrile art glass and leaded-glass lampshades are universally known and collected. His international reputation overshadowed only slightly those of his contemporaries—Will H. Bradley, whose posters were widely acclaimed, and Artus Van Briggle, the Denver, Colorado, potter whose celebrated Lorelei vase was offered for sale in Paris in 1901. American furniture was seldom constructed with the same flowing forms and curvilinear outline so popular in Europe. The Mission style, or the "New Style" as it was sometimes called, was less expensive to produce and more acceptable to a public wishing to escape the exaggerated eclecticism of the nineteenth century.

832. Right: Art Nouveau settee. Probably Grand Rapids. 1891. Cherry. H. 38¼″, D. 26″, L. 46½″. (Grand Rapids Public Museum)

833. Below: Art Nouveau side chair. Probably Grand Rapids. 1891. Cherry. H. 40″, W. 19½″, D. 17¾″. During the 1890's Art Nouveau-inspired, mass-produced furniture was made by firms in an effort to capitalize on the interest in the "French style." These pieces were not handcrafted. (Grand Rapids Public Museum)

834. Above: Art Nouveau chair and desk. Designed by William Codman and manufactured by the Gorham Silver Company. Providence. Ca. 1904. Ebony and boxwood encrusted with silver-and-ivory inlay. Chair height 30″. These pieces were crafted especially for exhibition at the 1904 St. Louis Exposition where they won a grand prize. (Gorham Silver Company)

835. Near left: Illustration from a trade catalogue of a "L'Art Nouveau Parlor Rocker." The Bishop Furniture Company. Grand Rapids. 190?. These chairs were available constructed of "golden oak and mahoganized birch" and were sold in the Grand Rapids area during the early 1900's for $6.89, cash with order. (The Metropolitan Museum of Art)

836. Right: Art Nouveau upholstered armchair. Made by the Tiffany Glass and Decorating Company. New York. 1890–1900. Maple and ash, with metal inlay. H. 35⅝″, W. 26⅛″, D. 25¼″. The design of this chair is attributed to Tiffany since the piece is similar in shape and decoration to examples made by him for H. O. Havemeyer. All four legs terminate with brass claw feet grasping a glass ball. The top rail is elaborately carved with a floral motif. (The Metropolitan Museum of Art)

The furniture illustrated on these two pages is from a 1907 catalogue published by S. Karpen & Brothers of Chicago and New York. "The Karpen factories and salesrooms form an organization for the manufacture and sale of upholstered furniture and special furniture equaled nowhere in the world." The pieces illustrated in the catalogue were in the styles of "Louis XIV (Quatorze) 1643–1715; Empire 1804–1814; Colonial 1558–1800; German, Deutsche Kunst (Modern); Louis XV (Quinze) 1715–1774; Chippendale 1760–1820; L'Art Nouveau 1898 to date (1907); Modern; Louis XVI (Seize) 1774–1793; Italian, Spanish Renaissance 1400–1643; English (Modern) and Mission (Arts and Crafts)." The emphasis, however, was on L'Art Nouveau furniture which could be purchased in "solid Cuban Mahogany," covered in "genuine gold leaf #'s 150, 200 and 250."

837. Far left, top; 838. Left; 839. Right: Illustrations from a sales catalogue published by S. Karpen & Brothers. Chicago, Illinois, and New York City. 1907. These three pieces are from their Catillya L'Art Nouveau suite which captured a Grand Prix at the 1904 St. Louis Exposition. The armchair sold for $250.00; the window bench, or settee, for $150.00. (Henry Ford Museum)

840. Below, center; 840a. Left; 841. Right:
Illustrations from a sales catalogue published by
S. Karpen & Brothers. Chicago and New York City.
1907. This "triumph of artists skilled in woodcraft"
was "the most artistic and beautiful example of
this school of decoration ever produced." The
complete suite of three pieces could be purchased
for $660.00. (Henry Ford Museum)

842. Above: Sculpture of Loie Fuller by Raoul
François Larche. French. Ca. 1900. Bronze. H. 18".
During the early 1900's, representations of Loie
Fuller (1862–1928), a renowned American dancer,
were incorporated into the design of silver,
glass, and pottery. The top rails of figures 840
and 841 are carved with a dancing woman
probably intended to represent this popular beauty.
(The Museum of Modern Art, New York)

463

843. Above. Portrait of Elbert Hubbard. American. 1914. Oil on canvas. Dimensions unavailable. (Current whereabouts unknown)

The innovator and originator of "Craftsman furniture," Gustav Stickley (1857–1942), rebelled against "conventionalized plant forms" of the Art Nouveau. The designs for his furniture, which was made by hand in workshops near Syracuse, New York, and marketed in his own Craftsman Building in New York City, were based upon functionalism. There were numerous imitators of Stickley's style, including the fabled "Fra" Elbert Hubbard (1856–1915). Hubbard's diverse activities centered around the manufacture of "Craft-Style" furniture in his Roycroft shops at East Aurora, New York. Other competitors in the Mission market included Stickley's brothers in Grand Rapids, Michigan. Stickley considered Tiffany glass and lamps compatible with his oak-crafted pieces. He not only illustrated them in his periodical, *The Craftsman Magazine*, but also exhibited them in showrooms in his Craftsman Building.

CHAPTER 14
THE MISSION STYLE
1890-1915

844. Above: Design for an Inglenook. By Gustav Stickley. American. Published in *Craftsman Homes* by Gustav Stickley. 1907. (New York Society Library)

845. Right: Caricature of Elbert Hubbard, *The Fra DeLuxe*, taken from *Art and Glory* by Freeman Champney. American. (Freeman Champney)

846. Design for a chair by Will H. Bradley. American. 1901–1902.
An excellent example of a Bradley design in the new Mission style.
(The Metropolitan Museum of Art)

847. Left: Illustration of an easy chair from *Arts and Crafts Summer Furniture*. Published by the Charles P. Limbert Company. Grand Rapids and Holland, Michigan. 1907. This reclining chair, which cost $28.00, was fitted with elastic cotton felt cushions covered in hard-finished goatskin. (Privately owned)

848. Above: Illustration of a footstool from *Arts and Crafts Summer Furniture*. Published by the Charles P. Limbert Company. 1907. Limbert furniture was made by the Dutch at "quaint Holland in America." When the evils of cosmopolitan life infringed upon the productivity of the Limbert operation at Grand Rapids, the firm moved westward to the more picturesque and secluded Holland. (Privately owned)

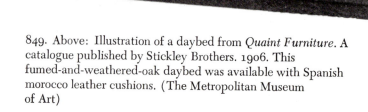

849. Above: Illustration of a daybed from *Quaint Furniture*. A catalogue published by Stickley Brothers. 1906. This fumed-and-weathered-oak daybed was available with Spanish morocco leather cushions. (The Metropolitan Museum of Art)

850. Below, center: Mission sofa. American. 1900–1913. Oak. H. 39″, D. 33½″, L. 71″. Bright, gaily printed fabrics were often used on heavy oak Mission furniture. The seat of this piece is covered with a textile woven with fraternal motifs. (Henry Ford Museum)

851. Below: Mission side chair. American. 1890–1910. Oak. H. 35″, W. 17″, D. 22″. Gustav Stickley's handcrafted furniture was aggressively imitated and mass-produced by competitors who forced him into bankruptcy in 1915. (The Brooklyn Museum)

852. Left; 852a. Below: Mission card and chair-table. Illustrated in a trade catalogue published by the H. T. Cushman Manufacturing Company. North Bennington, Vermont. Early twentieth century. The top of this piece was constructed from quartered oak and the seat covered with roanskin. This form has remained popular since the seventeenth century. See figures 27 and 27a. (The Metropolitan Museum of Art)

853. Left: Photograph of the Bleecker Street Subway Station, New York City. Early twentieth century. This station, which is located at Lafayette and Bleecker Streets, was equipped with an oak settee for weary travelers. In many stations these solid forms still serve New York's rapid transit customers. (Museum of the City of New York)

854. Above: Mission rocking chair. American. 1915. Cherry with mahoganized stain. H. 35½″, W. 24½″, D. 32″. The slip-seat of this piece is constructed with coil springs. (Henry Ford Museum)

855. Below: Museum installation. The "Craftsman" chairs, desk, and table are from Gustav Stickley's Eastwood, New York, plant, ca. 1905. (Chairs, tables, lamps: Mr. and Mrs. Terence Leichti; desk: Eric M. Schindler; photograph courtesy The Metropolitan Museum of Art)

856. Left: Mission armchair. Designed by Frank Lloyd Wright. American. Early twentieth century. Oak. H. 32″, W. 23″. This chair was used in the Darwin Martin residence at Buffalo, New York. (Albright–Knox Art Gallery)

857. Right: Mission side chair. Designed by Frank Lloyd Wright. American. Ca. 1895. Poplar. H. 42 1/16″, W. 16½″, D. 17⅜″. "The clean cut, straight-line forms that the machine can render far better than would be possible by hand" expressed Frank Lloyd Wright's final rejection of the Arts and Crafts movement in 1910. "Bring out the nature of the materials, let this nature intimately into your scheme. Strip the wood of varnish and let it alone—stain it." This chair is finished with brown stain. (Edgar J. Kaufmann, Jr.)

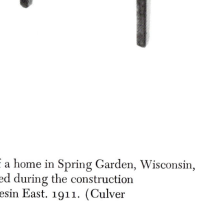

858. Far right, top: Interior of a home in Spring Garden, Wisconsin, where Frank Lloyd Wright lived during the construction of his famed studio-home, Taliesin East. 1911. (Culver Picture Service)

859. Far right, bottom: Mission armchair. Designed by Frank Lloyd Wright. American. Ca. 1895. Poplar. H. 29⅛″, W. 24¾″, D. 25½″. The Milwaukee, Wisconsin, cabinetmaker, George Neidecken, crafted many of Wright's progressive furniture designs. This chair is probably from his shop. It is possible that Wright used the piece in a studio near his home in Oak Park, Illinois. (Edgar J. Kaufmann, Jr.)

The opinion that Frank Lloyd Wright (1869–1959) expressed about seating furniture in 1954 has not, in many instances, proven accurate. "My early approach to the chair was something between contempt and a desperation. Because I believe sitting to be in itself an unfortunate necessity not quite elegant yet, I do not yet believe in any such thing as a 'natural' chair for an unnatural posture. The only attractive posture of relaxation is that of reclining. So I think the ideal chair is one which would allow the would-be 'sitter' to gracefully recline. Even the newest market chairs are the usual machines-for-sitting. Now I do not know if whatever God may be ever intended you or me to fold up on one of these—but, if so, let's say that fold-up or double-up ought to make you look more graceful. It ought to look as though it were intended for you to look and be just that.

"We now build well-upholstered benches and seats in our houses, trying to make them all part of the building. But still you must bring in and pull up the casual chair. There are many kinds of 'pull-up' chairs to perch upon—lightly. They're more easy. They're light. But the big chair wherein you may fold up and go to sleep reading a newspaper (all that kind of thing) is still difficult. I have done the best I could with this 'living room chair' but, of course, you have to call for somebody to help you move it. All my life my legs have been banged up somewhere by the chairs I have designed. But we are accomplishing it now. Someday it will be well done. But it will not have metal spiderlegs nor look the way most of the steel furniture these days looks to me.

". . . Yet every chair must eventually be designed for the building it is to be used in. Organic architecture calls for this chair which will not look like an apparatus but instead be seen as a gracious feature of its environment which can only be the building itself. So the stuffed-box-for-sitting-in is not much better than the machine-for-setting-it-in.

". . . When the house-interior absorbs the chair as in perfect harmony, then we will have achieved not so minor symptoms of a culture of our own."

How appalled Wright would be at the merchandise in today's furniture stores.

860. Left: Modern armchair. Designed by Frank Lloyd Wright. American. 1904. Pine. H. 32¼". Though Wright professed to detest Mission furniture, his early furniture is many times indistinguishable from that movement. The bottom stretchers of this piece extend through the legs. This method of construction was also practiced by Gustav Stickley. (The Museum of Modern Art, New York)

861. Left: Photograph of the exterior of the Frederick Robie house designed by Frank Lloyd Wright. The dawn of the "Modern" furniture movement in terms of American furniture is synonymous with the ascent of Wright's international reputation. This concrete house on Chicago's south side was completed in 1908. It was furnished with square-shaped, oak, Mission-inspired furniture. (Chicago Architectural Photo Co.)

862. Right: Modern side chair. Designed by Frank Lloyd Wright. American. 1904. Oak. H. 36″, W. 15″ D. 18½″. Wright collected Japanese prints. The design for this chair indicates how strongly he was influenced by Oriental artifacts. (The Museum of Modern Art, New York)

863. Left: Room interior. "International style" furniture has always been popular with architects and designers. This interior, from the Connecticut home of American architect, Phillip Johnson, is furnished with Mies Van Der Rohe furniture. (Knoll International)

864. Below: Barcelona stool. 865. Right: Barcelona chair. Designed by Ludwig Mies Van Der Rohe and manufactured by Knoll International. 1929. Polished stainless steel. Saddle-leather straps with foam-rubber cushions covered with top-grain leather. 864. H. 14½", W. 23", D. 22". 865. H. 29½", W. 29½", D. 29½". (Knoll International)

CHAPTER 15
THE INTERNATIONAL STYLE
1915-1970

In this section we have grouped some of the splendid chair forms that have been developed in the twentieth century in metal, wood, and plastics by an international group of designers, several of them world-famous architects. These seating pieces exhibit an astonishing range of elegant solutions to the problem of creating a successful chair, and many of them are just as handsome and satisfying today as when they were first created.

The chairs of the German-born architect, designer, and teacher, Ludwig Mies Van Der Rohe (born 1886) are perhaps more widely known than those of any other "International style" designer. His elegant metal-and-leather seating piece, the Barcelona chair, was originally designed for use in the German Pavilion at the International Exposition of 1929 in Barcelona, Spain. It represents a modern interpretation of the old Roman curule form. Onetime director of the Bauhaus in Dessau, Germany, Mies joined the Armour Institute (now Illinois Institute of Technology) in 1938. The American buildings he created are monuments of modern design. His master plan for the I.I.T. campus, the 860-900 Lake Shore Drive, Chicago, Illinois, apartments, the Cullinan Museum in Houston, and the Seagram Building in New York all demonstrate the highly innovative nature of this man's unique talent.

In 1920 the eighteen-year-old youth, Marcel Breuer, joined the Bauhaus in Weimar, Germany, as a student. By 1923 his creative abilities were sufficiently recognized for him to be considered one of the "new men." While director of the furniture workshop in 1925, he designed the Wassily lounge chair, figure 866. His furniture for the assembly hall, dining room, and students' rooms in the newly constructed Bauhaus at Dessau was also made of tubular steel, a medium that Breuer was to use successfully throughout his long career. "A piece of furniture is not an arbitrary composition; . . . In itself impersonal, it takes on meaning only from the way it is used or as part of a complete scheme." Breuer attempted to impose a standardization on the production of furniture which he intended to be compatible with any interior.

866. Wassily lounge chair. Designed by Marcel Breuer.
Manufactured by Knoll International. Ca. 1926. Tubular-steel frame, double-faced cowhide or reinforced canvas slings. H. 23⅛″, W. 27½″, D. 31⅛″. (Knoll International)

867. Above: Contour chaise longue. Designed by Richard
Schultz. Manufactured by Knoll International. 1967.
Cast and extruded aluminum. Woven Dacron mesh sling
with vinyl straps. H. 33¾″, D. 24½″, L. 58″. Schultz, a
sculptor, feels that his work with furniture "sharpens the
eye and heightens sensivity to form and proportion in other
design problems." Examples of both his furniture and
sculpture are in the permanent collections of museums
throughout the world. (Knoll International)

868. Below: "Chaise Longue LC/4." Designed by
LeCorbusier and Charlotte Perriand. 1927. Chromium-plated
steel-tube frame, pony skin. H. 33½″, W. 23¼″, L. 63″.
Referring to this lounge, in 1931 a critic lamented the
policies of the furniture manufacturers "where standardisation
in production is the main object of experiméntalism."
(Herman Miller, Inc.)

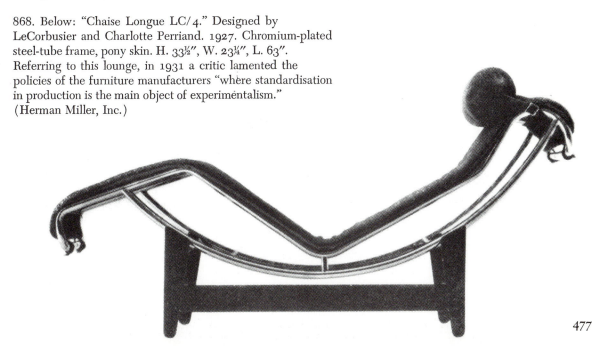

869. Left, top: Armchair. Designed by Ludwig Mies Van Der Rohe. Manufactured by Estler–Regale G.m.b.H. 1927. Tubular-steel frame with leather. H. 32″. (The Museum of Modern Art, New York)

870. Left, bottom: Cesca side chair. Designed by Marcel Breuer. Manufactured by Gebrüder Thonet A.G. 1928. Tubular steel, wood and cane. H. 32″, W. 18½″, D. 23⅝″. (The Museum of Modern Art, New York)

871. Above: Couch. Designed by George Nelson. Manufactured by Herman Miller. 1963. Steel, leather. H. 29¾″, L. 87″. (The Museum of Modern Art, New York)

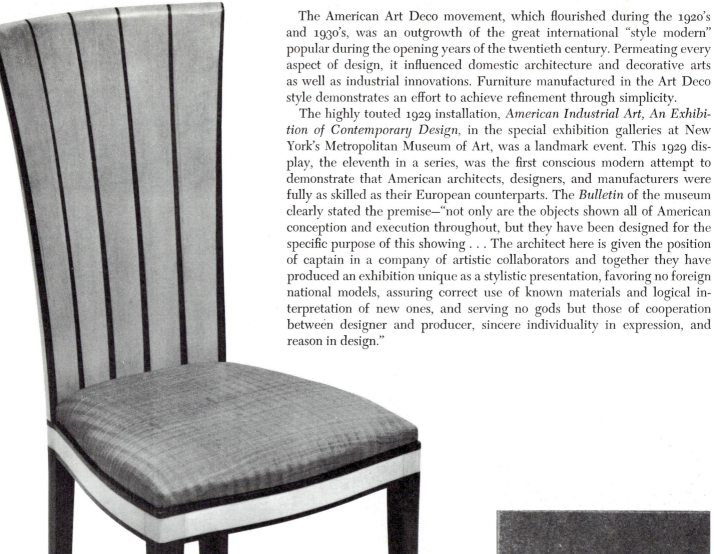

The American Art Deco movement, which flourished during the 1920's and 1930's, was an outgrowth of the great international "style modern" popular during the opening years of the twentieth century. Permeating every aspect of design, it influenced domestic architecture and decorative arts as well as industrial innovations. Furniture manufactured in the Art Deco style demonstrates an effort to achieve refinement through simplicity.

The highly touted 1929 installation, *American Industrial Art, An Exhibition of Contemporary Design*, in the special exhibition galleries at New York's Metropolitan Museum of Art, was a landmark event. This 1929 display, the eleventh in a series, was the first conscious modern attempt to demonstrate that American architects, designers, and manufacturers were fully as skilled as their European counterparts. The *Bulletin* of the museum clearly stated the premise—"not only are the objects shown all of American conception and execution throughout, but they have been designed for the specific purpose of this showing . . . The architect here is given the position of captain in a company of artistic collaborators and together they have produced an exhibition unique as a stylistic presentation, favoring no foreign national models, assuring correct use of known materials and logical interpretation of new ones, and serving no gods but those of cooperation between designer and producer, sincere individuality in expression, and reason in design."

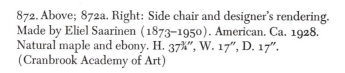

872. Above; 872a. Right: Side chair and designer's rendering. Made by Eliel Saarinen (1873–1950). American. Ca. 1928. Natural maple and ebony. H. 37¾", W. 17", D. 17". (Cranbrook Academy of Art)

873. Right: Gondola chairs and matching table. By Emile-Jacques Ruhlmann. French. 1925. Burl walnut. Chair height 36″, W. 21″, D. 19½″. This furniture, which was exhibited and much heralded at the Paris Exposition of 1925, was the inspiration for countless copies produced by American manfacturers. (Lillian Nassau Ltd.)

874. Below: Museum installation. The American designer, Raymond M. Hood, was responsible for this 1929 business executive's office. His use of aluminum for the construction of chairs, settees, and other furniture was considered advanced in relationship to European designers who were "accused of still using metal pipe structures" for such seating pieces. (The Metropolitan Museum of Art)

875. Above: Museum installation. 1929. Writing in a Metropolitan
Museum of Art *Bulletin*, Charles R. Richard described this Man's Den
by Joseph Urban in glowing terms—"The fine proportions and
severe and strongly articulated wood surfaces of wall cabinet and
bookcase, desk and chairs give this small alcove rare distinction and
character." (The Metropolitan Museum of Art)

876. Right; 876a. Below, center: Museum installation. The interior and furnishings designed by Robert T. Walker for a man's study for a country house in the 1929 exhibition were considered "thoroughly masculine but not in the least degree heavy." (The Metropolitan Museum of Art)

877. Below: Museum installation. 1929. The woman's bedroom designed by John Wellborn Root was fitted with gray pleated wall covering, "exquisite" white patterned glass curtains and soft-toned draperies. One critic felt that the furniture for this room setting was "tricky" and "the emphasis in this case seems to have been placed upon novelty of design and ornament." (The Metropolitan Museum of Art)

Despite the national disaster of a financial depression, the Metropolitan Museum in 1934 mounted another exhibition devoted to *Contemporary American Industrial Art*. Through the installations, which were still essentially Art Deco and "limited to objects of contemporary design," the institution hoped "to aid the modern style in arriving at a more definite formulation of principles." It acknowledged the continuing public interest in modern furnishings and "desired to inspire a steadily increasing number of firms to favor modern objects produced in large volume."

878. Left, top: Museum installation. Dining room designed by Walter Dorwin Teague. 1934. (The Metropolitan Museum of Art)

879. Left, bottom: Museum installation. Dining room designed by Donald Deskey, who also designed the furniture for New York's Radio City Music Hall. 1934. (The Metropolitan Museum of Art)

880. Right: Museum installation. Detail of a room for a lady, designed by the noted architect, Eliel Saarinen, of Cranbrook Foundation. 1934. (The Metropolitan Museum of Art)

881. Below: Museum installation. Dining room designed by Eugene Schoen, architect. 1934. (The Metropolitan Museum of Art)

882. Left: Armchair. Designed by Gerrit Rietveld (1888–1964). Holland. 1918. Beech plywood, painted, red back, blue seat. H. 34¼″, W. 26″, D. 32⅗″. The De Stijl movement was a group attempt by early twentieth-century Dutch artists to integrate totally painting, sculpture, and architecture. Rietveld, an independent cabinetmaker, joined this modern art group in 1917. Like the paintings of the famous De Stijl artist, Piet Mondrian, this red-and-blue chair, the result of a commission from the Dutch architect, Robert vant Hoff, is composed of square members in vivid colors with the separateness of the jointings emphasized. Prophesying in the journal, *De Stijl,* Rietveld said, "Our chairs . . . will become the abstract, real artifacts of future interiors." (Stedelyk Museum, Amsterdam)

883. Below, left: Side chair. Designed by T. H. Robsjohn–Gibbings. Manufactured by Saridis S.A. Athens, Greece. June, 1961. Greek walnut. H. 33⅞″, W. 20½″, D. 22″. Good chair design is ageless. The klismos form, first popular in ancient Greece and revived in the early nineteenth century, served as the basis for this modern chair. (Saridis of Athens)

884. Below, center: "Round" chair. Designed by Hans J. Wegner. Manufactured by Knoll International. Denmark. 1949. Beech with cane seat. H. 30″, W. 24½″, D. 20½″. This chair, the most famous of the "Danish modern," was developed after Wegner saw a Chinese child's chair in a Copenhagen museum. It is first roughed by machine and later finished by skilled craftsmen using age-old cabinetmaking techniques that limit the production to three a day. (Knoll International)

885. Right: Reclining chair. Designed by Marcel Breuer. Manufactured by Isokon Furniture Company in England. 1935. Laminated beech plywood, upholstered. H. 31½″, L. 53″. Breuer studied architecture at the famous Bauhaus in Weimar, Germany, and on graduation became the first master of its furniture workshops. His work in wood demonstrates clarity of structure, form, and visual balance. (Privately owned)

886. Below: Armchair. Designed by Hammond Kroll. American. Ca. 1930. Wood and parchment. H. 32″, W. 24″, D. 20″. Kroll, during the 1920's and 1930's, preferred the properties of wood over the new metals being used by architect designers. (Cooper–Hewitt Museum of Design, Smithsonian Institution)

887. Below; 887a. Bottom: 670/71 lounge chair and ottoman. Designed by Charles Eames. Manufactured by Herman Miller, Inc. American. 1956. Rosewood veneer, molded plywood, metal, with leather cushions. 887. H. 32¼″, W. 33¼″, D. 34½″. 887a. H. 17⅓″, W. 25½″, D. 21″. Charles Eames and Eero Saarinen experimented with molded furniture while at Michigan's Cranbrook Academy of Art. Their efforts won first prize at the 1941 Modern Furniture Competition sponsored by The Museum of Modern Art, New York. Forty-seven different hand operations are involved in the manufacture of this lounge chair. (Herman Miller, Inc.)

888. Left: Side chair. Designed by Charles Eames. American. 1946. Plywood and steel. H. 29½″, W. 19¼″, D. 20½″. While designing for the United States Navy special equipment to support war-injured men, Eames developed his molded-plywood techniques which he later used for the construction of furniture. He was also one of the first to use Fiberglas-reinforced plastic for seating pieces. (Henry Ford Museum)

889. Above: Side chair and table. Designed by Charles Eames. American. 1946. Plywood and steel. Height of chair: 29½″. Eames designed a seemingly endless array of lightweight chair shells which could be attached to different bases of steel tubes or wire. (Herman Miller, Inc.)

890. Below: Lounge chair. Designed by Alvar Aalto. Manufactured by Artek OY, Finland. 1934. Molded and bent birch plywood. H. 25½″. (The Museum of Modern Art, New York)

891. Above: Room interior with boat-shaped conference table designed by Florence Knoll and easy chair designed by Eero Saarinen. Two of the leading American manufacturers of International-style chairs are Knoll International and Herman Miller, Inc. Knoll International was founded in 1945 by Hans and Florence Knoll, in collaboration with Van Der Rohe. The CBS Building in New York City, one of Eero Saarinen's last projects, was furnished with pieces designed both by Florence Knoll, who was responsible for the interiors, and by the master himself. (Knoll International)

892. Above: Easy chair and ottoman. Designed by Eero Saarinen. American. 1948. Reinforced plastic shell with steel-rod base and foam-rubber upholstery. Chair height 35½″, W. 40″, D. 34″. (Knoll International)

893. Above: Room interior featuring the Catenary Group. Designed by George Nelson. American. 1963. These chrome-plated, steel-frame chairs were hung with pillows suspended on cables. (Herman Miller, Inc.)

894. Left: Marshmallow love seat. Designed by George Nelson. American. 1956. Metal and foam. H. 32½″, D. 33″, L. 52″. The oldest "Modern furniture" manufacturer in America is Herman Miller. His efforts in the 1930's revolutionized American interior design. George Nelson joined the Miller firm in 1946. (Herman Miller, Inc.)

895. Above, left: Side chair. Designed by Harry Bertoia. American. 1950's. Welded steel wire and steel rod; upholstered with foam rubber and a detachable cover. H. 30", W. 21", D. 22½". Bertoia's welded steel-wire side chairs and high-backed chairs have been manufactured in a variety of finishes. Bertoia considers his chairs "studies in space, form and metal." (Knoll International)

896. Center, left: High-backed chair. Designed by Harry Bertoia. American. 1950's. Welded steel wire and steel rod. Upholstered with foam rubber. H. 39⅛", W. 38½", D. 34½". (Knoll International)

897. Bottom, left: Dining chair. Designed by Warren Platner. American. 1965. Steel wire. Upholstered with polyester fiber over a rubber core. H. 29", W. 26½", D. 22". Platner's welded and plated steel-wire chair, which he developed while on a grant from the Graham Foundation, creates a "picket-fence" illusion. (Knoll International)

898. Above: Butterfly chair. American. Introduced in 1938. Iron frame with leather or canvas cover. H. 38". These chairs were originally priced for the carriage trade; however, adaptations are today offered for under $15.00 by department stores across the country. (Privately owned)

899. Right: Small diamond chair. Designed by Harry Bertoia. American. 1950's. Seat and back, welded steel wire; base, welded steel rod. H. 30½", W. 33¾", D. 28". Italian-born Harry Bertoia came to the United States at the age of fifteen. His famous "wire-shell" chairs relate to the metal screens he designs as space dividers for modern buildings. (Knoll International)

900. Left: Room interior with oval dining table and chairs designed by Eero Saarinen. (Knoll International)

901. Right: Armchair. Designed by Eero Saarinen. American. 1956. Molded-plastic shell with cast-metal base finished with plastic. H. 32¾″, W. 26″, D. 23½″. The graceful, plastic shells of Eero Saarinen's pedestal chairs achieve their creator's desire "to make the chair all one thing again." Revolutionary in 1956 and 1957, his cast-plastic concept is much imitated today. (Knoll International)

902. Right: Blow-up lounge chair. By
Scolari D'Urbino, Lomazzi & De Pas of
Milan, Italy. 1967. PVC plastic. H. 34″,
W. 50″, D. 41″. Pop artists during the
1960's developed inflatable sculpture.
Following in their footsteps, today's chair
manufacturers offer a varied selection of
"blow-up" furniture. This example is sold
with a foot pump and patch kit. (Selig
Manufacturing Co.)

903. Below: Museum installation. Strong,
undulating curves emphasize the molded-
plastic forms of this distinctive furniture
manufactured by Studio Artemide. Plastic,
once considered second-rate, today
dominates the innovational furniture market.
(City Art Museum of St. Louis)

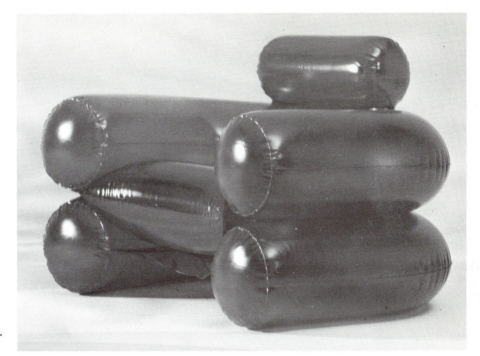

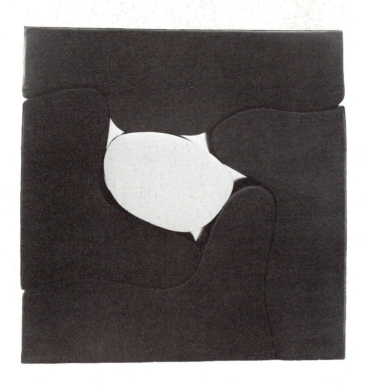

905. Top, right: Suzanne double lounge chair. Designed by Kazuhide Takahama. 1969. Frame, tubular steel. Upholstered with separate foam cushions. H. 26¾″, D. 29⅞″, L. 58⅝″. The Suzanne designs also include a single lounge chair and sofa. (Knoll International)

906. Center, right: Marcel sofa and lounge chair. Designed by Kazuhide Takahama. 1969. Aluminum frame with separate polyurethane cushions. Sofa length 97⅝″. Lounge chair height 25½″. (Knoll International)

907. Bottom, right: Raymond lounge chair. Designed by Kazuhide Takahama. 1969. Base and back support, reinforced Fiberglas and plastic. Upholstered foam cushions. H. 24¾″, D. 29½″, L. 31⅛″. Japanese-born Takahama now resides in Italy where his designs for Dino Gavina have received international attention. His sofas and lounge chairs with upholstered polyurethane cushions are striking statements of contemporary living. (Knoll International)

904. Above; 904a. Below: Malitte lounge. Designed by Sebastian Matta. 1969. Foam polyurethane blocks, covered in stretch wool. H. 63″ assembled. This unusual seating suite is composed of sculptured foam blocks which have been covered in vivid primary-color fabrics. (Knoll International)

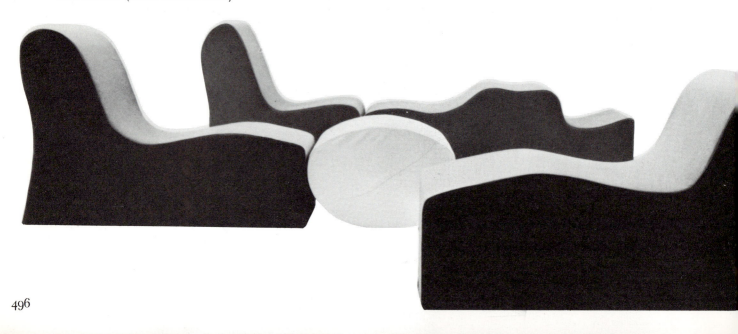

908. Above: Settee. Made by Sam Maloof. American. 1948. Black walnut. H. 31″, D. 23″, L. 44″. (Sam Maloof)

909. Right, top: Bench and stool. Made by Sam Maloof. American. 1948 and 1949. Black walnut. Bench height 16″. Stool height 28″. (Sam Maloof)

910. Right, bottom: A gaggle of chairs all made by Sam Maloof. (Sam Maloof)

"The designer and craftsman cannot, should not be separated. . . . Not only should a man be a designer on paper, but he should also be able to use his hands to create that which he has designed." Designer, craftsman, and perhaps philosopher, Sam Maloof, born in California in 1916, fashions, on a commission basis, limited-production and one-of-a-kind pieces for the home and office. His clean-lined chairs, while totally original in concept, remind one of Windsors from the mid-nineteenth century. His subtle designs and the great skill he demonstrates in their execution have earned for him the reputation of being one of the leading American creators of handsome furniture.

911. Left: Dining chair. Made by Sam Maloof. American. 1948. Black walnut. H. 31″, W. 24″, D. 23″. (Sam Maloof)

912. Right: Spindle-back rocking chair. Made by Sam Maloof. American. 1959. Black walnut. H. 45″, W. 28″, D. 45″. (Sam Maloof)

914. Right: Settee. Made by Sam Maloof. American. 1958. Black walnut. H. 42″, D. 22″, L. 45″. (Sam Maloof)

913. Left: Flat spindle occasional chair. Made by Sam Maloof. American. 1969. Black walnut. H. 44″, W. 29″, D. 26″. (Sam Maloof)

915. Right: Dining chair. Made by Sam Maloof. American. 1967. Black walnut. H. 30″, W. 21½″, D. 24″. (Sam Maloof)

916. Below: Conoid chair and table. Designed by George Nakashima. American. 1962. Available in walnut or cherry. H. 35″. W. 20″, D. 16½″. During his long career, Nakashima has created some twenty different chair designs. (Photograph courtesy G. William Holland)

George Nakashima (born 1905) is one of the most original handcraftsmen working in the United States today. Though the designs for his chairs show no formal influences from modern achitecture, they are entirely comfortable in the most avant-garde interiors. The ultimate form of Nakashima's furniture is often dictated by the materials at hand. A large slice of knotted wood becomes a chair seat, a bench seat, or even a table top. Though his Oriental-inspired forms are handcrafted, they are intended for a wide market.

917. Above: High Mira chair. Designed by George Nakashima. American. 1952. Available in walnut or cherry. Tall chair: H. 37″, W. 19¼″, D. 16½″. Short chair: H. 35″, W. 19¼″, D. 16½″. (Photograph courtesy G. William Holland)

918. Below: Conoid cushion chair. Designed by George Nakashima. American. 1962. Available in walnut or cherry. H. 33½″, W. 22″, D. 19″. (Photograph courtesy G. William Holland)

919. Left: Conoid bench with back. Designed by George Nakashima. American. 1962. English walnut, with hickory spindles. H. 29½″, D. From 24″ to 36″, L. 84″. Similar seating pieces are crafted from black walnut and Circassian walnut. (Photograph courtesy Time-Life, Inc.)

920. Above: Bench with back. Designed by George Nakashima. American. 1958. Available in walnut or cherry, with hickory spindles. H. 35″, D. 21″, L. 72″. The turned legs on this piece are similar to those created by craftsmen in Shaker communities across the United States during the nineteenth century. (Photograph courtesy G. William Holland)

921. Below: Lounge chair. Designed by George Nakashima. American. 1962. Available in walnut or cherry. H. 33½″, W. 23½″, D. 19″. This chair with a single arm resembles writing-arm Windsors of the eighteenth and nineteenth centuries. The seat is deeply shaped or "saddled," much like the seats on those earlier forms. (Photograph courtesy G. William Holland)

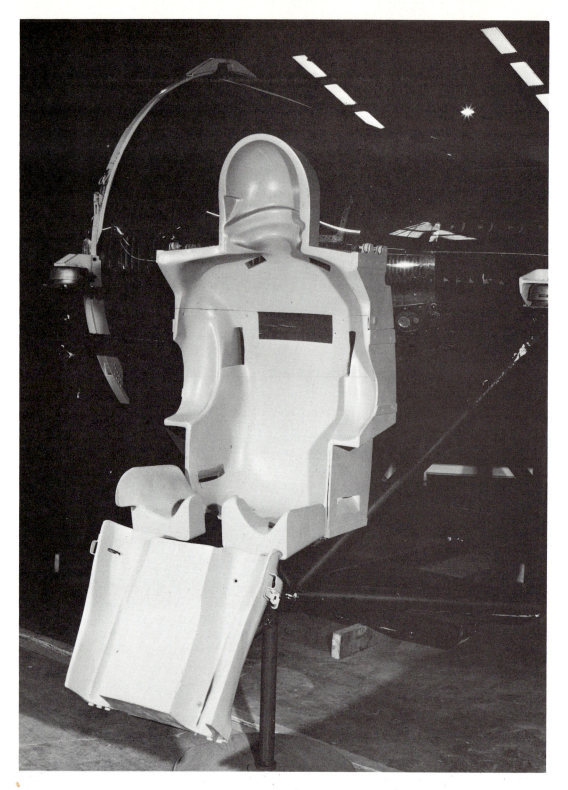

922. Above: Astronaut contour seat. American. 1962. Painted Fiberglas. H. 40″, W. 24″, D. 12″. Molded contour seats, such as this Fiberglas example used by Colonel John G. Glenn, Jr., U.S.M.C., first American astronaut to orbit the earth, perhaps anticipate the direction of seating pieces in the space age. (National Air and Space Museum, Smithsonian Institution)

923. Right: Museum installation. *Mirrored Room*. Designed by Lucas Samaras. American. 1966. Mirrors. Room size: H. 10′, W. 8′, D. 8′. The Greek-born artist, Lucas Samaras, has placed a mirror-covered Parsons-type table and square-back chair in the center of this room. Mirrored panels applied to the ceiling, walls and floor (here reflecting the photographer's flash) produce a sense of infinite, starry space, such as one would encounter on an interplanetary flight. (Albright–Knox Art Gallery)

SELECTED BIBLIOGRAPHY

SELECTED BIBLIOGRAPHY

This selected bibliography represents books and catalogues which were used in the preparation of this work. Listing the scholarly articles that have appeared over the years in *The Magazine* ANTIQUES would in itself comprise a book and, therefore, they have not been included.

Adams, Mary E. *Legrand Lockwood (1820–1872)*. Norwalk, Conn.: The Lockwood–Mathews Mansion Museum of Norwalk, Inc., 1969.

Amaya, Mario. *Art Nouveau*. New York: E. P. Dutton & Co., Inc., 1966.

America's Arts and Skills. New York: The American Federation of Arts, 1969.

Andrews, Edward Deming, and Andrews, Faith. *Shaker Furniture*. New Haven, Conn.: Yale University Press, 1937.

———. *The People Called Shakers*. New York: Oxford University Press, 1953.

Aronson, Joseph. *The Encyclopedia of Furniture*. New York: Crown Publishers, Inc., 1938.

Auchincloss, Louis. *Three Hundred Years of New York City Families*. New York: Wildenstein & Co., Inc., 1966.

Bailey, Thomas A. *The American Spirit*, vol. I. Boston: D. C. Heath and Company, 1967.

Baltimore Furniture, 1760–1810. Baltimore, Md.: The Baltimore Museum of Art, 1947.

Barbour, Frederick K. *The Stature of Fine Connecticut Furniture*. Privately published, 1959.

Bell, J. Munro, ed. *The Furniture Designs of Chippendale, Hepplewhite and Sheraton*. New York: Robert M. McBride & Company, 1938.

Benjamin, Asher. *The American Builder's Companion*. New York: Dover Publications, Inc., Reprint, 1969.

Biddle, James. *American Art from American Collections*. New York: The Metropolitan Museum of Art, 1963.

Bjerkoe, Ethel Hall. *The Cabinetmakers of America*. Garden City, N.Y.: Doubleday & Company, Inc., 1957.

Blackie and Son. *The Victorian Cabinet-Maker's Assistant*. New York: Dover Publications, Inc., Reprint, 1970.

Brainard, Newton C. *Connecticut Chairs in the Collection of The Connecticut Historical Society*. Hartford, Conn.: The Connecticut Historical Society, 1956.

Buchwald, Dr. Hans. *Form from Process —The Thonet Chair*. Cambridge, Mass.: Carpenter Center for the Visual Arts, 1967.

The Buffalo Fine Arts Academy. *Annual Report, 1966–1967*. Buffalo, N.Y.: Albright-Knox Art Gallery, October, 1967.

Burroughs, Paul H. *Southern Antiques*. New York: Bonanza Books, 1931.

Burton, E. Milby. *Charleston Furniture 1700–1825*. Charleston, S.C.: The Charleston Museum, 1955.

Butler, Joseph T. *American Antiques 1800–1900*. New York: The Odyssey Press, 1965.

Carpenter, Ralph E., Jr. *The Arts and Crafts of Newport, Rhode Island*. Newport, R.I.: The Preservation Society of Newport County, 1954.

Chippendale, Thomas. *The Gentleman and Cabinet-Maker's Director*. New York: Dover Publications, Inc., Reprint of the 3rd edition, 1966.

Chorley, Kenneth. *The Prentis Collection*. Concord, N.H.: New Hampshire Historical Society, 1958.

City Art Museum of Saint Louis *Bulletin*, vol. VL, no. L., May–June, 1970.

Comstock, Helen. *100 Most Beautiful Rooms in America*. New York: The Viking Press, 1958.

———. *American Furniture, Seventeenth, Eighteenth, and Nineteenth Century Styles*. New York: The Viking Press, Inc., 1962.

Cornelius, Charles Over. *Furniture Masterpieces of Duncan Phyfe*. New York: Dover Publications, Inc., Reprint, 1970.

Craig, James H. *The Arts and Crafts in North Carolina 1699–1840*. Winston-Salem, N.C.: The Museum of Early Southern Decorative Arts, Old Salem, Inc., 1965.

Cummings, Abbott Lowell. *Rural Household Inventories 1675–1775*. Boston: The Society for the Preservation of New England Antiquities, 1964.

Davidson, Marshall B. *Life in America*. Boston: Houghton Mifflin Company, 1951.

———. *American Heritage History of Colonial Antiques*. New York: American Heritage Publishing Co., Inc., 1967.

———. *American Heritage History of American Antiques from the Revolution to the Civil War*. New York: American Heritage Publishing Co., Inc., 1968.

———. *American Heritage History of Antiques from the Civil War to World War I*. New York: American Heritage Publishing Co., Inc., 1969.

Dow, George Francis. *The Arts and Crafts of New England 1704–1775*. Topsfield, Mass.: The Wayside Press, 1927.

Downing, A. J. *The Architecture of Country Houses*. New York: Dover Publications, Inc., Reprint, 1969.

Downs, Joseph. *Picturebook of the American Wing*. New York: The Metropolitan Museum of Art, 1946.

———. *American Furniture—Queen Anne and Chippendale Periods*. New York: The Macmillan Company, 1952.

Drepperd, Carl W. *Handbook of American Chairs*. Garden City, N.Y.: Doubleday & Company, Inc., 1948.

Durant, Mary. *American Heritage Guide to Antiques*. New York: American Heritage Publishing Co., Inc., 1970.

Early Furniture Made in New Jersey 1690–1870. Newark, N.J.: The Newark Museum, 1958.

Eastlake, Charles L. *Hints on Household Taste: in Furniture, Upholstery and Other Details*. New York: Dover Publications, Inc., Reprint, 1969.

Edwards, Ralph. *Sheraton Furniture Designs*. London: Alec Tiranti, 1949.

———. *The Shorter Dictionary of English Furniture*. London: County Life Limited, 1964.

Elder, William Voss, III. *Maryland Queen Anne and Chippendale Furniture of the Eighteenth Century*. Baltimore, Md.: The Baltimore Museum of Art, 1968.

Fales, Dean A., Jr. *Essex County Furniture*. Salem, Mass.: Essex Institute, 1965.

Fastnedge, Ralph. *English Furniture Styles from 1500 to 1830*. New York: A. S. Barnes & Company, Inc., 1964.

Fede, Helen Maggs. *Washington Furniture at Mount Vernon*. Mount Vernon, Va.: The Mount Vernon Ladies' Association of the Union, 1966.

Freeman, John Crosby. *The Forgotten Rebel*. Watkins Glen, N.Y.: Century House, 1966.

Frost, Sister Marguerite. "The Prose and the Poetry of Shakerism." The Philadelphia Museum *Bulletin*, Spring, 1962.

Gardner, Albert Ten Eyck, and Feld, Stuart P. *American Paintings, a Catalogue of the Collection of The Metropolitan Museum of Art*. New York: The Metropolitan Museum of Art, 1965.

Giedion, Siegfried. *Mechanization Takes Command*. New York: W. W. Norton & Company, Inc., 1969.

Gloag, John. *The Chair, Its Origins, Design and Social History*. New York: A. S. Barnes & Company, Inc., 1967.

Gottesman, Rita Susswein. *The Arts and Crafts in New York, 1726–1776*. New York: The New-York Historical Society, 1938.

———. *The Arts and Crafts in New York, 1777–1799*. New York: The New-York Historical Society, 1954.

Gowans, Alan. *Images of American Living*. Philadelphia: J. B. Lippincott, 1963.

Graham, John M., II. *The Glen–Sanders Collection*. Williamsburg, Va.: Colonial Williamsburg, 1966.

Hale, William Harlan. *The Horizon Book of Ancient Greece*. New York: American Heritage Publishing Co., Inc., 1965.

Hall, John. *The Cabinet-Maker's Assistant*. Baltimore, Md., 1840.

Halsey, R. T. H., and Tower, E. *The Homes of Our Ancestors.* Garden City, N.Y.: Doubleday, Page, & Company, 1925.

Harris, Eileen. *The Furniture of Robert Adam.* London: Alec Tiranti, 1963.

Hepplewhite, George. *The Cabinet-Maker and Upholsterer's Guide.* New York: Dover Publications, Inc., Reprint, 1969.

Heuvel, Johannes. *The Cabinetmaker in Eighteenth-Century Williamsburg.* Williamsburg, Va.: Colonial Williamsburg, 1963.

Hillier, Bevis. *Art Deco.* New York: E. P. Dutton & Co., Inc., 1968.

——. *The World of Art Deco.* An Exhibition Organized by The Minneapolis Institute of Arts. New York: E. P. Dutton & Co., Inc., 1971.

Hinckley, F. Lewis. *Directory of the Historic Cabinet Woods.* New York: Crown Publishers, Inc., 1960.

Hipkiss, Edwin J. *Eighteenth-Century American Arts: The M. and M. Karolik Collection.* Published for the Museum of Fine Arts, Boston. Cambridge, Mass.: Harvard University Press, 1941.

Hogarth, William. *The Analysis of Beauty.* London, 1753.

Hornor, William MacPherson, Jr. *Blue Book, Philadelphia Furniture, William Penn to George Washington.* Philadelphia: Privately printed, 1935.

Ince and Mayhew. *The Universal System of Household Furniture, 1762.* London: Alec Tiranti, Reprint, 1960.

Iverson, Marion Day. *The American Chair 1630–1890.* New York: Hastings House Publishers, 1957.

The John Brown House Loan Exhibition of Rhode Island Furniture. Providence, R.I.: The Rhode Island Historical Society, 1965.

Joy, Edward T. *The Book of English Furniture.* South Brunswick, N.J.: A. S. Barnes & Company, Inc., 1965.

——. *The Country Life Book of Chairs.* London: Country Life Limited, 1967.

Kettel, Russel H. *The Pine Furniture of Early New England.* New York: Doubleday, Doran & Co., Inc., 1929.

Kimball, Fiske. *The Elias Hasket Derby Mansion in Salem.* Salem, Mass.: Essex Institute, 1924.

Kirk, John T., and Maynard, Henry P. *Connecticut Furniture—Seventeenth and Eighteenth Centuries.* Hartford, Conn.: Wadsworth Atheneum, 1967.

——. *Early American Furniture: How to Recognize, Buy, and Care for the Most Beautiful Pieces—High-Style, Country, Primitive, and Rustic.* New York: Alfred A. Knopf, 1970.

Kovel, Ralph, and Terry. *American Country Furniture 1780–1875.* New York: Crown Publishers, Inc., 1965.

Lafever, Minard. *The Modern Builder's Guide.* New York: Dover Publications, Inc., Reprint of the 1st (1833) edition, 1969.

Larkin, Oliver W. *Art and Life in America.* New York: Rinehart & Company, 1949.

Lea, Zilla Rider. *The Ornamented Chair, Its Development in America, 1700–1890.* Rutland, Vt.: Charles E. Tuttle Company, 1960.

Lockwood, Luke Vincent. *Colonial Furniture in America.* 2 vols. New York: Charles Scribner's Sons, 1926.

The Lockwood–Mathews Mansion. Norwalk, Conn.: The Lockwood–Mathews Mansion Museum of Norwalk, Inc., 1969.

McClelland, Nancy. *Duncan Phyfe and the English Regency 1795–1830.* New York: William R. Scott, Inc., 1939.

The Metropolitan Museum of Art Guide to the Collections: The American Wing. New York: The Metropolitan Museum of Art, 1961.

The Metropolitan Museum of Art. *Pennsylvania German Arts and Crafts, A Picture Book.* New York: The Metropolitan Museum of Art, 1946.

Miller, Edgar G., Jr. *American Antique Furniture.* New York: Dover Publications, Inc., Reprint, 1966.

Miller, F. Isabelle. *Furniture by New York Cabinetmakers 1650–1680.* New York: Museum of the City of New York, 1957.

Modern Chairs 1918–1970. Boston: Boston Book & Art Publishers, 1970.

Montgomery, Charles F. *American Furniture, The Federal Period 1785–1825.* New York: The Viking Press, Inc., 1966.

Moody, Ella. *Modern Furniture.* New York: E. P. Dutton & Co., Inc., 1966.

Mount Vernon, An Illustrated Handbook. Mount Vernon, Va.: The Mount Vernon Ladies' Association of the Union, 1968.

Naylor, Gillian. *The Bauhaus.* New York: E. P. Dutton & Co., Inc., 1968.

Nutting, Wallace. *Furniture of the Pilgrim Century.* Framingham, Mass.: Old American Company, 1921–1924.

——. *Furniture Treasury.* 2 vols. New York: The Macmillan Company, 1928.

Ormsbee, Thomas H. *Field Guide to Early American Furniture.* Boston: Little, Brown and Company, 1951.

——. *Field Guide to American Victorian Furniture.* Boston: Little, Brown and Company, 1952.

——. *The Windsor Chair.* N.P.: Deerfield Books, Inc., 1962.

Otto, Celia Jackson. *American Furniture of the Nineteenth Century.* New York: The Viking Press, Inc., 1965.

Palardy, Jean. *The Early Furniture of French Canada.* Toronto, Canada: Macmillan of Canada, 1965.

Pallottino, Massimo. *Etruscan Painting.* Geneva, Switzerland: Albert Skira, 1952.

Parsons, Charles S. *The Dunlaps and Their Furniture.* Manchester, N.H.: The Currier Gallery of Art, 1970.

Payne, Gilbert. *The Horizon Book of Ancient Rome.* New York: American Heritage Publishing Co., Inc., 1966.

Payson, William Farquhar. *Mahogany, Antique and Modern.* New York: E. P. Dutton & Co., Inc., 1926.

Ramson, Frank E. *The City Built on Wood, a History of the Furniture Industry in Grand Rapids, Michigan, 1850–1950.* Privately published, 1955.

Randall, Richard H., Jr. *The Decorative Arts of New Hampshire, 1725–1825.* Manchester, N.H.: The Currier Gallery of Art, 1964.

——. *American Furniture in the Museum of Fine Arts.* Boston: Boston Museum of Fine Arts, 1965.

Rice, Norman S. *New York Furniture Before 1840.* Albany, N.Y.: Albany Institute of History and Art, 1962.

Robinson, Wahneta T. *Seven Decades of Design.* Long Beach, Calif.: California Arts Commission, 1967.

Sack, Albert. *Fine Points of Early American Furniture.* New York: Crown Publishers, Inc., 1950.

Sack, Israel. *American Antiques from Israel Sack Collection.* Washington, D.C.: Highland House Publishers, Inc., 1969.

Schiffer, Margaret Berwind. *Furniture and Its Makers of Chester County, Pennsylvania.* Philadelphia: University of Pennsylvania Press, 1966.

Schwartz, Marvin D. *Country Style.* Brooklyn, N.Y.: The Brooklyn Museum, 1956.

——. *Victoriana.* Brooklyn, N.Y.: The Brooklyn Museum, 1960.

——. *American Interiors 1675–1885.* Brooklyn, N.Y.: The Brooklyn Museum, 1968.

——. *Please Be Seated.* New York: The American Federation of Arts, Cooper–Hewitt Museum and the Smithsonian Institution, 1968.

Shea, John G. *The American Shakers and Their Furnishings.* New York: Van Nostrand Reinhold Company, 1971.

Shelley, Donald A. *Lewis Miller, Sketches and Chronicles, 1796–1882.* York, Pa.: The Historical Society of York County, 1966.

Sheraton, Thomas. *Cabinet-Maker and Upholsterer's Drawing Book.* London, 1791–1794.

——. *The Cabinet Dictionary.* London: W. Smith, 1803.

Smith, George. *The Cabinet-Maker and Upholsterer's Guide: Being a Complete Drawing Book.* London: Jones and Co., 1826.

Stalker, John, and Parker, George A. *Treatise of Japanning and Varnishing.* London: Alec Tiranti, Reprint, 1960.

Speltz, Alexander. *The Styles of Ornament.* New York: Dover Publications, Inc., 1959.

Stillman, Damie. *Decorative Work of Robert Adam.* New York: Transatlantic Arts, 1966.

Stoneman, Vernon C. *John and Thomas Seymour, Cabinetmakers in Boston 1794–1816.* Boston: Special Publications, 1959.

——. *A Supplement to John and*

Thomas Seymour, Cabinetmakers in Boston 1794–1816. Boston: Special Publications, 1965.

Sweeney, John A. H. *Winterthur Illustrated*. New York: Chanticleer Press, 1963.

Tracy, Berry B. "19th Century American Furniture in the Collection of The Newark Museum." *The Museum*, vol. 13, no. 4, Fall 1961.

———, and Gerdts, William H. *Classical America, 1815–1845*. Newark, N.J.: The Newark Museum, 1963.

———; Johnson, Marilynn; Schwartz, Marvin D.; and Boorsch, Suzanne. *19th Century American Furniture and Other Decorative Arts*. New York: The Metropolitan Museum of Art, 1970.

White, Margaret E. *Early Furniture Made in New Jersey, 1690–1870*. Newark, N.J.: The Newark Museum, 1958.

Whitehill, Walter Muir. *George Crowninshield's Yacht* Cleopatra's Barge *and a Catalogue of the Francis B. Crowninshield Gallery*. Salem, Mass.: Peabody Museum, 1959.

Williamson, Scott Graham. *The American Craftsman*. New York: Bramhall House, 1940.

Winchester, Alice. *How to Know American Antiques*. New York: Signet Books, 1951.

———. *The Antiques Treasury*. New York: E. P. Dutton & Co., Inc., 1959.

———. *Living With Antiques*. New York: E. P. Dutton & Co., Inc., 1963.

Wright, Louis B.; Tatum, George B.; McCoubrey, John W.; and Smith, Robert C. *The Arts in America, The Colonial Period*. New York: Charles Scribner's Sons, 1966.

CREDITS

CREDITS

ALBANY INSTITUTE OF HISTORY AND ART: 45—Bequest of Ledyard Cogswell, Jr.

ALBRIGHT-KNOX ART GALLERY: 192—Charles Clifton Fund; 856—Gift of Darwin R. Martin; 923—Gift of Seymour H. Knox.

THE ART INSTITUTE OF CHICAGO: 33—Sewell L. Avery Purchase Fund; 107—R. T. Crane, Jr., Memorial Fund; 275—Bequest of Elizabeth R. Vaughan.

THE BALTIMORE MUSEUM OF ART: Page 4—George C. Jenkins Fund; 318—Judge Irwin Untermeyer Purchase Fund; 506—Gift of Mrs. Henry V. Ward.

BOWDOIN COLLEGE MUSEUM OF ART: 2—Gift of E. Wilder Farley.

THE BROOKLYN MUSEUM: 472—Dick S. Ramsay Fund; 586—Gift of Miss Eleanor Curnow in memory of Mary Griffith Curnow; 595—Gift of Doctor Dorothea Curnow; 645—Gift of William J. Berry; 719—Gift of Herbert Hemphill; 805—Bequest of Laura L. Barnes; 821—Gift of Mrs. Otto Goetze; 851—Gift of Mrs. Charles Slaughter.

THE CORCORAN GALLERY OF ART: 266—Gift of Eva Markus through The Friends of the Corcoran.

LOS ANGELES COUNTY MUSEUM OF ART: 263—Colonel and Mrs. George J. Denis Fund.

THE METROPOLITAN MUSEUM OF ART: 10—Gift of Mrs. J. Insley Blair, 1951; 15—Rogers Fund, 1941; 26, 42, 54, 376, 392—Gift of Mrs. Russell Sage, 1909; 36—Bequest of Herbert Lee Pratt, 1945; 55—Gift of Mrs. J. Insley Blair, 1947; 56—Gift in memory of Mrs. J. Amory Haskell by her children, Mrs. Henry M. Post, Mrs. Lewis E. Waring, and Amory L. Haskell, through Mrs. Post, 1945; 60—Gift of Mrs. J. Insley Blair, 1946; 61—Rogers Fund, 1925; 62—Rogers Fund, 1962; 65—Harris Brisbane Dick Fund, 1938; 76—The Sylmaris Collection, Gift of George Coe Graves, 1930; 83—Gift of Mr. and Mrs. Paul Moore, 1945; 120—Bequest of Maria P. James, 1911; 125—Rogers Fund, 1925; 128—Gift of Mrs. J. Insley Blair, 1950; 139—Rogers Fund, 1920; 154—Gift of Samuel P. Avery, 1897; 172—Bequest of George Willett van Nest, 1917; 175—Victor Wilbour Fund, 1955; 176—Gift of Mrs. Robert Newlin Verplanck, 1940; 190—Gift of Mrs. Paul Moore, 1939; 213—Gift of Edgar William and Bernice Chrysler Garbisch, 1963; 214—Morris K. Jesup Fund, 1924; 218—Gift of Mrs. George Coe Graves, 1930; 238—Anonymous gift, 1948; 342—Gift of C. Ruxton Love, 1960; 349—Purchase, 1938, Joseph Pulitzer Bequest; 399—Rogers Fund, 1947; 425—Bequest of Maria P. James, 1911; 433—Rogers Fund, 1945; 446—Harris Brisbane Dick Fund, 1930; 449—Gift of Mrs. Paul Moore, 1965; 456—Gift of Mrs. Bayard Verplanck, 1940, in memory of Dr. James Sykes Rumsey; 461—Rogers Fund, 1953; 463—Rogers Fund, 1954; 480—Gift of Mrs. Bayard Verplanck, 1940; 513—Bequest of May Blackstone Huntington (Mrs. Austin); 515, 516, 517, 518—Purchase, L. E. Katzenbach Fund Gift, 1966; 539—Chair: Edgar J. Kaufmann Charitable Foundation Fund, 1968; Stand: Gift of Ronald S. Kane, 1967; 544, 556—Gift of Mr. and Mrs. Lowell Ross Burch and Miss Jean McLean Morron, 1951; 561—Gift of Mrs. Douglas Williams, 1969; 563, 565—Gift of Mrs. Charles Reginald Leonard, 1957, in memory of Edgar Welch Leonard, Robert Jarvis Leonard, and Charles Reginald Leonard; 602—Edgar J. Kaufmann Charitable Foundation Fund, 1969; 603—Gift of Mrs. D. Chester Noyes, 1968; 605—Gift of Josephine M. Fala, 1968; 609—Gift of the Artist, 1881; 610, 611—Gift of Mrs. D. Chester Noyes, 1968; 612—Gift of Ronald S. Kane, 1968; 613—Gift of James Graham and Sons, Inc., 1965; 624—Funds from various donors, 1970; 625—Rogers Fund, 1967; 661—Gift of Mrs. Florence Weyman, 1967; 836—Gift of Mr. and Mrs. Georges E. Seligmann, 1964.

MILWAUKEE ART CENTER: 743—Friends of Art Gift.

MUNSON-WILLIAMS-PROCTOR INSTITUTE: 562—Gift of Mrs. Erving Pruyn.

MUSEUM OF FINE ARTS, BOSTON: 4—Samuel Putnam Avery Fund; 74—Gift of Maxim Karolik; 103, 146, 156, 173, 302, 329, 330, 341, 374, 394, 407, 470, 502, 573—M. and M. Karolik Collection; 358—Gift of Mrs. Charles Gaston Smith's Group; 375—Gift of Mr. and Mrs. Guy Warren Walker; 389, 459—Gift of Mrs. Horatio A. Lamb in memory of Mr. and Mrs. Winthrop Sargent; 403—Decorative Arts Special Fund; 418—J. H. and E. A. Payne Fund; 418—Bequest of Mrs. E. H. Howe.

THE MUSEUM OF MODERN ART: 860, 862—Gift of Frank Lloyd Wright; 869, 890—Gift of Edgar J. Kaufmann, Jr.

MUSEUM OF THE CITY OF NEW YORK: 53—Gift of Mrs. Screven Lorillard; 325—Gift of Mrs. J. Amory Haskell; 455—Bequest of Helen Van Praag Tallmadge (Mrs. Henry O.); 536—Gift of Joseph B. Davis; 542—Gift of Mrs. Edward C. Moen; 545—Gift of Mr. and Mrs. Ernest Gunther Vietor; 585—Gift of Mrs. Henry De Bevoise Schenck; 614, 615—Gift of John Hall Morgan and Lancaster Morgan; 621—Gift of Mrs. Carnegie Miller in memory of her mother, Mrs. Andrew Carnegie; 646—Gift of Mrs. Franklin B. Dwight and W. Phoenix Belknap, Jr.; 648, 649—Gift of Mrs. Emalie Pottier Heckard; 650—Gift of Mr. and Mrs. Roswell Skeel, Jr.; 654—Gift of John D. Rockefeller, Jr.

THE NEWARK MUSEUM: 435—Mary I. Taylor Bequest, 1942; 549, 550, 551, 552—Gift from Florence P. Eagleton Estate; 617—Purchase, 1959, Wallace M. Scudder Bequest; 618, 622—Susan Dwight Bliss Bequest; 642—Gift of Mrs. Percy Ballantine, 1946; 786—Gift of Madison Alling, 1923.

THE TOLEDO MUSEUM OF ART: 216—Gift of Stephen Salisbury III; 217—Gift of Florence Scott Libbey, 1950; 221—Anonymous Donor, 1956.

YALE UNIVERSITY ART GALLERY: 5—Bequest of Charles Wyllys Betts; 64—Gift of Isaac Lothrop; 286—The John Hill Morgan Collection; 451—Mabel Brady Garvan Collection.

INDEX

INDEX

Note: All references are to page numbers, not figure numbers.